SHAKESPEARE
AND THE
FOLKTALE

SHAKESPEARE AND THE FOLKTALE

AN ANTHOLOGY OF STORIES

EDITED BY

CHARLOTTE ARTESE

PRINCETON UNIVERSITY PRESS

PRINCETON AND OXFORD

Owing to limitations of space, all acknowledgments for permission to reprint previously published material can be found starting on page 375.

Requests for permission to reproduce material from this work should be sent to permissions@press.princeton.edu

Published by Princeton University Press
41 William Street, Princeton, New Jersey 08540
6 Oxford Street, Woodstock, Oxfordshire OX20 1TR

press.princeton.edu

LCCN 2019937197
ISBN 9780691190853
ISBN (pbk.) 9780691190860

British Library Cataloging-in-Publication Data is available

Editorial: Anne Savarese and Jenny Tan
Production Editorial: Sara Lerner
Text Design: Leslie Flis
Cover Design: Faceout Studio, Derek Thornton
Production: Merli Guerra
Publicity: Jodi Price and Katie Lewis
Copyeditor: Jennifer Harris

Cover Credit: Peter Jackson (1922–2003), *When They Were Young: William Shakespeare* / Private Collection / © Look and Learn / Bridgeman Images

This book has been composed in Arno Pro with Estilo display.

Printed on acid-free paper. ∞

Printed in the United States of America

10 9 8 7 6 5 4 3 2 1

CONTENTS

ೕഌ

Acknowledgments   ix

INTRODUCTION   1

I. THE TAMING OF THE SHREW   10

Taming of the Shrew   14
Svend Grundtvig, "The Most Obedient Wife"   14
Angus MacLellan, "How a Bad Daughter Was Made a
   Good Wife"   21

Lord for a Day   27
Anonymous Ballad, "The Frolicksome Duke: Or, The
   Tinker's Good Fortune"   27
From *The Thousand and One Nights*, "Asleep and Awake"   30

*The Wicked Queen Reformed by Whipping
   by a Cobbler*   52
Rachel Harriette Busk, "The Queen and the Tripe-Seller"   52

II. THE COMEDY OF ERRORS   59

The Twins or Blood-Brothers   62
Giambattista Basile, "The Enchanted Doe"   62
D.L.R. and E. O. Lorimer, "The Story of the Two Golden
   Brothers"   69
Roger D. Abrahams, "Black Jack and White Jack"   76

III. TITUS ANDRONICUS 82

The Revenge of the Castrated Man   88
Mas'udi, "Revenge"   88
Gerald of Wales, "The Scene of Sorrows"   89
Anonymous Ballad, "The Lady and the Blackamoor"   91

The Maiden without Hands   98
Jacob and Wilhelm Grimm, "The Maiden without Hands"   98
Peter Buchan, "The Cruel Stepmother"   105
W. Henry Jones and Lewis L. Kropf, "The Envious Sisters"   110
Italo Calvino, "Olive"   115
Aleksandr Afanas'ev, "The Armless Maiden"   124

IV. THE MERCHANT OF VENICE   130

A Pound of Flesh   133
Johannes de Alta Silva, "The Creditor"   133
Yolando Pino-Saavedra, "White Onion"   137
Dov Noy, "The Cruel Creditor"   142
Meherjibhai Nosherwanji Kuka, "Fareed and the Kázi"   146

Three Caskets   149
Patrick Kennedy, "The Maid in the Country Underground"   149

V. ALL'S WELL THAT ENDS WELL   155

The Man Who Deserted His Wife   159
Giovanni Francesco Straparola, "Ortodosio, Isabella, Argentina"   159
Italo Calvino, "Catherine the Wise"   167

Inea Bushnaq, "The Sultan's Camp Follower" 175

Saṅgēndi Mahāliṅgam Naṭeṣa Ṣāstrī, "The Talisman of
Chastity" 180

VI. KING LEAR 202

Love Like Salt 206

Joseph Jacobs, "Cap o' Rushes" 206

Jean-François Bladé, "The Turkey-Girl" 211

Jean-Baptiste Frédéric Ortoli, "Marie, the King's Daughter" 220

Naki Tezel, "The Gift of God" 224

Jacob and Wilhelm Grimm, "The Goose Girl at the Spring" 229

VII. CYMBELINE 241

The Wager on the Wife's Chastity 251

Yolando Pino-Saavedra, "The Wager on the Wife's Chastity" 251

Kurt Ranke, "The Innkeeper of Moscow" 257

Italo Calvino, "Wormwood" 262

J. M. Synge, "The Lady O'Conor" 269

Snow White 274

Yolando Pino-Saavedra, "Blanca Rosa and the Forty Thieves" 274

Violet Paget, "The Glass Coffin" 279

Alan Bruford, "Lasair Gheug, the King of Ireland's
Daughter" 283

The Maiden Who Seeks Her Brothers 292

Peter Christian Asbjørnsen and Jørgen Moe, "The
Twelve Wild Ducks" 292

VIII. THE TEMPEST 300

The Magic Flight 304

Joseph Jacobs, "Nix Nought Nothing" 304

Peter Buchan, "Green Sleeves" 309

Jacob and Wilhelm Grimm, "The Two Kings' Children" 320

Zora Neale Hurston, "Jack Beats the Devil" 329

Marie-Catherine d'Aulnoy, "The Bee and the Orange Tree" 335

Bibliography 365
Index 369
Text Credits 375

ACKNOWLEDGMENTS

Many communities supported me as I worked on this book. My students at Agnes Scott College, who have read and discussed folktales and Shakespeare's plays with me over the past decade, never cease to dazzle me with their insight, industry, and irreverence. This book is dedicated to them. Members of the Agnes Scott English Department, past and present, have unstintingly supported my scholarship and teaching on Shakespeare's folktales: Christine Cozzens, Amber Dermont, Jim Diedrick, Alan Grostephan, Steve Guthrie, Waqas Khwaja, Bobby Meyer-Lee, Aisha Moon, Jamie Stamant, Nicole Stamant, Peggy Thompson, Willie Tolliver, and Rachel Trousdale. I would also like to thank Kerry Pannell and Emily Kandetski of the Academic Affairs division. I am grateful for support from Agnes Scott's Humanities Fund and Holder Fund for Faculty Innovation.

One of the many pleasures of working on this project has been that it has brought me in touch with an exciting group of scholars who have generously offered their knowledge and insight: Dan Ben-Amos, Jan Brunvand, Bill Carroll, Kent Cartwright, Paddy Fumerton, Donald Haase, Bill Hansen, Isaac Lévy, David Nee, Jonathan Roper, Patrick Ryan, Penelope Meyers Usher, Melissa Walter, Valerie Wayne, and Rosemary Lévy Zumwalt.

It was my great good fortune to have worked with Anne Savarese and Thalia Leaf of Princeton University Press on this book. I also appreciate the responses of two anonymous readers.

Friends and family have patiently offered listening ears and thoughtful advice, especially Megan Drinkwater, Alan Koch, Amy

Lovell, Jenny Mullen, Tom Mullen, Hod Nalle, and Jim Wiseman. My parents, Jack and Cynthia Williams, and my brother, Jason, have walked by my side over the peaks and into the valleys. My husband, Brian Artese, and our son, Leo, are the lights by which I find my way.

SHAKESPEARE
AND THE
FOLKTALE

INTRODUCTION

In 1898, the writer J. M. Synge visited the Aran Islands, seeking to improve his Irish. In a cottage kitchen, an old man seated in the chimney-corner told a story to Synge and the others who crowded around while dinner was cooking. In this tale, a young farmer named O'Conor borrows money from a strange little man who demands five pounds of O'Conor's flesh should he fail to repay the loan in a year's time. Later, O'Conor enters into an ill-advised wager with a ship's captain who claims he can seduce O'Conor's wife.

Those who know their Shakespeare will find this story familiar, with its clear resemblances to *The Merchant of Venice*, in which a man uses a pound of his flesh as collateral for a loan, and *Cymbeline*, in which a man bets on his wife's fidelity. Synge relates, "It gave me a strange feeling of wonder to hear this illiterate native of a wet rock in the Atlantic telling a story that is so full of European associations."[1] I was similarly struck when I first read the Chilean folktale "White Onion," a story about a young man who faces the prospect of having a kilogram of flesh cut from his rump when he fails to repay a loan on time. The story bears a marked resemblance to *The Merchant of Venice*, and yet the folktale—which features such earthy details as a grubby old man and woman as helpers and the identifying mark of three golden hairs growing from the heroine's waist—does not seem to be an adaptation of the play. We can recognize a connection between "White Onion" and *Merchant* just as we can recognize both a literary seventeenth-century French tale

---

1. Synge, *Aran Islands*, 24. For some background on Synge's travels in the Aran Islands, see Skelton, *Four Plays*, viii–ix.

involving glass slippers and a pumpkin coach and a Chinese story about an abused young girl and her pet fish as "Cinderella."

Part of the wonder I felt was over how stories separated by differences in time, place, culture, language, and genre can nevertheless resemble each other closely. I feel something of the birdwatcher's joy when she identifies a bird well-known or rare when I find "The Maiden without Hands," which I know from the Brothers Grimm, in a collection of Russian or Italian folktales. When I encountered "White Onion," I saw *The Merchant of Venice*, even though the antagonist is the feckless young man's godfather, not a Jewish moneylender. The Chilean folktale and the play resemble each other because both descend from earlier "Pound of Flesh" tales. We know such stories predate Shakespeare because medieval versions survive. Generations of Shakespeare scholars have examined his literary sources, but his folktale sources remain largely neglected. Yet just as birds and alligators help us to imagine their ancestors the dinosaurs, so folktales collected in the modern world (the nineteenth century and after) can give us insight into the stories Shakespeare and his audiences might have known. But just as a chicken is not an archaeopteryx, so the folktales in this volume are not Shakespeare's exact sources, but later members of the genus of his sources. Shakespeare may have known multiple versions of the story he then used as material for his plays, and so each folktale type is here represented by several examples.

In the case of *The Merchant of Venice*, we can be virtually certain that Shakespeare knew a version of the "Pound of Flesh" folktale published in a fourteenth-century Italian collection of stories by Giovanni Fiorentino, *The Dunce* (*Il Pecorone*). I have not included this story, although I have included an earlier medieval "Pound of Flesh" tale, because Ser Giovanni's story is generally accepted as Shakespeare's source and so is readily available in Geoffrey Bullough's indispensable eight-volume *Narrative and Dramatic*

Sources of Shakespeare and elsewhere.[2] This anthology aims to augment our knowledge of Shakespeare's sources and influences by supplying examples of his folktale sources rather than revisiting his acknowledged literary ones.

The larger question one might ask about *The Merchant of Venice*'s sources is, if we are nearly certain that Shakespeare knew the story in *The Dunce*, why should we interest ourselves in other versions of the same story? In what sense is "White Onion," a Chilean folktale collected in 1951, a "source" for a play written and performed in London around 1597? One answer focuses on Shakespeare: he might have known a number of versions of the "Pound of Flesh" folktale, some of them from oral tradition. Attending to the folktale in its many guises can give us a clearer sense of the story tradition available to Shakespeare, although we cannot reconstruct it exactly. Shakespeare's audience, moreover, may have also known the story in many forms, and unlike the playwright, many of them were illiterate, and so the oral tradition may have been all they knew.

Folktales often served as common ground in Shakespeare's theater. The playwright and some members of his audience would have read literary versions of a play's folktale source, and those who could not read might have heard those tales told. In our own culture, when a movie or television show (or short story or novel) adapts a fairy tale, the creator knows the expectations the audience will bring, and the audience knows that the creator knows. The audience waits to see how this version of a well-known story will conform to tradition and how it will vary. Will Red Riding Hood fall in love with the wolf? Will the evil fairy repent and rescue Sleeping Beauty? When we learn the folktale traditions that Shakespeare adapts, we can join this interplay between playwright and audience.

2. Bullough, *Narrative and Dramatic Sources*, 1.463–76.

Both folktales and Shakespeare's plays are cultural survivors, thriving in scores of languages and cultures through the ages. Just as modern writers, playwrights, and filmmakers endlessly adapt Shakespeare's plays, so Shakespeare drew from the tales in the culture of the time. Macbeth becomes a samurai in Akira Kurosawa's film *Throne of Blood*; Snow White becomes a bullfighter in Pablo Berger's film *Blancanieves*. The title of Catherine Belsey's 2007 book poses an essential question: *Why Shakespeare?* Why have Shakespeare's plays been so durably successful? Belsey concludes that the resemblances between Shakespeare's plays and folk narratives help to explain Shakespeare's place at the center of the Western literary canon. By absorbing the narrative traditions on which Shakespeare drew, we may peer into the heart of what makes him great: a profound connection to his audiences through the centuries and around the world.

This book defines narrative traditions using two concepts from folktale studies, "types" and "motifs." A folktale type is a generalized plot drawn from many different versions of what seems to be the same kind of story; a motif is a small narrative unit, or "those details out of which full-fledged narratives are composed."[3] The standard reference work, Hans-Jörg Uther's *The Types of International Folktales*, provides a title and a plot description for each folktale type, and assigns each type a number with the prefix ATU. "A Pound of Flesh," for example, is ATU 890. The entry in *The Types of International Folktales* for the folktale most of us know as "Bluebeard" is:

> [ATU] 312: *Maiden-Killer (Bluebeard)* ... An odd-looking rich man (e.g. with a blue beard [S62.1]) takes his bride to his splendid castle. She is forbidden to open a certain room, but she disobeys and finds it full of the dead bodies of her predecessors

3. Thompson, *Motif-Index*, 1.10.

[C611]. The husband wants to kill her for her disobedience [C920], but she is able to delay the punishment (three times) [K551]. She (her sister) calls their brother (three brothers) who kills the husband (sometimes with help from a dog or other animal) and rescues his sister(s) [G551.1, G652].

Common variations in the story tradition are noted parenthetically, and motifs are indicated in square brackets. The motifs are listed and defined in another essential reference work for folktale studies, Stith Thompson's *Motif-Index of Folk-Literature*. It catalogues folktale motifs and assigns them a number beginning with a letter. In the description of "Maiden-Killer," Motif C611 is "Forbidden chamber." Tale types and motifs are helpful tools, but studying multiple versions of a folktale type or motif can help readers understand the range of narrative possibilities for a traditional story.

Oral tradition played a greater role in Shakespeare's culture than in our own.[4] His plays themselves refer to storytelling. In *The Winter's Tale*, Queen Hermione calls her young son Mamillius to her to tell her a story. He obliges, saying, "A sad tale's best for winter. I have one / Of sprites and goblins" (2.1.22–26). In *Macbeth*, Lady Macbeth castigates her husband for being afraid of illusions, as if he were frightened by a "woman's story at a winter's fire" (3.4.62). Sometimes characters refer to specific folktales. In *Much Ado about Nothing*, Benedict cites "the old tale" with the lines "It is not so, nor 'twas not so: but indeed, God forbid it should be so!" (1.1.200–201). This chorus appears in an English folktale, "Mr. Fox," included in Joseph Jacobs's great nineteenth-century collection *English Fairy Tales*.[5] Edgar, disguised as a mad beggar in *King Lear*, intones "Childe Rowland to the dark tower came, / His word was still 'Fie,

4. On literacy rates in early modern England, see Fox, *Oral and Literate Culture*, 18–19.

5. Jacobs, *English Fairy Tales*, 151.

foh and fum, / I smell the blood of a British man'" (3.4.178–80), a reference to the folktale "Childe Rowland," also in Joseph Jacobs's collection.[6] In *Hamlet*, Ophelia in her madness utters, "They say the owl was a baker's daughter" (4.5.42–43), which refers to a traditional story in which Jesus and St. Peter, disguised as beggars, ask a baker's daughter for some bread. When she refuses, Jesus turns her into an owl.[7] Shakespeare seems to have expected his audiences to recognize folktales and other traditional stories from the briefest references to them. We might also recall that the theater itself is in large measure an oral form, with actors delivering lines they have learned in front of an audience, not unlike a storyteller.

I have used this collection as a textbook for my "Shakespeare and the Folktale" course, which I have taught regularly since 2010 at Agnes Scott College. The folktale sources can be an excellent point of entry into Shakespeare. They are less intimidating than the Bard, provide a partial preview of the play's plot, and allow a course on Shakespeare to include texts from many cultures. I also hope that this book will bring pleasure to those who enjoy Shakespeare, folktales, or both. Each section includes tales related to a specific play, with a brief introduction to point out the connections. Within each chapter, the stories are ordered in a way that follows the introduction's discussion of these connections. Those who would like more extended analysis can consult my 2015 book, *Shakespeare's Folktale Sources*.

Shakespeare's Folktale Sources considers seven plays: *The Taming of the Shrew*, *Titus Andronicus*, *The Merry Wives of Windsor*, *The Merchant of Venice*, *All's Well That Ends Well*, *Measure for Measure*, and

6. Ibid., 123.

7. See Uther, *Types of International Folktales*, ATU 751A, "The Farmwife Is Changed into a Woodpecker," which notes variants in which the woman is a baker's daughter and the transformation is into an owl; and Thompson, *Motif-Index*, A1958.0.1, "The Owl Is a Baker's Daughter."

Cymbeline, which have one or more plots based directly on a folktale. This anthology also includes *King Lear*, which adapts a legendary history that includes folktales and folk narrative motifs; *The Comedy of Errors*, which is based on a classical Roman play that is in turn related to the "Twins or Blood-Brothers" folktale; and *The Tempest*, whose dependence on the "Magic Flight" folktale is partial and incomplete, but fascinating nonetheless. I did not include *The Merry Wives of Windsor* or *Measure for Measure* here because of a dearth of relevant folktales available in English.

While other Shakespeare plays, such as *A Midsummer Night's Dream* and *Macbeth*, include supernatural elements, and others, such as *The Winter's Tale* and *Pericles*, include folktale motifs, they do not follow the plot of any one folktale type. The plays that Shakespeare bases on specific folktales tend to focus on marriage and family instead of magical elements, and transform such elements in traditional tales into a more recognizable reality. *Titus Andronicus* adapts the "Maiden without Hands" folktale, in which the maimed heroine's hands always grow back; not so for *Titus's* heroine Lavinia. In the "Snow White" plot of *Cymbeline*, there is nothing magical about how Imogen falls into a death-sleep and then awakens: she simply takes a drug that later wears off, much like the one Juliet takes in *Romeo and Juliet*. *The Tempest* is the exception to this trend, but even in this play the magic in the folktale source, "The Magic Flight," is curtailed, ending not with a sorcerers' showdown but with Prospero's renunciation of magic. For this reason, I prefer to use the term "folktale" rather than "fairy tale" when speaking of Shakespeare's traditional sources, since "fairy tale" suggests magical elements, and in contemporary culture can suggest the whimsical, inconsequential, and naïve.

In deciding which versions of the folktales to include in each chapter, I considered first how close the connections were between the play in question and the versions of the folktale. I also selected stories for how well they were told, and my final consideration was diversity of the cultures represented. Since I teach in the United States, I am always especially pleased to come upon New World folktales that speak to Shakespeare's plays. I have not restricted my selections to English or even European folktales, because folktales show a remarkable ability to transcend cultural and linguistic boundaries. Many literary stories that scholars accept as Shakespeare's sources are Italian and French. Orally transmitted tales recorded in very different places can be quite similar. A folktale told in Iraq in the twentieth century participates in the same tradition Shakespeare drew on for his plays, and so might provide evidence about how the folktale appeared in seventeenth-century London. I am convinced that what we gain by examining these folktale traditions justifies this inevitably speculative enterprise. We cannot know exactly how these stories were told in Shakespeare's day, but we can learn about the story traditions themselves.

The folktales herein primarily come from the geographical expanse from India to Ireland that folktale scholars consider to be a "traditional area"—that is, a region in which very similar versions of a given tale can be found.[8] Thus, with a few exceptions, most of the stories in this collection come from Europe, the Middle East, and India. Morocco, situated close to Europe on the Mediterranean, supplies a Jewish folktale related to *The Merchant of Venice*, and I also include two stories from African diasporic cultures, "Black Jack and White Jack" and "Jack Beats the Devil." These last two stories come from the New World, as do three Chilean stories I have included. These stories seem to descend, at least partially, from European traditions conveyed by colonization, slavery, and other forms of cultural contact.

What can folktales teach us about Shakespeare? They might illuminate his creative processes. They might help us understand

8. Thompson, *Folktale*, 14.

why Shakespeare's plays have been so successful across time and space. They also may help us imagine what Shakespeare's audience might have brought with them into the theater, whether they were standing on the ground or seated in a privileged position on the stage, since folktales could have been available to those at a range of literacy levels. Shakespeare's folktale sources can reveal to us how he met his audience on common ground, and how he kept them there.

I. The Taming of the Shrew

The folktale "Taming of the Shrew" (ATU 901), named for Shakespeare's play, tells a story very similar to Katherine and Petruchio's. In a Danish version of the folktale, "The Most Obedient Wife," a stranger comes to town, and although he is warned against it, marries a woman known for being quarrelsome. He arrives for their wedding inappropriately dressed and then insists on leaving before the wedding reception. On the way to his house, he shoots his dog and horse for disobeying him, striking terror into his bride, who then must carry the dead horse's saddle the rest of the way. He further trains his new wife by requiring her to agree to his patently false statements. Eventually, they visit the wife's family, where her husband wins a wager by proving she is more obedient to her husband than her sisters are to theirs.[*]

Petruchio, likewise, appears in Padua at the beginning of Shakespeare's play and abruptly asks for the hand of the notorious Katherine. He makes a mockery of their wedding celebration and then "tames" his wife by uproariously mistreating her. He threatens to cancel their trip to the wedding of Katherine's sister, Bianca, unless Katherine agrees that the sun is the moon and that an old man is a young woman. When the newlyweds finally arrive at Katherine's family home, Petruchio wins a wager with his new brother-in-law, Lucentio, and Petruchio's friend, Hortensio, about whose wife is the most obedient.

One part of this story Shakespeare does not stage is the episode in which the groom kills his animals on the journey to his house.

---

[*] Jan Harold Brunvand's work on the "Taming of the Shrew" folktales is foundational. See his article "Folktale Origin," and his book *Taming of the Shrew*.

The play alludes to this episode, however. When Petruchio's servant Grumio begins relating the misadventures of Katherine and Petruchio's post-wedding trip to Curtis, his fellow servant, Curtis interrupts to ask if they were both riding one horse (4.1.61). This non sequitur nods to the folktale—Curtis anticipates the moment when the couple must walk, the bride carrying the horse's gear, which would not be the case if there were two horses. In a medieval Spanish version of the folktale, the groom's pretext for killing a dog is that he asks it to bring him water, which it of course does not do.* In what might be another allusion to the folktale, Petruchio, once home, calls for water and his dog Troilus in the same breath (4.1.136–41). Dog-lovers can breathe a sigh of relief, however: a servant brings the water, and the dog is never mentioned again.

The Scottish folktale included here, "How a Bad Daughter Was Made a Good Wife," ends with a somewhat risqué moment. In order to win the obedience wager, the bride must take off her dress in front of her husband and brothers-in-law and throw it on the fire. The boy actor playing Katherine on Shakespeare's stage could not have done this because the audience then would have beheld a naked boy instead of a naked woman, but Petruchio requires Katherine to throw her cap down on the floor at his command, and he has earlier mauled the new dress and cap tailor-made for Katherine to wear to her sister's wedding. This Scottish folktale also includes a shocking episode in which the groom humiliates and injures his domineering mother-in-law. In this tale, the groom subjects a person as well as animals to violence in order to intimidate the bride, whereas Petruchio harms no animals but farcically beats and berates his servants. The secondary taming of another troublesome

---

* Manuel, *Count Lucanor*. The episode with the dog occurs in the story "Of What Happened to a Young Man on His Wedding Day," 208–16. This collection also includes a second "Taming" story, "Of That Which Happened to the Emperor Frederick and Don Alvar Fanez, with Their Wives," 32–42.

woman, an older one, is perhaps suggested in the play by a reference to Petruchio's "taming school," where Hortensio will learn to tame the widow he has married (4.2.55), who appears in place of the folktale wife's second sister in the obedience wager at the end of the play.

Before the "Taming of the Shrew" plot has even begun, however, Shakespeare's audience encounters another folktale, "Lord for a Day" (ATU 1531). The opening scenes, known as Inductions and often cut in performance, tell the story of a tinker, Christopher Sly, booted out of a tavern for drunk and disorderly behavior. He falls in a stupor on the ground, and a passing nobleman, the Lord, decides to take him to his house, dress him in fine clothes, and convince him that he is a rich lord who has madly supposed himself to be a beggar for years. The Katherine-Petruchio plot with which we are more familiar is actually a play within a play, performed for Sly, the Lord, and his servants by a traveling troupe of actors. The "Lord for a Day" story appears in many oral and literary forms, including *The Thousand and One Nights*, in which the mischievous lord is none other than the famed caliph Haroun er Reshid, who makes many appearances. I've included the long tale from *The Thousand and One Nights*, "Asleep and Awake," because it not only is very funny but also includes some moments strikingly parallel to the *Shrew* Inductions. Just as Sly declares, "Upon my life, I am a lord indeed / And not a tinker, nor Christopher Sly" (Ind.2.70–71), breaking into blank verse in order to do so, Aboulhusn declares, "By Allah, I am in truth Commander of the Faithful!"* Aboulhusn dallies with the harem slave-girls with as much gusto as Sly, when presented with his fake wife, briskly orders, "Servants, leave me and her alone. / Madam, undress you and come now to bed" (Ind.2.113–

---

*Richard Burton's perhaps more familiar translation of the story renders the hero's name as Abu el-Hasan. *Supplemental Nights*, 1.1–29.

14). Sly addresses the lady by the absurd title "Madam wife" (Ind.2.109), just as Aboulhusn addresses a eunuch inappropriately as "chief."

Shakespeare's version of "Lord for a Day," strangely enough, has no ending—Sly is not heard from again after the second act, which means his story is only a partial frame for the "Taming of the Shrew" plot, an opening bracket without a closing one. In the folktales, the beggar is once again rendered unconscious, believing he is a lord, and deposited back into his former, impoverished life. Some versions of the tale end at this point, but the two included here, "Asleep and Awake" and the English ballad "The Frolicksome Duke," have the trickster lord making room for the dupe in his entourage.

I have included an example of a third folktale type, "The Wicked Queen Reformed by Whipping by a Cobbler" (ATU 905A*), because it combines themes from the "Taming" and "Lord for a Day" stories. A shrewish woman, the queen, trades places with the abused wife of a working-class man, who beats the haughty queen into submission. The patient wife of the cobbler, or, in the version presented here, the tripe-seller, enjoys a brief tenure as queen, like the dupe in "Lord for a Day." While the Lord who tricks Christopher Sly is not transformed into a tinker, in the "Taming" plot of the play, the gentlemen Lucentio and Hortensio transform themselves into tutors in order to have access to Katherine's sister, Bianca. Lucentio's servant Tranio has his own "Lord for a Day" episode when he poses as his master. The two men exchange clothes onstage, revealing the extent to which clothing signified rank in the Renaissance. Much attention is given in "The Queen and the Tripe-Seller" folktale to the exchange of the women's clothing, which is the first order of business for the meddlesome fairies who effect the trade.

These folktales provide context, but not answers, for two of the more baffling questions about Shakespeare's play: What happens to Sly and the Lord? Is Katherine really "tamed" at the end of the play? Seeing the play's basis in traditional stories provides a new perspective on its controversies.

TAMING OF THE SHREW

Svend Grundtvig
The Most Obedient Wife[*]

Long ago there was a rich farmer who had three daughters, all grown up and marriageable, and all three very pretty. The eldest of them was the prettiest, and she was also the cleverest, but she was so quarrelsome and obstinate, that there was never any peace in the house. She constantly contradicted her father, who was a kind, peace-loving man, and she quarreled with her sisters, although they were very good-natured girls.

Many wooers came to the farm, and one of them wished to marry the eldest daughter. The farmer said that he had no objection to him as a son-in-law, but at the same time he thought it his duty to tell the suitor the truth. Accordingly he warned him that his eldest daughter was so violent and strong-minded that no one could live in peace with her. As some compensation for these faults, she would receive three hundred pounds more in her dowry than would her two sisters. That was, of course, very attractive, but the young man thought over the matter and, after he had been visiting the house for some time, he altered his mind and asked for the hand of the second daughter. The daughter accepted him, and, as her

[*] Svend Grundtvig, *Danish Fairy Tales*, trans. Gustav Hein (London: George G. Harrap, 1914), 175–83, https://babel.hathitrust.org/cgi/pt?id=mdp.39015008544416; view=1up;seq=205 (accessed April 19, 2017).

father was willing, the two became man and wife and lived very happily together. Then came another wooer, from another part of the country, and he also wanted to marry the eldest daughter. The father warned him, as he had cautioned the first wooer; telling him that she would receive three hundred pounds more than her youngest sister, but that he must be careful, for she was so stubborn and quarrelsome that nobody could live in peace with her. So the second wooer changed his mind and asked for the hand of the youngest daughter. They married shortly after and lived happily and peacefully together.

The eldest sister was now alone with her father, but she did not treat him any better than before, and grew even more ill-humored because her two sisters had found favor in the eyes of the first two wooers. She was obstinate and quarrelsome, violent and bad-tempered, and she grew more so from day to day.

At last another wooer came, and he was neither from their own district nor even from their country, but from a distant land. He went to the farmer and asked for the hand of his eldest daughter. "I do not want her to marry at all," said the father, "it would be a shame to allow her to do so; she is so ill-tempered and violent that no human being could live in peace with her and I do not want to be the cause of such unhappiness." But the wooer remained firm; he wanted her, he said, whatever her faults might be. At length the father yielded, provided that his daughter were willing to marry the young man, for, after all, he would be glad to get rid of her, and as he had told the suitor the whole truth about her, his conscience was clear. Accordingly the young man wooed the girl, and she did not hesitate long, but accepted the offer, for she was tired of sitting at home a despised and spurned spinster.

The wooer said that he had no time to remain with them just then, as he must return home at once, and, as soon as the wedding-day was fixed, he rode away. He also told them not to wait for him at the farm on the day of the wedding, he would appear in good time at the church. When the day came the farmer drove with his daughter to the church, where a great company of wedding guests had assembled; the bride's sisters and brothers-in-law were there, and all the village people arrived in their Sunday clothes. The bridegroom was there also, but in ordinary traveling garments; and so the couple walked up to the altar and were married.

As soon as the ceremony was over, the bridegroom took his young wife by the hand and led her out of the church. He sent a message to his father-in-law asking him to excuse their absence from the marriage feast, as they had no time to waste. He had not driven in a coach, as is the custom at weddings, but traveled on horseback, on a fine big gray horse, with an ordinary saddle, and a couple of pistols in the saddlebags. He had brought no friends or relations with him, only a big dog, that lay beside the horse during the ceremony. The bridegroom lifted his bride onto the pommel, as if she had been a feather, jumped into the saddle, put the spurs to his horse, and rode off with the dog trotting behind. The marriage party standing at the church door looked after them, and shook their heads in amazement. Then they got into their carriages, drove back to the house, and partook of the marriage feast without bride or bridegroom.

The bride did not like this at all, but as she did not want to quarrel with her bridegroom so soon, she held her tongue for a time; but as he did not speak either, she at last broke the ice and said that it was a very fine horse they were riding. "Yes," he replied; "I have seven other horses at home in my stables, but this is my favorite; it is the most valuable of all, and I like it best." Then she remarked that she liked the beautiful dog also. "It is indeed a jewel of a dog," he said, "and has cost me a lot of money."

After a while they came to a forest, where the bridegroom sprang from his horse and cut a thin switch from a willow-tree. This he wound three times round his finger, then tied it with a thread and gave it to his bride, saying: "This is my wedding gift to you. Take good care of it, and carry it about you always! You will not repent it." She thought it a strange wedding gift, but put it in her pocket, and they rode on again. Presently the bride dropped her glove, and the bridegroom said to the dog: "Pick it up, Fido!" But the dog took no notice, and left the glove on the ground. Then his master drew his pistol from the holster, shot the dog, and rode on, leaving it lying dead. "How could you be so cruel?" said his bride. "I never say a thing twice," was the reply, and they journeyed on in silence.

After some time they came to a running stream that they had to cross. There being only a ford, and no bridge, the man said to his horse: "Take good care! Not a drop must soil my bride's dress!" When they had crossed, however, the dress was badly soiled, and the husband lifted his bride from the horse, drew out the other pistol and shot the horse, so that it fell dead to the ground. "Oh, the poor horse!" cried the bride. "Yes, but I never say a thing twice," answered her husband. Then he took saddle, bridle, and cover from the horse; bridle and cover he carried himself, but the saddle he gave to his young wife, and said: "You can carry that; we shall soon be home." He walked on in silence, and the bride quickly put the saddle on her back and followed him; she had no desire to make him say it twice.

Soon they arrived at his dwelling-place, a very fine farm. The menservants and maidservants rushed to the door and received them, and the husband said to them: "See, this is my wife and your mistress. Whatever she tells you, you are to do, just as if I had ordered it." Then he led her indoors and showed her everything—

living-rooms and bedrooms, kitchen and cellar, brewhouse and dairy—and said to her: "You will look after everything indoors, I attend to everything out-of-doors," and then they sat down to supper, and soon after went to bed.

Days, weeks, and months passed; the young wife attended to all household matters while her husband looked after the farm, and not a single angry word passed between them. The servants had been accustomed to obey their master implicitly, and now they obeyed their mistress likewise, and so six months passed without there having arisen any necessity for the husband to say the same thing twice to his wife. He was always kind and polite to her, and she was always gentle and obedient.

One day he said to her: "Would you not like to visit your relations?" "Yes, dear husband, I should like to do so very much, if it is convenient," she replied. "It is quite convenient," he said, "but you have never mentioned it. It shall be done at once; get ready, while I have the horses put to the carriage." He went to the stable and saw to everything, while his wife ran upstairs to dress as quickly as possible for the journey. The husband drove up, cracked his whip and asked: "Are you ready?" "Yes, dear," came the reply, and she came running out and entered the carriage. She had not quite finished dressing and carried some of her things in her hand, and these she put on in the carriage.

Then they started. When they had driven nearly half the distance, they saw a great flock of ravens flying across the road. "What beautiful white birds!" said the husband. "No, they are black, dear!" said his wife. "I think it is going to rain," he said, turned the horses, and drove home again. She understood perfectly why he had done so; it was the first time that she had contradicted him, but she showed no resentment, and the two conversed in quite a friendly fashion all the way home. The horses were put into the stable—and it did not rain.

When a month had passed, the husband said one morning: "I believe it is going to be fine today. Would you not like to visit your relations?" She wished to do so very much indeed, and she hastened a little more than the last time, so that when her husband drove up and cracked his whip, she was quite ready and mounted the carriage beside him. They had driven considerably more than half the distance, when they met a large flock of sheep and lambs. "What a fine pack of wolves!" said the husband. "You mean sheep, dear!" said the wife. "I think it will rain before evening," said the husband, looking up at the sky. "It will be better for us to drive home again." With these words he turned the horses and drove back home. They conversed in a friendly manner until they reached home; but it did not rain.

When another month had passed, the husband said one morning to his wife: "We really must see whether we cannot manage to visit your relations. What do you say to our driving across today? It looks as though the day would be fine." His wife thought so too; she was ready very soon and they set out. They had not traveled far when they saw a great flock of swans flying along over their heads. "That was a fine flock of storks," said the husband. "Yes, so it was, dear," said his wife, and they drove on; there was no change in the weather that day, so that they reached her father's farm in due course. He received them joyfully and sent at once for his two other daughters and their husbands, and a very merry family meeting it was.

The three married sisters went into the kitchen together, because they could talk more freely there, and they had a great deal to tell each other; the two younger ones in particular had many questions to ask their elder sister, because they had not seen her for a very long time. Then they helped to prepare the dinner: it goes without saying that nothing was too good for this festive occasion.

The three brothers-in-law sat meanwhile with their father-in-law in the sitting-room and they, too, had much to tell and ask each other. Then said the old farmer: "This is the first time that you have all three been gathered together under my roof, and I should like to ask you frankly how you are pleased with your wives." The husbands who had married the two younger, good-tempered sisters said at once that they were perfectly satisfied and lived very happily. "But how do you get on with yours?" the father-in-law asked the husband of the eldest sister. "Nobody ever married a better wife than I did," was the reply. "Well, I should like to see which of you has the most obedient wife," said the father-in-law, and then he fetched a heavy silver jug and filled it to the top with gold and silver coins. This he placed in the middle of the table before the three men, and said that he would give it to him who had the most obedient wife.

They put the matter to the test at once. The husband who had married the youngest sister went to the kitchen door and called: "Will you come here a moment, Gerda, please; as quickly as possible!" "All right, I am coming," she answered, but it was some time before she came, because as she explained, she had first to talk about something with one of her sisters. "What do you want with me?" she asked. The husband made some excuse, and she went out again.

Now it was the turn of the man who had married the middle sister. "Please come here a moment, Margaret!" he called. She also answered: "Yes, I am coming at once," but it was a good while before she came; she had had something in her hands and was compelled to put it down first. The husband invented some excuse, and she went out again.

Then the third husband went to the kitchen door, opened it slightly and just said: "Christine!"—"Yes!" she answered, as she stood there with a large dish of food in her hands. "Take this from me!" she said quickly to her sisters, but they looked at her in amazement and did not take the dish. Bang! she dropped it right on the middle of the kitchen floor, rushed into the room and asked: "What do you wish, dear?"—"Oh, I only wanted to see you," he said, "but since you are here, you may as well take that jug standing on the table; it is yours, with all that is in it.—You might also show us what you got from me as a marriage gift on our wedding day."—"Yes, dear, here it is," she said, and drew the willow ring from her bosom, where she had kept it ever since. The husband handed it to his father-in-law and asked: "Can you put that ring straight?"—No, that was impossible without breaking it. "Well, you see now," said the husband, "if I had not bent the twig when it was green, I could not have made it into this shape."

After that they sat down to a merry meal, then the husband of the oldest sister returned home with her, and they lived for many years very happily together.

Angus MacLellan

How a Bad Daughter Was Made a Good Wife*

Once there was a rich farmer who had three sons. When he died, he left his farm to them to carry on for as long as they chose to stick together. Each of them had a right in the house and in the land.

The eldest of them married a gentleman's daughter, and was well off; and the second married a wife who was as well born as his brother's. The youngest of them, who was a carpenter, was then the only one of them left unmarried. He decided to marry. His brothers

*Angus MacLellan, *Stories from South Uist*, trans. John Lorne Campbell (London: Routledge and Kegan Paul, 1961), 65–69.

told him that if he got married, he must get a wife who was just as well born as theirs were.

"No, I won't," he said. "I'll get the daughter of a bad mother, as bad as I can find."

"Well, she mustn't come here!"

"Yes, she will, and she has as good a right to come here as your wives had!"

He took his pony and his dog, and went away, not knowing how far he would go. The day was bad, and snow was falling. What did he see on his way but an old man at work plowing in a field. He went over to him and said:

"Oh, oh! you've got a bad day for plowing!"

"Well," said the old fellow, "indeed, it isn't good!"

"Why do you have to work outside on a day like this?"

"Well, there's no one else to go out but myself, and the work has to be done, and I must keep on with it."

"Is there no one but yourself?"

"Oh yes, I have my wife along with me at home, and my daughter."

"Well, indeed, I'd think they wouldn't let you work outside on a day like this."

"Well, my good lad," said the old man, "and you look like one to me, you are right enough there. If there was a way I could stay at home, I wouldn't come out myself; but I'd rather to be outside, than indoors listening to the womenfolk."

"Indeed," said the youngest son, "is that the way of it?"

"Yes, it is," said the old man.

"Well, I'd think your own daughter wouldn't want you to be out of doors (in weather like this)."

"If her mother is bad, my daughter is seven times worse."

"May I marry her?" asked the young man.

"My goodness, mother, why did you bring them? Not one of those you gave me ever reached the house! If only you knew what he did to me!"

"What did he do to you?"

"We hadn't gone far before his dog went off after a hare, and as it had disobeyed him, he shot it when it did come back to him. Next he came to the river with the pony, and no beast could have gotten across at the place he was trying to put the pony across. When the pony wouldn't cross the river, he shot it, and I can tell you that I had to carry the saddle home myself on my back!"

"Oh, the devil!" said her mother, "if only I had been there! He wouldn't have done that to me! Weren't you soft with him!"

When the farmer's youngest son heard that, he jumped in and caught the old woman and stripped her and slashed her backside with his knife and put salt in the wounds he had made, and then let her go. The mother-in-law went off lamenting. When she got home, the old man was sitting at the fire, having a rest; he hadn't had to be outside! She went up to him and put her arms around his neck.

"My darling husband," she said, "of all the men in the world! In spite of everything I ever did to you, you never treated me the way our son-in-law has; he's slashed me and injured me! I'll never say a cross word to you again!"

The young man had tamed the mother, and he had tamed the daughter! The daughter would do anything he asked her to do. One day when the three of them, he and his two elder brothers, were at home, he said to them:

"You've now got the daughters of big rich men; but I'll wager they won't do what you ask them as well as my wife will for me."

"Yes, they will, they'll do anything we ask them."

"I'll bet a hundred pounds that they won't."

"Right enough," said the other brothers, "we'll bet the same. How are you going to test them?"

"Well, there's a good fire in the room here. Ask your wife to come down and take off her dress and put it in the fire and see if she'll do it."

The eldest brother called for his wife to come down. When she came, she asked him, "What do you want me for?"

"Nothing much. Take off that dress you have on and put it in the fire, so we can see if it'll burn."

"Aye, aye! Haven't you anything better to do than that?" she said, leaving the room.

"Here," he said to his second brother, "you go and get your wife and ask her to do the same thing."

The second brother's wife was sent for, and asked to do the same thing.

"Oh, you should have something better to do than this sort of thing," she said, "you don't know what you're thinking of."

The youngest brother went and brought down his own wife.

"I want you," he said, "to take off that dress you've got on and put it in the fire so we can see how well it burns."

She looked at him. "Indeed," she said, "it cost too much for me to go and burn it in front of you."

"Won't you do it at all?" he said.

"Oh, of course, if it pleases you; I'll do anything to please you." She took off her dress and put it on the fire.

"Very good," he said, "you'll get a much better dress than that." He turned to his brothers:

"Who's right now?" he said. "Pay me the hundred pounds!" He took a hundred pounds from each of his brothers, neither of whose wives would do for them what the daughter of a bad mother did for him!

LORD FOR A DAY

Anonymous Ballad

The Frolicksome Duke:
Or, The Tinker's Good Fortune[*]

Now as famed as report, a young duke keeps a court,
One that pleases his fancy with frolicsome sport:
Now amongst all the rest, here is one I protest,
Which make you to smile when you hear the true jest:
A poor tinker he found, lying drunk on the ground,
As secure in a sleep as if laid in a shroud.

The duke said to his men, "William, Richard, and Ben,
Take him home to my palace, We'll sport with him then";
O'er a horse he was laid, and with care soon conveyed
To the palace, although he was poorly arrayed;
Then they stripped off his clothes, both his shirt, shoes,
    and hose
And they put him to bed for to take his repose.

Having pulled off his shirt, which was all over dirt,
They did give him clean holland,[†] this was no great hurt;
On a bed of soft down, like a lord of renown,
They did lay him to sleep the drink out of his crown;
In the morning when day, he admiring lay
For to see the rich chamber both gaudy and gay.

---

[*] Magdalene College Pepys Ballads 4.235, EBBA 21895, in *English Broadside Ballad Archive*, ed. Patricia Fumerton, http://ebba.english.ucsb.edu/ballad /21895/xml (accessed April 25, 2017). Date published: 1664–1703? I have modernized the spelling and punctuation.

[†] Linen clothing.

Now he lay something late, in his rich bed of state,
Till at last knights and squires, they on him did wait;
And the chamberlain bare,* then did likewise declare,
He desired to know what apparel he'd wear:
The poor tinker amazed, on the gentleman gazed.
And admired how he to this honor was raised.

Though he seemed something mute, yet he chose a
    rich suit,
Which he straightways put on without longer dispute;
With a star on his side, which the tinker oft eyed,
And it seemed for to swell him a little with pride;
For he said to himself, "Where is Joan my sweet wife?
Sure she never did see me so fine in her life!"

From a convenient place, the right duke his good grace
Did observe his behavior in every case;
To a garden of state, on the tinker they wait,
Trumpets sounding before him, thought he, this is great,
Where on horses or two, pleasant walks he did view,
With commanders and squires in scarlet and blue.

A fine dinner was dressed, both for him and his guest,
He was placed at the table above all the rest,
In a rich chair of state, lined with fine crimson red,
With a rich golden canopy over his head;
As he sat at his meat, the music played sweet,
With the choicest of singing his joys to complete.

While the tinker did dine, he had plenty of wine,
Rich canary with sherry, and tent† superfine;

---

* Bare-headed as a sign of respect.
† A Spanish red wine.

Like a right honest soul, faith, he took off his bowl,[*]
Till at last he began for to tumble and roll
From his chair to the floor, where he sleeping did snore
Being seven times drunker than ever before.

Then the duke did ordain, they should strip him amain,[†]
And restore him his old leather garments again;
'Twas a point next the worst, yet perform it they must,
And they carried him straight where they found him at first
Then he slept all the night, as indeed well he might,
But when he did awaken his joys took their flight.

For the height of his glory so pleasant did seem,
That he thought it to be but a mere golden dream,
Till at length being brought, to the duke where he sought
For a pardon, as fearing he had set them at naught:[‡]
But his Highness he said, "Thou'rt a jolly bold blade,
Such a frolic before I think never was played."

Then his highness bespoke him a new suit and a cloak,
Which he gave for the sake of this frolicsome joke,
Nay, and five hundred pound, with ten acres of ground
"Thou shalt never," said he, "range the countries round,
Crying old brass to mend, for I'll be thy good friend,
Nay, and Joan thy sweet wife shall my duchess attend."

Then the tinker replied, "What, must Joan my sweet bride
Be a lady, in chariots of pleasure to ride?
Must we have gold and land, every day at command?
Then I shall be a squire I well understand.

[*] Drank up his bowl of wine.
[†] With force.
[‡] Disrespected them.

Well, I thank your good grace, and your love I embrace,
I was never before in so happy a case."

From *The Thousand and One Nights,*
*Translated by John Payne**

Asleep and Awake†

There was once [at Baghdad], in the Khalifate of Haroun er Reshid,
a man, a merchant, who had a son by name Aboulhusn el Khelia.‡
The merchant died and left his son great store of wealth, which he
divided into two parts, one of which he laid up, and spent of the
other half; and he fell to companying with Persians§ and with the
sons of the merchants and gave himself up to good eating and good
drinking, till all that he had with him of wealth¶ was wasted and
gone; whereupon he betook himself to his friends and comrades

*John Payne, *Tales from the Arabic of the Breslau and Calcutta (1814–18) Editions
of the Book of the Thousand Nights and One Night Not Occurring in the Other Printed
Texts of the Work*, 3 vols. (London, 1884), 1.5–31, https://babel.hathitrust.org/cgi
/pt?id=hvd.hn52pv;view=1up;seq=17 (accessed April 20, 2017). The story con-
tinues with another narrative about Aboulhusn and his wife until p. 42. The notes
that follow are Payne's.

† Breslau Text, vol. iv, pp. 134–89, Nights cclxxii–ccxci. This is the story familiar
to readers of the old *Arabian Nights* as "Abou Hassan, or the Sleeper Awakened"
and is the only one of the eleven tales added by Galland to his version of the
(incomplete) *MS. of the Book of the Thousand Nights and One Night* procured by
him from Syria, the Arabic original of which has not yet been discovered. (See my
Book of the Thousand Nights and One Night, vol. IX, pp. 264 et seq.) The preceding
title is of course intended to mark the contrast between the everyday (or waking)
hours of Aboulhusn and his fantastic life in the Khalifa palace, supposed by him
to have passed in a dream, and may also be rendered "The Sleeper and the Waker."

‡ That is, "the Wag."

§ Always noted for debauchery.

¶ That is, the part he had taken for spending money.

and boon-companions and expounded to them his case, discovering to them the failure of that which was in his hand of wealth; but not one of them took heed of him neither inclined unto him.

So he returned to his mother (and indeed his spirit was broken), and related to her that which had happened to him and what had betided him from his friends, how they had neither shared with him nor requited him with speech. "O Aboulhusn," answered she, "on this wise are the sons* of this time: if thou have aught, they make much of thee,† and if thou have nought, they put thee away [from them]." And she went on to condole with him, what while he bewailed himself and his tears flowed and he repeated the following verses:

> An if my substance fail, no one there is will succor me,
>   But if my wealth abound, of all I'm held in amity.
> How many a friend, for money's sake, hath companied
>   with me!
>   How many an one, with loss of wealth, hath turned mine
>   enemy!

Then he sprang up [and going] to the place wherein was the other half of his good, [took it] and lived with it well; and he swore that he would never again consort with those whom he knew, but would company only with the stranger nor entertain him but one night and that, whenas it morrowed, he would never know him more. So he fell to sitting every night on the bridge‡ and looking on every one who passed by him; and if he saw him to be a stranger, he made friends with him and carried him to his house, where he caroused with him till the morning. Then he dismissed him and

---

* That is, "those," a characteristic Arab idiom.
† Literally, draw thee near [to them].
‡ That is, that over the Tigris.

would never more salute him nor ever again drew near unto him neither invited him.

On this wise he continued to do for the space of a whole year, till, one day, as he sat on the bridge, according to his custom, expecting who should come to him, so he might take him and pass the night with him, behold, [up came] the Khalif and Mesrour, the swordsman of his vengeance, disguised [in merchants' habits] as of their wont. So he looked at them and rising up, for that he knew them not, said to them, "What say ye? Will you go with me to my dwelling-place, so ye may eat what is ready and drink what is at hand, to wit, bread baked in the platter* and meat cooked and wine clarified?" The Khalif refused this, but he conjured him and said to him, "God on thee, O my lord, go with me, for thou art my guest this night, and disappoint not my expectation concerning thee!" And he ceased not to press him till he consented to him; whereat Aboulhusn rejoiced and going on before him, gave not over talking with him till they came to his [house and he carried the Khalif into the] saloon. Er Reshid entered and made his servant abide at the door; and as soon as he was seated, Aboulhusn brought him somewhat to eat; so he ate, and Aboulhusn ate with him, so eating might be pleasant to him. Then he removed the tray and they washed their hands and the Khalif sat down again; whereupon Aboulhusn set on the drinking vessels and seating himself by his side, fell to filling and giving him to drink and entertaining him with discourse.

His hospitality pleased the Khalif and the goodliness of his fashion, and he said to him, "O youth, who art thou? Make me acquainted with thyself, so I may requite thee thy kindness." But Aboulhusn smiled and said, "O my lord, far be it that what is past

---

* "Platter bread," that is, bread baked in a platter, instead of, as usual with the Arabs, in an oven or earthen jar previously heated, to the sides of which the thin cakes of dough are applied, "is lighter than oven-bread, especially if it be made thin and leavened."—Shecouri, a medical writer quoted by Dozy.

should recur and that I be in company with thee at other than this time!" "Why so?" asked the Khalif. "And why will thou not acquaint me with thy case?" And Aboulhusn said, "Know, O my lord, that my story is extraordinary and that there is a cause for this affair." Quoth the Khalif, "And what is the cause?" And he answered, "The cause hath a tail." The Khalif laughed at his words and Aboulhusn said, "I will explain to thee this [saying] by the story of the lackpenny and the cook. Know, O my lord, that

STORY OF THE LACKPENNY AND THE COOK

One of the good-for-noughts found himself one day without aught and the world was straitened upon him and his patience failed; so he lay down to sleep and gave not over sleeping till the sun burnt him and the foam came out upon his mouth, whereupon he arose, and he was penniless and had not so much as one dirhem. Presently, he came to the shop of a cook, who had set up therein his pans* [over the fire] and wiped his scales and washed his saucers and swept his shop and sprinkled it; and indeed his oils† were clear‡ and his spices fragrant and he himself stood behind his cooking-pots [waiting for custom]. So the lackpenny went up to him and saluting him, said to him, 'Weigh me half a dirhem's worth of meat and a quarter of a dirhem's worth of kouskoussou§ and the like of bread.' So the cook weighed out to him [that which he sought] and the lackpenny entered the shop, whereupon the cook set the food before him and he ate till he had gobbled up the whole

---

* Or cooking-pots.
† Or fats for frying.
‡ Or clarified.
§ *Taam*, literally, "food," the name given by the inhabitants of Northern Africa to the preparation of millet flour (something like semolina) called kouskoussou, which forms the staple food of the people.

and licked the saucers and abode perplexed, knowing not how he should do with the cook concerning the price of that which he had eaten and turning his eyes about upon everything in the shop.

Presently, he caught sight of an earthen pan turned over upon its mouth; so he raised it from the ground and found under it a horse's tail, freshly cut off, and the blood oozing from it; whereby he knew that the cook adulterated his meat with horses' flesh. When he discovered this default, he rejoiced therein and washing his hands, bowed his head and went out; and when the cook saw that he went and gave him nought, he cried out, saying, 'Stay, O sneak, O slink-thief!' So the lackpenny stopped and said to him, 'Dost thou cry out upon me and becall [me] with these words, O cuckold?' Whereat the cook was angry and coming down from the shop, said, 'What meanest thou by thy speech, O thou that devourest meat and kouskoussou and bread and seasoning and goest forth with "Peace* [be on thee!]," as it were the thing had not been, and payest down nought for it?' Quoth the lackpenny, 'Thou liest, O son of a cuckold!' Wherewith the cook cried out and laying hold of the lackpenny's collar, said, 'O Muslims, this fellow is my first customer† this day and he hath eaten my food and given me nought.'

So the folk gathered together to them and blamed the lackpenny and said to him, 'Give him the price of that which thou hast eaten.' Quoth he, 'I gave him a dirhem before I entered the shop'; and the cook said, 'Be everything I sell this day forbidden‡ to me, if he gave me so much as the name of a piece of money! By Allah, he gave me nought, but ate my food and went out and [would have] made off, without aught [said!]' 'Nay,' answered the lackpenny, 'I gave thee a

---

* Or "in peace."

† Eastern peoples attach great importance, for good or evil omen, to the first person met or the first thing that happens in the day.

‡ Or "attributed as sin."

dirhem,' and he reviled the cook, who returned his abuse; whereupon he dealt him a cuff and they gripped and grappled and throttled each other. When the folk saw them on this wise, they came up to them and said to them, 'What is this strife between you, and no cause for it?' 'Ay, by Allah,' replied the lackpenny, 'but there is a cause for it, and the cause hath a tail!' Whereupon, 'Yea, by Allah,' cried the cook, 'now thou mindest me of thyself and thy dirhem! Yes, he gave me a dirhem and [but] a quarter of the price is spent. Come back and take the rest of the price of thy dirhem.'

"For that he understood what was to do, at the mention of the tail; and I, O my brother," added Aboulhusn, "my story hath a cause, which I will tell thee."

The Khalif laughed at his speech and said, "By Allah, this is none other than a pleasant tale! Tell me thy story and the cause." "With all my heart," answered Aboulhusn. "Know, O my lord, that my name is Aboulhusn el Khelia and that my father died and left me wealth galore, of which I made two parts. One I laid up and with the other I betook myself to [the enjoyment of the pleasures of] friendship [and conviviality] and consorting with comrades and boon-companions and with the sons of the merchants, nor did I leave one but I caroused with him and he with me, and I spent all my money on companionship and good cheer, till there remained with me nought [of the first half of my good]; whereupon I betook myself to the comrades and cup-companions upon whom I had wasted my wealth, so haply they might provide for my case; but, when I resorted to them and went round about to them all, I found no avail in one of them, nor broke any so much as a crust of bread in my face. So I wept for myself and repairing to my mother, complained to her of my case. Quoth she, 'On this wise are friends; if thou have aught, they make much of thee and devour thee, but, if thou have nought, they cast thee off and chase thee away.' Then I brought out the other half of my money and bound myself by an oath that I would never more entertain any, except one night, after which I would never again salute him nor take note of him; hence my saying to thee, 'Far be it that what is past should recur!' For that I will never again foregather with thee, after this night."

When the Khalif heard this, he laughed heartily and said, "By Allah, O my brother, thou art indeed excused in this matter, now that I know the cause and that the cause hath a tail. Nevertheless, if it please God, I will not sever myself from thee." "O my guest," replied Aboulhusn, "did I not say to thee, 'Far be it that what is past should recur! For that I will never again fore gather with any'?" Then the Khalif rose and Aboulhusn set before him a dish of roast goose and a cake of manchet-bread and sitting down, fell to cutting off morsels and feeding the Khalif therewith. They gave not over eating thus till they were content, when Aboulhusn brought bowl and ewer and potash* and they washed their hands.

Then he lighted him three candles and three lamps and spreading the drinking-cloth, brought clarified wine, limpid, old, and fragrant, the scent whereof was as that of virgin musk. He filled the first cup and saying, "O my boon-companion, by thy leave, be ceremony laid aside between us! I am thy slave; may I not be afflicted with thy loss!" drank it off and filled a second cup, which he handed to the Khalif, with a reverence. His fashion pleased the Khalif and the goodliness of his speech and he said in himself, "By Allah, I will assuredly requite him for this!" Then Aboulhusn filled the cup again and handed it to the Khalif, reciting the following verses:

Had we thy coming known, we would for sacrifice
    Have poured thee out heart's blood or blackness of the
        eyes;

---

*A common Eastern substitute for soap.

Ay, and we would have spread our bosoms in thy way,
> That so thy feet might fare on eyelids, carpet-wise.

When the Khalif heard his verses, he took the cup from his hand and kissed it and drank it off and returned it to Aboulhusn, who made him an obeisance and filled and drank. Then he filled again and kissing the cup thrice, recited the following verses:

Thy presence honoreth us and we
> Confess thy magnanimity;
If thou forsake us, there is none
> Can stand to us instead of thee.

Then he gave the cup to the Khalif, saying, "Drink [and may] health and soundness [attend it]! It doth away disease and bringeth healing and setteth the runnels of health abroach."

They gave not over drinking and carousing till the middle of the night, when the Khalif said to his host, "O my brother, hast thou in thy heart a wish thou wouldst have accomplished or a regret thou wouldst fain do away?" "By Allah," answered he, "there is no regret in my heart save that I am not gifted with dominion and the power of commandment and prohibition, so I might do what is in my mind!" Quoth the Khalif, "For God's sake, O my brother, tell me what is in thy mind!" And Aboulhusn said, "I would to God I might avenge myself on my neighbors, for that in my neighborhood is a mosque and therein four sheikhs, who take it ill, whenas there cometh a guest to me, and vex me with talk and molest me in words and threaten me that they will complain of me to the Commander of the Faithful, and indeed they oppress me sore, and I crave of God the Most High one day's dominion, that I may beat each of them with four hundred lashes, as well as the Imam of the mosque, and parade them about the city of Baghdad and let call before them, 'This is the reward and the least of the reward of whoso exceedeth [in talk] and spiteth the folk and troubleth on them their joys.' This is what I wish and no more."

Quoth the Khalif, "God grant thee that thou seekest! Let us drink one last cup and rise before the dawn draw near, and tomorrow night I will be with thee again." "Far be it!" said Aboulhusn. Then the Khalif filled a cup and putting therein a piece of Cretan henbane, gave it to his host and said to him, "My life on thee, O my brother, drink this cup from my hand!" "Ay, by thy life," answered Aboulhusn, "I will drink it from thy hand." So he took it and drank it off; but hardly had he done so, when his head forewent his feet and he fell to the ground like a slain man; whereupon the Khalif went out and said to his servant Mesrour, "Go in to yonder young man, the master of the house, and take him up and bring him to me at the palace; and when thou goest out, shut the door."

So saying, he went away, whilst Mesrour entered and taking up Aboulhusn, shut the door after him, and followed his master, till he reached the palace, what while the night drew to an end and the cocks cried out, and set him down before the Commander of the Faithful, who laughed at him. Then he sent for Jaafer the Barmecide and when he came before him, he said to him, "Note this young man and when thou seest him tomorrow seated in my place of estate and on the throne of my Khalifate and clad in my habit, stand thou in attendance upon him and enjoin the Amirs and grandees and the people of my household and the officers of my realm to do the like and obey him in that which he shall command them; and thou, if he bespeak thee of anything, do it and hearken unto him and gainsay him not in aught in this coming day." Jaafer answered with, "Hearkening and obedience,"* and withdrew, whilst the Kha-

---

*This common formula of assent is an abbreviation of "Hearkening and obedience are due to God and to the Commander of the Faithful" or the other person addressed.

lif went in to the women of the palace, who came to him, and he said to them, "Whenas yonder sleeper awaketh tomorrow from his sleep, kiss ye the earth before him and make obeisance to him and come round about him and clothe him in the [royal] habit and do him the service of the Khalifate and deny not aught of his estate, but say to him, 'Thou art the Khalif.' " Then he taught them what they should say to him and how they should do with him and withdrawing to a privy place, let down a curtain before himself and slept.

Meanwhile, Aboulhusn gave not over snoring in his sleep, till the day broke and the rising of the sun drew near, when a waiting-woman came up to him and said to him, "O our lord [it is the hour of] the morning prayer." When he heard the girl's words, he laughed and opening his eyes, turned them about the place and found himself in an apartment the walls whereof were painted with gold and ultramarine and its ceiling starred with red gold. Around it were sleeping-chambers, with curtains of gold-embroidered silk let down over their doors, and all about vessels of gold and porcelain and crystal and furniture and carpets spread and lamps burning before the prayer-niche and slave-girls and eunuchs and white slaves and black slaves and boys and pages and attendants. When he saw this, he was confounded in his wit and said, "By Allah, either I am dreaming, or this is Paradise and the Abode of Peace!"* And he shut his eyes and went to sleep again. Quoth the waiting-woman, "O my lord, this is not of thy wont, O Commander of the Faithful!"

Then the rest of the women of the palace came all to him and lifted him into a sitting posture, when he found himself upon a couch, stuffed all with floss-silk and raised a cubit's height from the

* *Dar es Selam,* one of the seven "Gardens" into which the Mohammedan Paradise is divided.

ground.* So they seated him upon it and propped him up with a pillow, and he looked at the apartment and its greatness and saw those eunuchs and slave-girls in attendance upon him and at his head, whereat he laughed at himself and said, "By Allah, it is not as I were on wake, and [yet] I am not asleep!" Then he arose and sat up, whilst the damsels laughed at him and hid [their laughter] from him; and he was confounded in his wit and bit upon his finger. The bite hurt him, and he cried "Oh!" and was vexed; and the Khalif watched him, whence he saw him not, and laughed.

Presently Aboulhusn turned to a damsel and called to her; whereupon she came to him and he said to her, "By the protection of God, O damsel, am I Commander of the Faithful?" "Yes, indeed," answered she; "by the protection of God thou in this time art Commander of the Faithful." Quoth he, "By Allah, thou liest, O thousandfold strumpet!" Then he turned to the chief eunuch and called to him, whereupon he came to him and kissing the earth before him, said, "Yes, O Commander of the Faithful." "Who is Commander of the Faithful?" asked Aboulhusn. "Thou," replied the eunuch, and Aboulhusn said, "Thou liest, thousandfold catamite that thou art!" Then he turned to another eunuch and said to him, "O my chief,† by the protection of God, am I Commander of the Faithful?" "Ay, by Allah, O my lord!" answered he. "Thou in this time art Commander of the Faithful and Vicar of the Lord of the Worlds." Aboulhusn laughed at himself and misdoubted of his reason and was perplexed at what he saw and said, "In one night I am become Khalif! Yesterday I was Aboulhusn the Wag, and today I am Commander of the Faithful." Then the chief eunuch came up to him and said, "O Commander of the Faithful (the name of God encompass thee!), thou art indeed Commander of the Faithful

---

* That is, a mattress eighteen inches thick.

† Complimentary form of address to eunuchs, generally used by inferiors only.

and Vicar of the Lord of the Worlds!" And the slave-girls and eunuchs came round about him, till he arose and abode wondering at his case.

Presently, one of the slave-girls brought him a pair of sandals wrought with raw silk and green silk and embroidered with red gold, and he took them and put them in his sleeve, whereat the slave cried out and said, "Allah! Allah! O my lord, these are sandals for the treading of thy feet, so thou mayst enter the draft-house." Aboulhusn was confounded and shaking the sandals from his sleeve, put them on his feet, whilst the Khalif [well-nigh] died of laughter at him. The slave forewent him to the house of easance, where he entered and doing his occasion, came out into the chamber, whereupon the slave-girls brought him a basin of gold and an ewer of silver and poured water on his hands and he made the ablution.

Then they spread him a prayer-carpet and he prayed. Now he knew not how to pray and gave not over bowing and prostrating himself, [till he had prayed the prayers] of twenty inclinations,* pondering in himself the while and saying, "By Allah, I am none other than the Commander of the Faithful in very sooth! This is assuredly no dream, for all these things happen not in a dream." And he was convinced and determined in himself that he was Commander of the Faithful; so he pronounced the Salutation† and made an end‡ of his prayers; whereupon the slaves and slave-girls came round about him with parcels of silk and stuffs§ and clad him

* The morning prayer consists of four inclinations (*rekäat*) only. A certain fixed succession of prayers and acts of adoration is called a *rekah* (singular of *rekäat*) from the inclination of the body that occurs in it.
† That is, the terminal formula of prayer, "Peace be on us and on all the righteous servants of God!"
‡ That is, said "I purpose to make an end of prayer."
§ Or "linen."

in the habit of the Khalifate and gave him the royal dagger in his hand. Then the chief eunuch went out before him and the little white slaves behind him, and they ceased not [going] till they raised the curtain and brought him into the hall of judgment and the throne-room of the Khalifate. There he saw the curtains and the forty doors and El Ijli and Er Recashi* and Ibdan and Jedim and Abou Ishac† the boon-companions and beheld swords drawn and lions‡ encompassing [the throne] and gilded glaives and death-dealing bows and Persians and Arabs and Turks and Medes and folk and peoples and Amirs and viziers and captains and grandees and officers of state and men of war, and indeed there appeared the puissance of the house of Abbas§ and the majesty of the family of the Prophet.

So he sat down upon the throne of the Khalifate and laid the dagger in his lap, whereupon all [present] came up to kiss the earth before him and called down on him length of life and continuance [of glory and prosperity]. Then came forward Jaafer the Barmecide and kissing the earth, said, "May the wide world of God be the treading of thy feet and may Paradise be thy dwelling-place and the fire the habitation of thine enemies! May no neighbor transgress against thee nor the lights of fire die out for thee,¶ O Khalif of [all] cities and ruler of [all] countries!"

Therewithal Aboulhusn cried out at him and said, "O dog of the sons of Bermek, go down forthright, thou and the master of the police of the city, to such a place in such a street and deliver a hun-

---

* A well-known poet of the time.

† That is, Ibrahim of Mosul, the greatest musician of his day.

‡ That is, doughty men of war, guards.

§ The Abbaside Khalifs traced their descent from Abbas, the uncle of Mohammed, and considered themselves, therefore, as belonging to the family of the Prophet.

¶ That is, "May thy dwelling-place never fall into ruin."

dred dinars to the mother of Aboulhusn the Wag and bear her my
salutation. [Then, go to such a mosque] and take the four sheikhs
and the Imam and beat each of them with four hundred lashes and
mount them on beasts, face to tail, and go round with them about
all the city and banish them to a place other than the city; and bid
the crier make proclamation before them, saying, 'This is the reward and the least of the reward of whoso multiplieth words and
molesteth his neighbors and stinteth them of their delights and
their eating and drinking!'" Jaafer received the order [with submis-
sion] and answered with ["Hearkening and] obedience"; after
which he went down from before Aboulhusn to the city and did
that whereunto he had bidden him.

Meanwhile, Aboulhusn abode in the Khalifate, taking and giving, ordering and forbidding and giving effect to his word, till the
end of the day, when he gave [those who were present] leave and
permission [to withdraw], and the Amirs and officers of state departed to their occasions. Then the eunuchs came to him and calling down on him length of life and continuance [of glory and pros-
perity], walked in attendance upon him and raised the curtain, and
he entered the pavilion of the harem, where he found candles
lighted and lamps burning and singing-women smiting [on instruments of music]. When he saw this, he was confounded in his wit
and said in himself, "By Allah, I am in truth Commander of the
Faithful!" As soon as he appeared, the slave-girls rose to him and
carrying him up on to the estrade,* brought him a great table,
spread with the richest meats. So he ate thereof with all his might,
till he had gotten his fill, when he called one of the slave-girls and
said to her, "What is thy name?" "My name is Miskeh," replied she,
and he said to another, "What is thy name?" Quoth she, "My name

---

* That is, the raised recess situated at the upper end of an Oriental saloon,
wherein is the place of honor.

is Terkeh." Then said he to a third, "What is thy name?" "My name is Tuhfeh," answered she; and he went on to question the damsels of their names, one after another [till he had made the round of them all], when he rose from that place and removed to the wine-chamber.

He found it every way complete and saw therein ten great trays, full of all fruits and cakes and all manner sweetmeats. So he sat down and ate thereof after the measure of his sufficiency, and finding there three troops of singing-girls, was amazed and made the girls eat. Then he sat and the singers also seated themselves, whilst the black slaves and the white slaves and the eunuchs and pages and boys stood, and the slave-girls, some of them, sat and some stood. The damsels sang and warbled all manner melodies and the place answered them for the sweetness of the songs, whilst the pipes cried out and the lutes made accord with them, till it seemed to Aboulhusn that he was in Paradise and his heart was cheered and his breast dilated. So he sported and joyance waxed on him and he bestowed dresses of honor on the damsels and gave and bestowed, challenging this one and kissing that and toying with a third, plying one with wine and another with meat, till the night fell down.

All this while the Khalif was diverting himself with watching him and laughing, and at nightfall he bade one of the slave-girls drop a piece of henbane in the cup and give it to Aboulhusn to drink. So she did as he bade her and gave Aboulhusn the cup, whereof no sooner had he drunken than his head forewent his feet [and he fell down, senseless]. Therewith the Khalif came forth from behind the curtain, laughing, and calling to the servant who had brought Aboulhusn to the palace, said to him, "Carry this fellow to his own place." So Mesrour took him up [and carrying him to his own house], set him down in the saloon. Then he went forth from him and shutting the saloon-door upon him, returned to the Khalif, who slept till the morrow.

As for Aboulhusn, he gave not over sleeping till God the Most High brought on the morning, when he awoke, crying out and saying, "Ho, Tuffaheh! Ho, Rahet el Culoub! Ho, Miskeh! Ho, Tuhfeh!" And he gave not over calling upon the slave-girls till his mother heard him calling upon strange damsels and rising, came to him and said, "The name of God encompass thee! Arise, O my son, O Aboulhusn! Thou dreamest." So he opened his eyes and finding an old woman at his head, raised his eyes and said to her, "Who art thou?" Quoth she, "I am thy mother;" and he answered, "Thou liest! I am the Commander of the Faithful, the Vicar of God." Whereupon his mother cried out and said to him, "God preserve thy reason! Be silent, O my son, and cause not the loss of our lives and the spoiling of thy wealth, [as will assuredly betide,] if any hear this talk and carry it to the Khalif."

So he rose from his sleep and finding himself in his own saloon and his mother by him, misdoubted of his wit and said to her, "By Allah, O my mother, I saw myself in a dream in a palace, with slave-girls and servants about me and in attendance upon me, and I sat upon the throne of the Khalifate and ruled. By Allah, O my mother, this is what I saw, and verily it was not a dream!" Then he bethought himself awhile and said, "Assuredly, I am Aboulhusn el Khelia, and this that I saw was only a dream, and [it was in a dream that] I was made Khalif and commanded and forbade." Then he bethought himself again and said, "Nay, but it was no dream and I am no other than the Khalif, and indeed I gave gifts and bestowed dresses of honor." Quoth his mother to him, "O my son, thou sportest with thy reason: thou wilt go to the hospital and become a gazing-stock. Indeed, that which thou hast seen is only from the Devil and it was a delusion of dreams, for whiles Satan sporteth with men's wits in all manner ways."

Then said she to him, "O my son, was there any one with thee yesternight?" And he bethought himself and said, "Yes; one lay the night with me and I acquainted him with my case and told him my story. Doubtless, he was from the Devil, and I, O my mother, even as thou sayst truly, am Aboulhusn el Khelia." "O my son," rejoined she, "rejoice in tidings of all good, for yesterday's record is that there came the Vizier Jaafer the Barmecide [and his company] and beat the sheikhs of the mosque and the Imam, each four hundred lashes; after which they paraded them about the city, making proclamation before them and saying, 'This is the reward and the least of the reward of whoso lacketh of goodwill to his neighbors and troubleth on them their lives!' and banished them from Baghdad. Moreover, the Khalif sent me a hundred dinars and sent to salute me." Whereupon Aboulhusn cried out and said to her, "O old woman of ill-omen, wilt thou contradict me and tell me that I am not the Commander of the Faithful? It was I who commanded Jaafer the Barmecide to beat the sheikhs and parade them about the city and make proclamation before them and who sent thee the hundred dinars and sent to salute thee, and I, O beldam of ill-luck, am in very deed the Commander of the Faithful, and thou art a liar, who would make me out a dotard."

So saying, he fell upon her and beat her with a staff of almond-wood, till she cried out, "[Help], O Muslims!" and he redoubled the beating upon her, till the folk heard her cries and coming to her, [found] Aboulhusn beating her and saying to her, "O old woman of ill-omen, am I not the Commander of the Faithful? Thou hast enchanted me!" When the folk heard his words, they said, "This man raveth," and doubted not of his madness. So they came in upon him and seizing him, pinioned him and carried him to the hospital. Quoth the superintendent, "What aileth this youth?" And they said, "This is a madman." "By Allah," cried Aboulhusn, "they lie against me! I am no madman, but the Commander of the Faithful." And the superintendent answered him, saying, "None lieth but thou, O unluckiest of madmen!"

Then he stripped him of his clothes and clapping on his neck a heavy chain, bound him to a high lattice and fell to drubbing him two bouts a day and two anights; and on this wise he abode the space of ten days. Then his mother came to him and said, "O my son, O Aboulhusn, return to thy reason, for this is the Devil's doing." Quoth he, "Thou sayst sooth, O my mother, and bear thou witness of me that I repent [and forswear] that talk and turn from my madness. So do thou deliver me, for I am nigh upon death." So his mother went out to the superintendent and procured his release and he returned to his own house.

Now this was at the beginning of the month, and when it was the end thereof, Aboulhusn longed to drink wine and returning to his former usance, furnished his saloon and made ready food and let bring wine; then, going forth to the bridge, he sat there, expecting one whom he should carouse withal, as of his wont. As he sat thus, behold, up came the Khalif [and Mesrour] to him; but Aboulhusn saluted them not and said to them, "No welcome and no greeting to the perverters!* Ye are no other than devils." However, the Khalif accosted him and said to him, "O my brother, did I not say to thee that I would return to thee?" Quoth Aboulhusn, "I have no need of thee; and as the byword says in verse:

'Twere fitter and better my loves that I leave,
For, if the eye see not, the heart will not grieve.

And indeed, O my brother, the night thou camest to me and we caroused together, I and thou, it was as if the Devil came to me and troubled me that night." "And who is he, the Devil?" asked the Khalif. "He is none other than thou," answered Aboulhusn; whereat the Khalif smiled and sitting down by him, coaxed him and spoke him fair, saying, "O my brother, when I went out from thee, I forgot [to

* That is, the necromancers.

shut] the door [and left it] open, and belike Satan came in to thee." Quoth Aboulhusn, "Ask me not of that which hath betided me. What possessed thee to leave the door open, so that the Devil came in to me and there befell me with him this and that?" And he related to him all that had befallen him, from first to last, and there is no advantage in the repetition of it; what while the Khalif laughed and hid his laughter.

Then said he to Aboulhusn, "Praised be God who hath done away from thee that which irked thee and that I see thee in weal!" And Aboulhusn said, "Never again will I take thee to boon-companion or sitting-mate; for the byword saith, 'Whoso stumbleth on a stone and returneth thereto, blame and reproach be upon him.' And thou, O my brother, nevermore will I entertain thee nor use companionship with thee, for that I have not found thy commerce propitious to me."* But the Khalif blandished him and conjured him, redoubling words upon him with "Verily, I am thy guest; reject not the guest," till Aboulhusn took him and [carrying him home], brought him into the saloon and set food before him and friendly entreated him in speech. Then he told him all that had befallen him, whilst the Khalif was like to die of hidden laughter; after which Aboulhusn removed the tray of food and bringing the wine-tray, filled a cup and emptied it out three times, then gave it to the Khalif, saying, "O boon-companion mine, I am thy slave and let not that which I am about to say irk thee, and be thou not vexed, neither do thou vex me." And he recited these verses:

No good's in life (to the counsel list of one who's
  purpose-whole),
    An if thou be not drunken still and gladden not thy soul.

---

* Literally, "I have not found that thou hast a heel blessed (or propitious) to me."

Ay, ne'er will I leave to drink of wine, what while the night
   on me
   Darkens, till drowsiness bow down my head upon my
      bowl.
In wine, as the glittering sunbeams bright, my heart's
   contentment is,
   That banishes hence, with various joys, all kinds of care
      and dole.

When the Khalif heard these his verses, he was moved to ex-
ceeding delight and taking the cup, drank it off, and they ceased not
to drink and carouse till the wine rose to their heads. Then said
Aboulhusn to the Khalif, "O boon-companion mine, of a truth I
am perplexed concerning my affair, for meseemed I was Commander of the Faithful and ruled and gave gifts and largesse, and in
very deed, O my brother, it was not a dream." "These were the delusions of sleep," answered the Khalif and crumbling a piece of henbane into the cup, said to him, "By my life, do thou drink this cup."
And Aboulhusn said, "Surely I will drink it from thy hand." Then
he took the cup from the Khalif's hand and drank it off, and no
sooner had it settled in his belly than his head forewent his feet
[and he fell down senseless].

Now his parts and fashions pleased the Khalif and the excellence
of his composition and his frankness, and he said in himself, "I will
assuredly make him my cup-companion and sitting-mate." So he
rose forthright and saying to Mesrour, "Take him up," [returned to
the palace]. Accordingly, Mesrour took up Aboulhusn and carrying
him to the palace of the Khalifate, set him down before Er Reshid,
who bade the slaves and slave-girls encompass him about, whilst
he himself hid in a place where Aboulhusn could not see him.

Then he commanded one of the slave-girls to take the lute and
strike it at Aboulhusn's head, whilst the rest smote upon their

instruments. [So they played and sang,] till Aboulhusn awoke at the last of the night and heard the noise of lutes and tabrets and the sound of the pipes and the singing of the slave-girls, whereupon he opened his eyes and finding himself in the palace, with the slave-girls and eunuchs about him, exclaimed, "There is no power and no virtue but in God the Most High, the Supreme! Verily, I am fearful of the hospital and of that which I suffered therein aforetime, and I doubt not but the Devil is come to me again, as before. O my God, put thou Satan to shame!" Then he shut his eyes and laid his head in his sleeve and fell to laughing softly and raising his head [bytimes], but [still] found the apartment lighted and the girls singing.

Presently, one of the eunuchs sat down at his head and said to him, "Sit up, O Commander of the Faithful, and look on thy palace and thy slave-girls." Quoth Aboulhusn, "By the protection of God, am I in truth Commander of the Faithful and dost thou not lie? Yesterday, I went not forth neither ruled, but drank and slept, and this eunuch cometh to rouse me up." Then he sat up and bethought himself of that which had betided him with his mother and how he had beaten her and entered the hospital, and he saw the marks of the beating, where withal the superintendent of the hospital had beaten him, and was perplexed concerning his affair and pondered in himself, saying, "By Allah, I know not how my case is nor what is this that betideth me!"

Then he turned to a damsel of the damsels and said to her, "Who am I?" Quoth she, "Thou art the Commander of the Faithful;" and he said, "Thou liest, O calamity!* If I be indeed the Commander of the Faithful, bite my finger." So she came to him and bit it with her might, and he said to her, "It sufficeth." Then he said to the chief eunuch, "Who am I?" And he answered, "Thou art the Commander

---

* That is, "O thou who art a calamity to those who have to do with thee!"

of the Faithful." So he left him and turning to a little white slave, said to him, "Bite my ear"; and he bent down to him and put his ear to his mouth. Now the slave was young and lacked understanding; so he closed his teeth upon Aboulhusn's ear with his might, till he came near to sever it; and he knew not Arabic, so, as often as Aboulhusn said to him, "It sufficeth," he concluded that he said, "Bite harder," and redoubled his bite and clenched his teeth upon the ear, whilst the damsels were diverted from him with hearkening to the singing-girls, and Aboulhusn cried out for succor from the boy and the Khalif [well-nigh] lost his senses for laughter.

Then he dealt the boy a cuff and he let go his ear, whereupon Aboulhusn put off his clothes and abode naked, with his yard and his arse exposed, and danced among the slave-girls. They bound his hands and he wantoned among them, what while they [well-nigh] died of laughing at him and the Khalif swooned away for excess of laughter. Then he came to himself and going forth to Aboulhusn, said to him, "Out on thee, O Aboulhusn! Thou slayest me with laughter." So he turned to him and knowing him, said to him, "By Allah, it is thou slayest me and slayest my mother and slewest the sheikhs and the Imam of the Mosque!"

Then the Khalif took him into his especial favor and married him and bestowed largesse on him and lodged him with himself in the palace and made him of the chief of his boon-companions, and indeed he was preferred with him above them and the Khalif advanced him over them all. Now they were ten in number, to wit, El Ijli and Er Recashi and Ibdan and Hassan el Feresdec and El Lauz and Es Seker and Omar et Tertis and Abou Nuwas* and Abou Ishac en Nedim and Aboulhusn el Khelia, and by each of them hangeth a story that is told in other than this book. And indeed Aboulhusn became high in honor with the Khalif and favored above all, so that

* Abou Nuwas ibn Hani, the greatest poet of the time.

he sat with him and the Lady Zubeideh bint el Casim and married the latter's treasuress, whose name was Nuzhet el Fuad.

THE WICKED QUEEN REFORMED BY WHIPPING BY A COBBLER

Rachel Harriette Busk

The Queen and the Tripe-Seller[*]

They say there was a queen who had such a bad temper that she made everybody about her miserable. Whatever her husband might do to please her, she was always discontented, and as for her maids she was always slapping their faces.

There was a fairy who saw all this, and she said to herself, "This must not be allowed to go on"; so she went and called another fairy, and said, "What shall we do to teach this naughty queen to behave herself?" and they could not imagine what to do with her; so they agreed to think it over, and meet again another day.

When they met again, the first fairy said to the other, "Well, have you found any plan for correcting this naughty queen?"

"Yes," replied the second fairy; "I have found an excellent plan. I have been up and all over the whole town, and in a little dirty back lane I have found a tripe-seller as like to this queen as two peas."

"Excellent!" exclaimed the first fairy. "I see what you mean to do. One of us will take some of the queen's clothes and dress up the

---

[*]Rachel Harriette Busk, *The Folk-lore of Rome* (London: Longmans, Green, 1874), 348–54, https://babel.hathitrust.org/cgi/pt?id=hvd.32044024331308 ;view=1up;seq=380 (accessed April 19, 2017).

tripe-seller, and the other will take some of the tripe-seller's clothes and dress up the queen in them, and then we will exchange them till the queen learns better manners."

"That's the plan," replied the second fairy. "You have said it exactly. When shall we begin?"

"This very night," said the first fairy.

"Agreed!" said the second fairy; and that very night, while everyone else was gone quietly to bed they went, one into the palace and fetched some of the queen's clothes, and, bringing them to the tripe-seller's room, placed them by the side of her bed; and the other went to the tripe-seller's room and fetched her clothes, and took them and put them by the side of the queen's bed. They also woke them very early, and when each got up she put on the things that were by the side of the bed, thinking they were the things she had left there the night before. Thus the queen was dressed like a tripe-seller, and the tripe-seller like a queen.

Then one fairy took the queen, dressed like a tripe-seller, and put her down in the tripe-seller's shop, and the other fairy took the tripe-seller, dressed like a queen, and placed her in the palace, and both of them did their work so swiftly that neither the queen nor the tripe-seller perceived the flight at all.

The queen was very much astonished at finding herself in a tripe-shop, and began staring about, wondering how she got there.

"Here! Don't stand gaping about like that!" cried the tripe-man, who was a very hot-tempered fellow; "Why, you haven't boiled the coffee!"

"Boiled the coffee!" repeated the queen, hardly apprehending what he meant.

"Yes; you haven't boiled the coffee!" said the tripe-man. "Don't repeat my words, but do your work!" and he took her by the shoulders, put the coffee-pot in her hand, and stood over her looking so fierce that she was frightened into doing what she had never done or seen done in all her life before.

Presently the coffee began to boil over.

"There! Don't waste all the coffee like that!" cried the tripe-man, and he got up and gave her a slap, which made the tears come in her eyes.

"Don't blubber!" said the tripe-man; "but bring the coffee here and pour it out."

The queen did as she was told; but when she began to drink it, though she had made it herself, it was so nasty she didn't know how to drink it. It was very different stuff from what she got at the palace; but the tripe-man had his eye on her, and she didn't dare not to drink it.

"A halfp'th of cat's-meat!" sang out a small boy in the shop.

"Why don't you go and serve the customer?" said the tripe-man, knocking the cup out of the queen's hand. Fearing another slap, she rose hastily to give the boy what he wanted, but not knowing one thing in the shop from another, she gave him a large piece of the best tripe fit for a prince.

"Oh, what fine tripe today!" cried the small boy, and ran away as fast as he could.

It was in vain the tripe-man halloed after him; he was in too great a hurry to secure his prize to think of returning.

"Look what you've done!" cried the tripe-man, giving the queen another slap; "you've given that boy for a penny a bunch of tripe worth a shilling." Luckily, other customers came in and diverted the man's attention.

Presently all the tripe hanging up had been sold, and more customers kept coming in.

"What has come to you, today!" roared the tripe-man, as the queen stood not knowing what to do with herself. "Do you mean to say you haven't washed that other lot of tripe!" and this time he gave her a kick.

To escape his fury, the queen turned to do her best with washing the other tripe, but she did it so awkwardly that she got a volley of abuse and blows too.

Then came dinner-time, and nothing prepared, or even bought to prepare, for dinner. Another stormy scene ensued at the discovery, and the tripe-man went to dine at the inn, leaving her to go without any dinner at all, in punishment for having neglected to prepare it.

While he was gone she helped all the customers to the wrong things, and, when he came home, got another scolding and more blows for her stupidity. And all through the afternoon it was the same story.

But the tripe-seller, when she found herself all in a palace, with half-a-dozen maids waiting to attend her, was equally bewildered. When they kept asking her if there was nothing she pleased to want, she kept answering, "No, thank you," in such a gentle tone, the maids began to think that a reign of peace had come to them at last.

By-and-by, when the ladies came, instead of saying, as the queen had been wont, "What an ugly dress you have got; go and take it off!" she said, "How nice you look; how tasteful your dress is!"

Afterward the king came in, bringing her a rare nosegay. Instead of throwing it on one side to vex him, as the queen had been wont, she showed so much delight, and expressed her thanks so many times, that he was quite overcome.

The change that had come over the queen soon became the talk of the whole palace, and everyone congratulated himself on an improvement that made them all happy. The king was no less pleased than all the rest, and for the first time for many years he said he would drive out with the queen; for on account of her bad temper he had long given up driving with her. So the carriage came round with four prancing horses, and an escort of cavalry to ride before and behind it. The tripe-seller hardly could believe she was to drive in this splendid carriage, but the king handed her in before she knew where she was. Then, as he was so pleased with her gentle and grateful ways, he further asked her to say which way she would like to drive.

The tripe-seller, partly because she was too much frightened to think of any other place, and partly because she thought it would be nice to drive in state through her own neighborhood, named the broader street out of which turned the lane in which she lived, for the royal carriage could hardly have turned down the lane itself. The king repeated the order, and away drove the royal cortège.

The circumstance of the king and queen driving out together was sufficient to excite the attention of the whole population, and wherever they passed the people crowded into the streets; thus a volley of shouts and comments ran before the carriage toward the lane of the tripe-man. The tripe-man was at the moment engaged in administering a severe chastisement to the queen for her latest mistake, and the roar of the people's voices afforded a happy pretext for breaking away from him.

She ran with the rest to the opening of the lane just as the royal carriage was passing.

"My husband! my husband!" she screamed as the king drove by, and plaintive as was her voice, and different from her usual imperious tone, he heard it and turned his head toward her.

"My husband! my royal husband!" pleaded the humbled queen.

The king, in amazement, stopped the carriage and gazed from the queen in the gutter to the tripe-seller in royal array by his side, unable to solve the problem.

"This is certainly my wife!" he said at last, as he extended his hand to the queen. "Who then can you be?" he added, addressing the tripe-seller.

"I will tell the truth," replied the good tripe-seller. "I am no queen; I am the poor wife of the tripe-seller down the lane there; but how I came into the palace is more than I can say."

"And how come you here?" said the king, addressing the real queen.

"That, neither can I tell; I thought you had sent me hither to punish me for my bad temper; but if you will only take me back I will never be bad-tempered again; only take me away from this dreadful tripe-man, who has been beating me all day."

Then the king made answer: "Of course you must come back with me, for you are my wife. But," he said to the tripe-seller; "what shall I do with you? After you have been living in luxury in the palace, you will feel it hard to go back to sell tripe."

"It's true I have not many luxuries at home," answered the tripe-seller; "but yet I had rather be with my husband than in any palace in the world"; and she descended from the carriage, while the queen got in.

"Stop!" said the king. "This day's transformation, howsoever it was brought about, has been a good day, and you have been so well behaved, and so truth-spoken, I don't like your going back to be beaten by the tripe-man."

"Oh, never mind that," said the good wife; "he never beats me unless I do something very stupid. And, after all, he's my husband, and that's enough for me."

"Well, if you're satisfied, I won't interfere any further," said the king; "except to give you some mark of my royal favor."

So he bestowed on the tripe-man and his wife a beautiful villa, with a nice casino outside the gates, on condition that he never beat her any more.

The tripe-man was so pleased with the gifts that had come to him through his wife's good conduct that he kept his word, and was always thereafter very kind to her. And the queen was so frightened at the thought that she might find herself suddenly transformed into a tripe-seller again that she kept a strict guard over her temper, and became the delight of her husband and the whole court.

II. The Comedy of Errors

A report of a 1594 performance of *The Comedy of Errors* noted that it was "like to Plautus his Menechmus."* That is, the reporter recognized Shakespeare's play as an adaptation of *Menaechmi*, a second-century BCE Roman play by Plautus, whose title might be translated as *The Two Menaechmuses* or *The Brothers Menaechmus*. Some scholars agree, however, that Plautus's play was itself indebted to a folktale known as "The Twins or Blood-Brothers" (ATU 303).† Shakespeare, and those in his audience with as much or more formal education as he had, would have known the play, but those both less and more literate might well have known the folktale from oral tradition.

"The Twins or Blood-Brothers" folktale commonly begins with a supernatural conception, leading to the birth of two identical boys, either to one woman or to two different women. These two women are generally separated by class: one is a servant to the other, as in "The Enchanted Doe" from Giambattista Basile's seventeenth-century *The Tale of Tales*, and "Black Jack and White Jack," told in 1920 by a man from Antigua. Once the two boys are grown, one of them leaves their home, but leaves behind him a life token, a knife or a tree, say, that magically reveals when the departed brother is in difficulty. This first brother travels to a distant place and marries. He then encounters a witch or sorcerer who traps him, and he languishes in captivity. His life token reveals to

---

* Shakespeare, *Comedy of Errors*, 107.

† Hansen, *Ariadne's Thread*, 450–53, and "Oral Source"; and Trenkner, *Greek Novella*, 99–108.

his brother that he is in danger, so the brother sets out to find him. When the second brother arrives at the first brother's home, he is mistaken by everyone—including his brother's wife—for his absent twin. He finds the witch, kills her, and rescues his captive brother. Sometimes the second brother marries as well, to his sister-in-law's sister in "Black Jack," and unusually, to the witch in "The Two Golden Brothers," a Persian folktale.

The Comedy of Errors begins with an expository scene in which Egeus, a merchant from Syracuse, explains that many years ago, his wife gave birth to twin boys. At the very same time, a poor woman in the same inn also gave birth to twin boys. These births are not the result of supernatural conception, as in the folktales, but rather an uncanny coincidence. Egeus purchased the poor woman's sons to be slaves to serve his own sons. Rather than one set of twins, or two identical boys, one of high birth and one of lower, Shakespeare seems to select both options from the folktale: two sets of twins, one set of masters and one set of slaves. (*Menaechmi* features one pair of twins and a single slave.)

Egeus, his wife, and the four infants, however, had the mischance to meet a storm at sea, and were separated on the waves. He saved one of his sons and one of the slaves, but he has not seen his wife, his other son, or the other infant slave since. The twin brothers are separated, as in the folktale, but shortly after birth rather than as young men. Even so, and without prompting from a magical life indicator, Egeus's son Antipholus of Syracuse, now an adult, has set off in search of his missing twin, prompted by existential loneliness. He describes his quest in soliloquy:

I to the world am like a drop of water
That in the ocean seeks another drop;
Who, falling there to find his fellow forth,
Unseen, inquisitive, confounds himself.

So I, to find a mother and a brother,
In quest of them, unhappy, lose myself. (1.2.35–40)

He utters these lines just after his arrival in Ephesus with his slave,
Dromio of Syracuse. Unbeknownst to them, the two boys lost at
sea have settled in Ephesus. Improbably, they are also named Antipholus and Dromio, allowing the many complications that make
up the play's action to ensue. Antipholus of Ephesus's wife, Adriana, mistakes Antipholus of Syracuse for her husband, and Nell the
kitchen maid mistakes Dromio of Syracuse for her intended. Antipholus of Ephesus is locked out of his home because his household is already entertaining his twin, and he storms off to meet a
courtesan with whom he has been indulging in a flirtation. The
courtesan is perhaps reminiscent of the folktale sorceress as an al-
luring woman, as in the Persian tale "The Two Golden Brothers."
Later, Antipholus of Syracuse takes sanctuary in a convent, and the
abbess refuses to release him until she has plied him with her po-
tions and prayers, despite Adriana's entreaties: a stronger suggestion of the sorceress as an old witch, as in "Black Jack and White
Jack." (*Menaechmi* includes the courtesan but not the abbess.) All
four female characters in the play are at various moments accused
of being enchantresses.

Ultimately, the brothers find each other and the errors are
cleared up. We learn, in the final scene, that the duke of Ephesus
awarded Antipholus of Ephesus Adriana as his bride because of his
heroism in battle, just as Black Jack won the princess by rescuing
her from a monster. Antipholus of Syracuse will wed his sister-in-
law's sister, Luciana, just as White Jack does in "Black Jack." Luciana has been horrified at Antipholus of Syracuse's attempts to woo
her, because of course she thinks that he is her sister's husband, just
as Black Jack is horrified to learn that White Jack has slept with his
wife. The motif of a wife unknowingly sleeping with her husband's

twin is hinted at in the scene in which Adriana has dinner alone with Antipholus of Syracuse, while her husband bangs on the house's door. Fratricidal violence threatens to prevent the happy ending of this folktale, but it does not, while the play ends with the reunion of Egeus's long-scattered family (the abbess, it turns out, is his wife) and the prospect of two weddings.

THE TWINS OR BLOOD-BROTHERS

Giambattista Basile

The Enchanted Doe*

There was once a certain king of Long Pergola named Iannone who had a great desire to have children and was always praying to the gods to make his wife's belly swell up. And in the hope that they would move fast to content him, he was especially charitable with wayfarers, to whom he would have given the pupils of his eyes. But finally, when he saw that things were taking a long time and that there was no way they were going to sprout a bud, he hammered his door shut and shot at anyone who drew near.

It happened that a great bearded sage came passing through that land, and not knowing that the king had changed his tune, or else knowing about it and wanting to find a cure for it, he went to see Iannone and begged to be received in his home. With a dark face and a terrible scowl, the king said to him, "If this is the only candle

---

*Giambattista Basile, *The Tale of Tales, or Entertainment for Little Ones*, trans. Nancy L. Canepa (Detroit: Wayne State University Press, 2007), 108–14. The ninth entertainment of the first day. *The Tale of Tales*, whose Neapolitan title is *Lo cunto de li cunto*, is also known as *The Pentamerone*. It was first published in 1634–36. The notes that follow are adapted from Canepa's.

you have, you can go to bed in the dark! The time is past for Berta to spin!* The kittens have opened their eyes! There's no more mother now!" And when the old man asked the reason for this transformation, the king answered, "Out of my desire to have children, I spent and spread and threw away my belongings on all who came and went, and finally, when I saw I couldn't get a clean shave, I pulled my hand out and took up the anchor." "If that's all there is," replied the old man, "calm down; I'll get her pregnant for you straightaway or you can have my ears." "If you do," said the king, "I give you my word that I'll reward you with half of my kingdom."

The other answered, "Now listen carefully: if you want a good graft get the heart of a sea dragon and have it cooked by a young virgin who, at the mere odor coming from the pot, will find herself with swollen belly; when the heart is cooked, give it to the queen to eat, and you'll see that she'll immediately become pregnant, too, as if she were in her ninth month." "How can that be?" replied the king. "To tell you the truth, it seems pretty hard to swallow." "No need to marvel," said the old man, "since if you read the myths you can find that after brushing against a flower while passing through the Olenian Fields Juno's belly blew up and she gave birth." "If that's how it is," the king concluded, "let the dragon heart be found this very instant. After all, I've got nothing to lose."

And so he sent a hundred fishermen to sea, and they prepared harpoons, trawls, hooks, nets, traps, lines, and reels, and sailed around and searched far and wide until they finally caught a dragon. Then they ripped out its heart and brought it to the king, who gave it to a lovely lady-in-waiting to cook. She locked herself in a room, and no sooner had she put the heart on the fire and the vapor had started to rise from the stew then not only did the fair cook herself become pregnant but all the furniture in the room began to swell

---

* That is, it's no longer the good old days.

up, and at the end of a few days they were all delivered. The big canopy bed had a little bed, the strongbox a little chest, the big chairs little chairs, the big table a little table, and the chamber pot a little decorated chamber pot that was so pretty you could have eaten it. The cooked heart had barely been tasted by the queen before she felt her own belly growing large, and in four days she and her lady-in-waiting both gave birth at the same time to lovely strapping boys, the one such a spitting image of the other that you couldn't tell them apart. The two boys grew up together with such love that they became inseparable, and their fondness for each other was so intense that the queen began to feel a bit of envy, since her son showed greater affection for the son of one her servants than for herself, and she couldn't figure out how to remove that speck from her eye.

Now one day when the prince wanted to go hunting with his companions, he had a fire lit in the hearth in his cold room and began to melt down lead to make bullets, and since he was missing something or the other, he went to look for it in person. In the meantime, the queen came by to see what her son was doing, and when she found Canneloro, the son of the lady-in-waiting, alone in there, she thought she would remove him from the world, and threw some red-hot bullet mold in his face. He ducked, but it hit him on the eyebrow and left him with an ugly gash; the queen was already about to send off a second charge when Fonzo, her son, arrived. Pretending that she had come to see how he was, she gave him a few insipid caresses and left.

Canneloro pulled a hat down over his forehead so that Fonzo couldn't see what had happened, and he stood perfectly still even though he felt like he was frying with pain. And when he had finished rolling those balls like a cockroach,* he asked the prince's

---

*The comparison is between making bullets and "the pellets of feces that a certain type of beetle forms and rolls along the ground" (Canepa, 111 n. 5).

permission to leave town. Marveling at this sudden decision, Fonzo asked what the reason was, to which Canneloro answered, "Attempt to discover no more, my dear Fonzo. May it suffice you to know that I am forced to leave, and the heavens know that as I leave you, heart of mine, my soul plays tug-of-war with my breast, my spirit goes 'row your boat' away from my body, my blood plays 'beat it, Marco'* with my veins. But since there's nothing to be done, take care of yourself and remember me."

After they embraced, Canneloro went off to his room in a state of despair. There he put on a suit of armor and a sword, to which another weapon had given birth when the heart was cooking, and, completely armed, he got a horse from the stable and was just about to put his feet in the stirrups when Fonzo came in crying and asking him if, seeing as he intended to abandon him, he could at least leave him some sign of his love so that Fonzo could reduce the anguish caused by the other's absence. At these words Canneloro took his dagger in hand and drove it into the ground, and, when a lovely spring gushed forth, he said to the prince, "This is the best memento I can leave you, since from the course of this spring you will be able to tell the course of my life: if you see it run clear, you will know that my state is similarly clear and calm; if you see it muddy, you can imagine that I am in trouble; and if you find it dry (may the heavens will this not), you can assume that the oil of my lantern has burned off and that I will be where I have to pay my toll to nature." That said, he put his hand on his sword and, striking the ground, caused a myrtle bush to sprout, saying, "When you see that it is green, you will know that I am as green as garlic; if you see it withered, you can assume that my luck is not standing very tall; and if it becomes completely dry you can say a requiem of shoes and clogs† for your Canneloro."

---

* A nickname of a famous bandit, Marco Sciarra.

† Derived from a garbled form of the Latin for "rest in peace."

That said, they embraced again and Canneloro left. He walked far and wide, and after the occurrence of many things that it would take a long time to recount, such as fights with coachmen, swindles by innkeepers, assassinations of customs officers, the dangers of treacherous roads, and the diarrhea caused by fear of thieves, he finally arrived at Long Pergola* just when they were having a splendid joust, in which the daughter of the king was promised to the champion. Canneloro presented himself and performed so gallantly that he proved a great bother to all the knights who had come from many different countries to earn themselves a name. And for his feats he was given the king's daughter, Fenizia, for his wife, and great festivities were held.

After living for a few months in blessed peace, Canneloro got the melancholic urge to go hunting, and when he told the king, he in turn was told, "Watch out for your legs, my son-in-law, and see that Old Nick doesn't blind you! Keep your wits about you! Open your door, sir, for in these woods there's an ogre worse than the demon, who every day changes shape; now he appears as a wolf, now a lion, now a deer, now a donkey, and now one thing and now another, and with a thousand stratagems he drags the poor souls he encounters into a grotto where he eats them up. So, my son, don't put your health at risk, for you'll lose the rags off your back!"

Canneloro, who had left all fear in his mother's belly, paid no heed to his father-in-law's advice and went off hunting as soon as the Sun had cleared away the Night's soot with the straw broom of its rays. And when he got to the wood—where under the canopy of branches shadows congregated to form a monopoly and plot against the Sun—the ogre, who had seen him arrive, transformed himself into a lovely doe, which Canneloro began to pursue as soon

* Presumably a mistake, since Canneloro comes from Long Pergola.

as he saw it. The doe held him off and bounced him around from one place to another until it drove him to the heart of the wood, where it caused so much rain and snow to fall that it seemed like the sky was falling. And when Canneloro found himself in front of the ogre's grotto, he went in to save himself, and since he was numb with cold he gathered up some wood he found there and, pulling his flint out of his pocket, lit a great fire.

As he was standing there getting warm and drying his clothes, the doe appeared at the mouth of the grotto and said, "Oh, sir knight, give me leave to warm up a little, for I'm frozen stiff." Canneloro, who was courteous, said, "Come closer, and may you be welcome." "I'll come," answered the doe, "but I'm afraid that you'll kill me." "Have no fear," replied Canneloro. "Come, on my word." "If you want me to come," resumed the doe, "tie up those dogs so they won't bother me, and secure that horse so it won't kick me." And Canneloro tied up the dogs and tethered the horse. Then the doe said, "Yes, now I feel almost reassured; but if you don't fasten your sword I won't come in, on the soul of my grandpa!" And Canneloro, who enjoyed familiarizing with the doe, fastened his sword like a farmer going to the city does, for fear of the police. As soon as the ogre saw that Canneloro was defenseless, he took back his true shape, grabbed hold of him, lowered him into a ditch that was at the back of the grotto, and covered it with a rock so he could eat him later.

But when Fonzo, who morning and evening visited the myrtle bush and the spring for news of Canneloro, found the one withered and the other muddy, he immediately imagined that his friend was in trouble. Wanting to assist him, he got on his horse without asking leave of his father or mother, and, well armed and in the company of two enchanted dogs, he set off into the world. And he traveled and roamed in this direction and that until he finally arrived at Long Pergola.

He found the kingdom completely draped in black for the presumed death of Canneloro, and no sooner had he arrived in court than every person there, believing that he was Canneloro because of his resemblance to him, ran to ask Fenizia for their reward. Throwing herself headlong down the stairs, she hugged Fonzo and said, "My dear husband, my heart, where have you been all these days?" From this response Fonzo immediately suspected that Canneloro had come to this land and left it, and he decided to interrogate the princess very carefully in order to determine from her words where he might be. And, hearing it said that he had exposed himself to too great a danger in that accursed hunt, especially since he might have been discovered by the ogre, who was so terribly cruel with men, he immediately understood that that was what his friend had come up against. He feigned to know nothing about the matter, and when it was night he went off to bed.

Pretending to have made a vow to Diana not to touch his wife that night, he lay his unsheathed sword between him and Fenizia like a stockade. In the morning, he couldn't wait for the Sun to come out—and give some golden pills* to the heavens to make it shit its shadow—since as soon as he got out of bed he intended to go hunting, and neither Fenizia's pleas nor the king's orders could stop him.

After mounting his horse, he went to the woods with his enchanted dogs, and the same thing that had happened to Canneloro happened to him. He went into the grotto and saw Canneloro's weapons, dogs, and horse tied up, and he was then certain that that was where his friend had been snared. And when the doe told him to tie up his weapons, dogs, and horse, he sicced them on the doe and they tore it to shreds. As he was searching for some other trace of his friend, he heard moans coming from down in the ditch, and

---

*Laxatives.

after lifting the rock he pulled out Canneloro along with all the others the ogre had been keeping there, buried alive, in order to fatten them up. And so they embraced with great rejoicing and went home, where upon seeing those two identical men, Fenizia was not able to tell which of them was her husband. But when Canneloro lifted his hat she saw the scar and, recognizing him, she embraced him.

After spending a month in amusements in that land, Fonzo wanted to return home and see his own nest again. With Fonzo as his messenger, Canneloro wrote to his mother to come and take part in his greatness, which she did, and from that time on he wanted nothing more to do with either dogs or hunting, always remembering the saying that goes, *Miserable is he who is punished at his own expense.*

D.L.R. and E. O. Lorimer

The Story of the Two Golden Brothers[*]

Once upon a time there was a man called Malik Ahmad who had seven wives, but he had no children by any of them. "Here I have all this wealth," said he, "but I have no children, so what is the good of it to me?"

He was thinking thus one day when a Derwish[†] turned up. Malik Ahmad offered him all sorts of gifts and alms, but the Derwish declined to accept them. "I'm not a grabbing, take-things sort of man," said he. "I'm not a cadger. On the contrary, if any man wants a thing that I am able to bring to pass for him, I do it without

---

[*] D.L.R. and E. O. Lorimer, *Persian Tales, Written Down for the First Time* (London: Macmillan, 1919), 212–19, https://babel.hathitrust.org/cgi/pt?id=njp.32101076395944;view=1up;seq=256 (accessed April 20, 2017). No. 32.

[†] A dervish: a Muslim mystic.

reward." "Good," said Malik Ahmad, "there is a thing I want very much, and it's this: I have great wealth and I have married seven wives, but I have no children. I want a son."

"This wish of yours," replied the Derwish, "is easily satisfied, but there's a condition attaching to it."—"And what is the condition?" "It is this, Malik Ahmad," answered the Derwish, "I will give you a drug, but then any children who may come will belong half of them to me and half of them to you." Malik Ahmad agreed to this condition, for said he to himself: "Supposing children do come, I'll be able to satisfy this fellow with money or horses or mares." So they reduced the terms of their agreement to writing, and the Derwish put his hand in his pocket and drew out a pomegranate, and gave it to Malik Ahmad, saying: "Give this to your youngest wife to eat."

The Derwish went off, and Malik Ahmad gave the pomegranate to his wife, and they ate it together. After some days, she conceived, and after nine months and nine hours she gave birth to a pair of twin boys. The boys grew up till they reached the age of eighteen years. They learned to read and write, and were very strong, and there was nothing in which they were not perfect.

Now among themselves the family all said: "The Derwish went away, he'll never come back." One day, however, they were sitting at their ease when he suddenly made his appearance. He salaamed, and brought out the written document, and said: "I have come for my share." "Whatever wealth or property you want is yours," said Malik Ahmad, "you are welcome." "I want my share, and nothing but my share," replied the Derwish, and, argue as he might, Malik Ahmad could make no impression on him and had to give in.

Then the elder son said: "I will go with him," and the younger son said: "I will go." In the end the elder went, and when he was leaving he took a ring from his finger and gave it to his brother, saying: "Brother, whenever this ring gets loose on your finger and slips off and falls to the ground, you may know that I am in difficulties." So he left, and they all raised a great lamentation at his departure.

Now the Derwish and he went on their way till they arrived near a spring. The boy was going along behind when he saw an old graybeard standing in the road. "Oh young man," cried the graybeard, "why ever have you started out to travel with this fellow? Are you tired of life?" "He made an agreement with my father," said the boy, "so what can I do? Show me a way out of it all!" "Pay attention to all I say then," said the old man.—"On my eyes be it!" "Very well," continued the graybeard, "you will go to the spring and he will say to you: 'My child, put your mouth down to the water and drink,' then when you have stooped down he will cut off your head with his sword. After that he will mount your horse and plunge into the water, and the horse and saddle and he himself will turn into gold. Now, when you arrive at the water's edge and he has made his polite speech to you, do you say: 'Oh no! you are my father and I am your child, I will not drink before you.' Then when he puts his mouth down to the water, smite off his head. If you don't kill him, he will kill you."

When he had finished speaking, the graybeard vanished, and the lad followed on after the Derwish. "My child," said the Derwish, "why have you been so long in coming?"—"I had dismounted, and was tightening my horse's girths." They went up to the spring, and the Derwish said: "My child, now drink some water."—"Oh no, I could not show such disrespect before my elder and better. You are my father, drink first." And, despite all the Derwish's endeavors, he absolutely declined to drink first. "Well," thought the Derwish, "what does this boy know about it! I'll drink first, then he'll drink afterward."

So he went and put his mouth down to the water. While he was thus stooping, the lad struck him on the back of the neck with his sword and his head flew off and fell far away in the desert. Then the boy mounted the horse and struck into the blood-stained water and crossed to the other side, and he and his horse turned all into gold.

He went on till he came to a mountain on which there was a great deal of snow, and there he was caught in a snowstorm. Now, near the foot of the mountain there was a big village. The people looked out and saw a horseman caught in the snow, and they saw that he would perish if they were long in reaching him with help. So they raised a relief party, and some sturdy young men went out and succeeded in getting to him. They found that he was speechless, and they took him up on their shoulders and led his horse along, and carried him to the house of the Kadkhuda, or Headman, of the village. First, they took him to the baths, and he recovered his warmth, and then they brought him back, and they saw that he was a marvelously fine young man, every bit of him of gold.

"Good Heavens!" said they, "is this a man or a peri*?" and they asked who he was. "I am a stranger," said he, "and I lost my way." After he had stayed there some days, the Headman said to him: "Young man, I have a very fine daughter. If you ask for her, I will give her to you to wife, and all this wealth and property will also become yours. Do stay here, for I have only this one daughter and no son." "Very good," said the youth, and some days later they gave him the maiden, and they two were married.

One day he said: "I am getting very bored. Give me some men with me and let me go out hunting." "By all means," said his father-in-law, and he placed some hunters at his disposal, and they mounted and started off for the chase. They sighted a fine striped and dappled gazelle and surrounded it, and they agreed that the one in whose direction it might go should be allowed to follow it

---

* A supernatural being.

up alone. As it chanced, it made in the direction of the golden youth, whose name, by the way, was Malik Mahmad.

It gave a leap, bounded up, and fled away. "No one else must follow it but me!" cried the youth, and he galloped after it till it came to the mouth of a cave. Down it went into the cave, and after it went the youth. His companions waited and waited for him, but he didn't come back, and they didn't know where he had gone. "However are we to answer for him to the Kadkhuda?" said they. However, there was nothing they could do, so after some days they returned to the village.

When the Kadkhuda found that Malik Mahmad had not come back with them, he made great lamentation and said: "I was well pleased with this stranger, but he hasn't remained with me." The people said: "He was no human being. No one knows what he was. It is true he came in the shape and likeness of a man," and everyone had something of his own to say on the subject.

Now listen to a few words about Malik Mahmad. When he entered the cave he heard a sound of stringed instruments and drums and singing. And when he arrived at the place where the sounds were coming from, he found a beautiful lady sitting there with slave-girls standing round her, their hands laid on their breasts. "You are welcome," said the Lady, "come and sit down," and he went and sat down beside her.

After the evening meal they started conversing, and the maiden said: "What did you do with the gazelle?" "I'm blessed if I know what became of it," replied he; "it came into this cave, but I don't know where it went to then." "O golden youth," said the Lady, "I myself am that gazelle. Now I have a custom and it is this, that I wrestle with everyone who comes here. If you throw me to the ground, then I shall become your property, and if I throw you, you will become mine, and I will put you in chains and tie up your horse in my stable. I have a lot of prisoners already, and I'll put you along with the rest." "Very good," said he, and they got up and started wrestling. The Lady lifted him up and flung him to the ground, knocking him senseless, and then she threw him into prison.

All of a sudden the ring on his brother's finger turned loose and slipped off and fell to the ground. "Alack and alas!" cried Sultan Mahmad, "my brother is in trouble," and he went to his father and mother and told them what had happened, and said: "I am going to find my brother." Then he mounted his horse and set out after his brother, and they all raised mourning and lamentation after him as he went.

When he came to the place near the spring he saw the graybeard, and the old man said: "O Sultan Mahmad, are you going to look for your brother?" "How does he know where I'm going?" thought Sultan Mahmad. "He must certainly know where my brother is, for it must be he who has told him my name," but aloud he only said: "Yes." Then the old man said: "Your brother is a prisoner in such and such a place. He made a wager with a Lady, and she flung him to the ground and knocked him senseless, and threw him into prison. Now you will go on and cross the water, and you will turn into gold just as he did. Then when you get to the cave the Lady will wrestle with you, but you must put out your hands and catch her in such and such a way by the arms and fling her to the ground. For if you catch her thus, she will become limp and powerless."

"I'll do exactly as you say," said Sultan Mahmad, and he wished the old man good-bye and proceeded to the spring. He saw the place where the Derwish's blood had run into the water, and he crossed over and turned into gold. Then he followed in his brother's tracks and came to the snow mountain, and he too was caught in a snowstorm.

Now the people of the village looked out and they saw him and said: "What a stupid fool he is! He got caught once and we rescued him, now why has he gone and got caught again!" However, they raised a rescue party and went out and brought him in.

"My boy," said the Kadkhuda, "why ever did you go on to the mountain, so that you would get caught in the snow and the storm? But where have you been all these days?" "I just went somewhere," said Sultan Mahmad, who perceived that they were talking of his twin brother. Then a beautiful lady came and sat down beside him and they talked together. Now he understood that she was his brother's wife, and at night when they lay down to sleep he drew his sword from its scabbard and laid it between himself and the woman. "Why do you do that?" said she. "In the early days when I married you, you weren't like this." "We have a custom," he said, "to sleep like this for some days."

He stayed there a few days, and then he said: "Father, I want to go a-hunting."—"I'm afraid you may go off like the last time and be a long time in coming back." "Oh no," said Sultan Mahmad, "I'll come back soon." Some men went with him, and again the same gazelle appeared and they surrounded it. It came toward Sultan Mahmad, then it gave a leap, started aside, and bounded away, while Sultan Mahmad pursued it to the entrance of the cave. He found there was singing going on inside, and, advancing farther into the cave, he saw a beautiful lady, so beautiful that there was no one like her, sitting on a throne.

He made his salaams, and she said: "Come and sit down." He went and sat down by her, and she said: "O golden youth." "Yes," said he. "I have a wager," she went on, "that whoever can throw me to the ground, I and all I possess will become his. And there is a young man just like yourself who will become yours if you win. And if I throw you I'll send you after your brother." "All right," said Sultan Mahmad, and then they got up and started wrestling. Then Sultan Mahmad put out his hands and seized her by the arms in the way the old man had shown him, and put his leg in front of hers, and threw her to the ground and tied her hands.

"Don't tie my hands," said she, "I belong to you now."—"I won't agree to untie them till you show me my brother." "Go and get that bottle, then," said she, "and hold it to your brother's nose till he recovers consciousness; and you can do what you like with the other prisoners." He went and took the bottle and held it to his brother's nose, and he came to his senses, and they threw their arms round each other's neck and wept.

Then they got up and came to the Lady and untied her hands. After that they gave themselves up to mirth and jollity, and they told each other their stories. Then morning came, and they set the prisoners free and restored them to consciousness, and they loaded up everything they cared for and went off. The Lady too they took away with them, and Sultan Mahmad married her, and Malik Mahmad found his wife, the Kadkhuda's daughter, waiting for him in the village, and they all went off to their own country and settled down there in peace.

The story is ended.

Roger D. Abrahams
Black Jack and White Jack*

There were two ladies, one colored and one white, who came from foreign parts. The colored lady was supposed to be the maid of the

*Roger D. Abrahams, *African American Folktales: Stories from Black Traditions in the New World* (New York: Pantheon, 1985), 288–91. No. 98. Abrahams's source for this story is Johnson, "Folklore from Antigua," 40–83. In this article, "Black Jack and White Jack" is story no. 35, pp. 77–80. The storyteller was George B. Edwards, a fifty-year-old man from Greenbay, Antigua. Johnson recorded the story in a regional dialect, which Abrahams has rendered as standard academic English.

white lady. So they came to live in this strange land, where they didn't know anybody. On the first day that they were there, they went out for a walk. And they took with them a bottle of water each. They walked a mile. When the water was finished, they turned back. The second day, they went for another walk, and they took two bottles of water with them. This time they went for two miles. That water was finished, too, so they turned back. They went the third day, and they took three bottles of water. They went three miles, and when the water was all gone, they turned back again. Now on the fourth day, they took four bottles of water, and they went four miles, and the water was all gone again. But they didn't turn back his time. They went on for four more miles. They got thirsty, of course, and then they saw two ponds. One was running white water, and one was running black water. The white woman drank from the white pond, and the black woman drank from the black pond. Then they returned home, and both fell very sick. They called in the doctor, and the doctor said they were both pregnant. And they remained sick for the whole nine months. The time came for the babies to be delivered. The white woman had a white son, and the black woman had a black son. The white one called her son White Jack. The black woman called her son Black Jack. Well, they grew up together like brothers. They looked alike, except one was dark, the other light.

After they had grown up to be young men, Black Jack said one day, "Would you like to go out hunting?" And White Jack said that he would go along with him. Black Jack brought the knife, which he always carried with him. And they went out to hunt. They caught three different kinds of animals each—a lion, a unicorn, and a bear. They tamed them so that the animals would do anything they asked them to do.

One day, while they were walking in the woods, they came to a crossroad, where there was a large tree. Black Jack stuck his knife into that tree and said, "White Jack, if you come back and see that knife has dropped and is all rusty, then you'll know I'm dead." So they took their departure, each on one of the roads. They each had their three animals along.

Black Jack heard of a king that had a daughter. And every year a lion came there to destroy that girl. Any man who could kill that monster could have the girl to be his wife. So Black Jack made his way to the king's palace. He made arrangements that he would volunteer to kill the monster. The next day, the king sent his daughter in a coach out to the woods where this lion was, for this is what he had to do every year. And Black Jack was there, lying in ambush. When the monster came out after the girl, Black Jack said to one of his beasts, "Hold on, my lion, my unicorn, and my bear!" And his three beasts tore up this monster, and they killed him. Now Black Jack didn't want the king to know it was he who had killed the lion. So he asked the girl not to tell the father it was he, for he had some plan in his mind.

So, while they were going back, the coachman told the girl to say to the father that it was he that killed the lion. He threatened to kill her if she did not. So the girl told the father it was the coachman that killed the lion. And the king agreed to have the girl marry the coachman.

On the next day, Black Jack was passing by the palace, and the girl was looking out from the veranda. She saw Black Jack and she said to the King, "Ah, Papa! Papa! That was the man who really saved me from the lion." And the king called him in. And they hanged the coachman for telling a lie. Two days after that, Black Jack married the girl.

The day after they were married, they were both on the veranda looking out, and Black Jack saw a cottage far away. Black Jack asked his wife, "What is that place over there? I would like to go there."

"Many have gone there and haven't returned; for there is an old woman who lives there who eats people," his wife told him.

Black Jack replied, "I am not afraid. I will go." His wife could not persuade him not to go. After he went, she felt like she didn't have a husband, because she knew he would lose his life there.

Black Jack, with his lion, his unicorn, and his bear, walked about four miles till they reached a river. He met an old man with a boat in that river. He said to the old man, "Old Man, take me over this river, will you please?"

The old man said, "No sir! There is an old woman over there that eats people." Black Jack said, "Old Man, take me over the river, and I will give you a guinea." He said, "No sir, for many have gone and haven't returned."

Then Black Jack said, "Hold on, my lion, my unicorn, and my bear!" And his beasts took him over the river. He came to a gate, and he rapped on this gate. The name of this gate was Open-unto-me. Just then the old lady came along. She said to the gate, "Open-unto-me," and she and Black Jack went on in. But he left his three beasts outside. When he went in, the old woman said to herself, "Um, a pretty human this one is." Then she took him all through the house, you know. And when she got him to one certain room, she struck him dead with her magic, and she threw his body in a room with the many other bodies of the people she had killed before.

On that same day, White Jack returned from his journey and came to the tree. And he saw the knife on the ground and rusted. And he said to himself, "My brother, Black Jack, is dead. Wherever his body is, I must find him." So he set out in search of him. He walked all day till he came to the king's palace. He stopped and asked for a drink of water. Now the two Jacks, Black Jack and White Jack, looked so alike that this girl took him for her husband. And the father also. So White Jack slept with the girl that night. The next day, they were both on the same veranda looking out, and he asked her, "What place is that over yonder?" She told him, "You asked me that before. There is an old woman over there who eats people!" Then he said to the girl, "I want to go, and I will go." And he set off with his three beasts.

When he reached the river, he saw the same old man with the boat. He said, "Old Man, take me over this river, would you please?" He said, "No sir! I saw one man pass here like you, and he didn't come back."

White Jack said, "Old Man, if you take me over the river, I will give you ten guineas." He said, "No sir! There is an old woman over there who eats people."

White Jack said to his beasts, "Hold on, my lion, my unicorn, and my bear!" And his beasts took him over the river. When he got over the river, he saw the three beasts of Black Jack mourning. He was mad now. He rapped on the gate. The old woman said, "Open-unto-me!" and the gates opened and he went in. The old woman said, "Um, um, a pretty man to eat." With White Jack were the three beasts of Black Jack and his own beasts. When the old woman said "a pretty man to eat," he said, "The Devil and Hell, a man to eat! Go find my brother, Black Jack!" The old woman got scared, you know. She asked him to come into the rooms. He went, and took the beasts with him. When he reached that certain room, he would not go in. He started to threaten the old woman. She got so scared, and took up some of a bottled medicine to bring people back to life, and went to where Black Jack was, and used it on him till he came to life. As he got to life, White Jack said, "Hold on, my lion, my unicorn, and my bear!" And they tore the old woman to pieces.

They left the place. While they were on the way back, Black Jack did not tell White Jack that he was married to the king's daughter. So when they came near the king's palace, White Jack said he slept there last night with the daughter of the king. And Black Jack started to tell him it was his wife. But he was so mad that he hauled off and killed White Jack, because he had slept with his wife. Then he saw what he had done, killing this man who was like his brother and who had just saved his life. They had brought away with them the medicine that the old woman used. So Black Jack had it, and in his sorrow he brought back White Jack to life. Black Jack went home to his wife, and White Jack married the king's next daughter.

And I was to the weddin', and I got a glass a wine and a kick.

III. TITUS ANDRONICUS

Titus Andronicus dramatically declares its literary source, the story of Philomela from Ovid's *Metamorphoses* (8 CE). In Act 4, Scene 1, a copy of *Metamorphoses* is brought onstage, and Lavinia, Titus's raped and mutilated daughter, opens it up and points to the story, so that neither the characters nor the audience can mistake the parallel between Lavinia and Philomela, whose rapists have cut out their victims' tongues. Not that anyone would miss the connection: Lavinia has already been called Philomela twice, once by Aaron the Moor, who is plotting her tragedy (2.2.43), and once by her uncle Marcus, who discovers her after the attack (2.3.38–43). Lavinia undergoes even greater torture than Philomela: she has been raped by two men who have cut off her hands as well as her tongue. Later, Titus punishes these villains by baking them into pies that he serves to their mother, just as Philomela and her sister, Procne, punish Tereus, Philomela's attacker and Procne's husband, by feeding him the remains of his son. "Worse than Philomel you used my daughter," Titus says, "And worse than Progne I will be revenged" (5.3.194–95).

A play that reveals its classical influences so clearly might not seem the likeliest candidate for a folktale play. Just as *The Comedy of Errors* borrows from and one-ups its classical source while simultaneously suggesting a folktale, so *Titus Andronicus* is explicitly Ovidian, and implicitly folkloric. Its similarities to the folktale "The Revenge of the Castrated Man" (ATU 844*) are quite clear but not called out the way an authored literary text like *Metamorphoses* can be. Resemblances to another folktale, "The Maiden without

Hands" (ATU 706) are more diffuse, but detectable nonetheless. These two folktales, as their titles make clear, center on dismemberment, just as the story of Philomela does, which perhaps led Shakespeare to associate the three stories with one another.

"The Revenge of the Castrated Man" story is nasty, brutish, and short. The heart of its action is that a slave, prisoner, or servant is ill-treated by his master, and in revenge he takes the master's sons to the top of a high tower, and says he will throw them to their deaths if their father does not instantly mutilate himself. The frantic father cuts off part of his body, but the servant kills the children anyway. In *Titus Andronicus*, Aaron the Moor frames two of Titus's sons for murdering the emperor's brother, and they are condemned to death. Aaron then tells the distraught Titus that the emperor will grant his sons a reprieve if Titus cuts off his hand. But Titus's severed hand is returned to him, along with his sons' heads.

The "Revenge" folktale circulated in Arabic literature (represented here by a story taken from Mas'udi's *Meadows of Gold*), as an episode in a longer folktale in Jewish tradition, and in European texts. Included here are two versions of the story from Britain, the first from Gerald of Wales's twelfth-century travel narrative, and the other a sixteenth-century ballad. Aaron the Moor, who sets the "Revenge" plot in motion in *Titus*, seems to represent the folktale's geographical diversity in his person. Shakespeare's audience would have associated Moors with Islam, although Aaron declares himself irreligious. His name is Jewish, perhaps primarily associated for Elizabethans with Moses's brother. He belongs to the group of Goths whom Titus has taken prisoner, although the play never pauses to explain how a Moor came to live among these Northern Europeans. In the ballad "The Lady and the Blackamoor," the villain is black, and in Mas'udi's account he is Sindi, or Indian. Shakespeare may have been simply following his folktale source when he made his villain a Moor, because there seems to be no other explanation for Aaron's presence among the Goths.

The story in *Meadows of Gold* makes very clear how and why the slave was punished: the master caught his wife and his slave in bed together. In a fit of rage, the master castrated the slave, who bided his time until he could exact his awful revenge. Similarly, Aaron is having an affair with Tamora, queen of the Goths, who marries the Roman emperor at the beginning of the play. In "The Lady and the Blackamoor" ballad, the Moor rapes his master's wife as part of his vengeance, just as Aaron plans Lavinia's rape and brags about the other rapes he has committed. Curiously, the violence that passes between Moor and master remains vague in the ballad. The servant commits some "fault" and the master "corrects" him. While in Mas'udi's story, there is castration-for-castration justice, in "The Lady and the Blackamoor," we don't know the logic behind the slave's demand that the master cut off his nose. Gerald of Wales begins his account by telling us that the lord of a castle kept a prisoner whose eyes he had put out for an unspecified reason. This seems like an incomplete euphemization of castration when midway through the story we learn that the prisoner had also been castrated, and he demands that the lord castrate himself to save his child. While in the *Journey through Wales* and the ballad versions of the story, the father dies of grief, Titus responds to the entry of "a Messenger with two heads and a hand" (3.1.234sd) by gathering his wits and planning his revenge. He sends his son Lucius to raise an army of Goths that eventually apprehend Aaron and bring him to justice, but not until many more have died.

The "Revenge" plot of the play is concentrated, unfolding over two scenes, and fairly unmistakable, as befits the skill of its "chief architect and plotter" Aaron (5.3.121). "The Maiden without Hands" plot becomes visible when Chiron and Demetrius, Tamora's sons, rape Lavinia and cut off her tongue and hands. The removal of her hands is apparently Chiron and Demetrius's addition and response to Philomela's story. Because Philomela could no longer speak, she wove a tapestry accusing her rapist and sent it to her sister, who rescued her from captivity and planned their revenge on Tereus. Onstage, the only readily visible effect of Lavinia's brutalization might have been her missing hands, making her resemble the heroine of the "Hands" folktale. This folktale was popular and widespread, and was woven into medieval French romances and Renaissance Italian novella collections. I think, then, that Shakespeare and his audience would have been sensitive to the elements of the folktale that surface in the play, although they are not so tightly woven as the elements of the "Revenge" plot.

The heroines of the "Hands" folktale are mutilated for various reasons. In the Brothers Grimm's version, the heroine's father has unwittingly promised her to the devil, who commands him to cut off her hands. The young woman escapes the devil, but also decides she can no longer live in her father's house. Lavinia's troubles begin when, in the first scene of the play, her father promises to wed her to the emperor Saturninus, despite the fact that she is already engaged to the emperor's brother. Lavinia elopes and escapes the marriage with the ominously named ruler, but the Andronici become alienated from the emperor and prey to the Goths when Saturninus marries Tamora instead of Lavinia. In the Italian folktale "Olive," which has roots in medieval legend, Olive's hands are cut off by her Jewish father to punish her for being a Christian, a sectarian conflict also apparent in the play's faultlines between Moor, Roman, and Goth. In the Hungarian, Scottish, and Russian folktales included here, a female relative's enmity leads to the heroine's mutilation, although in the latter two, she induces a male relative to commit the actual violence. Tamora is related to Lavinia by marriage—she is her sister-in-law, like the villainess in the Russian version—and Tamora incites her sons to mutilate Lavinia.

Although the severing of Lavinia's hands may seem to be merely a development of elements borrowed from Philomela's story, there are folktale precedents for her severed tongue as well. In the Scottish story "The Cruel Stepmother," Beatrix's father cuts out her tongue when she reproaches him for cutting off her arm and leg. In the Grimms' version, a doe's tongue and eyes are presented as false evidence of the heroine's death.

In the folktales, after the heroine has been mutilated, she often takes refuge in the woods, and sometimes eats fruit hanging from tree branches in order to stay alive—how else can she feed herself without hands? A king finds her and marries her, but when she is again banished from her home and wandering in the woods, sometimes it is an older man who finds her, and in the Hungarian "The Envious Sisters," it is her own father. Lavinia is found in the woods by her uncle Marcus, a high-status man—a tribune—an older man, and her relative. He insistently identifies her with trees, calling her arms branches and comparing her lost hands to aspen leaves (2.3.18, 45).

The heroine of the "Hands" stories is often accused of bearing monstrous children, as in the German, Hungarian, and Russian versions included here, or of killing an infant, as in the Scottish and Russian versions. Lavinia endures no such calumnies, but her nemesis, Tamora, plots to kill her own newborn. In the Russian folktale, the villainess fabricates a claim that the heroine has mated with the beasts of the forest, and has given birth to a half-dog, half-bear creature as a result. Tamora's lover, Aaron, is constantly equated with animals—a raven, a fly, a dog—making her union with him bestial in the eyes of the Romans, and the Goths call the child that Tamora bears him "the tadpole" and "as loathsome as a toad" (4.2.87, 69).

Tamora attempts or metaphorically does the horrible things of which the "Hands" heroine is accused.

Perhaps this provides some compensatory justice, because Lavinia never gets her happy ending, as the folktale heroines inevitably do. Lavinia's folktale counterparts ultimately regain both their husbands and their hands. Lavinia's husband is dead, killed by her own attackers, and will never return. While in four of the folktales presented here, the maiden's hands are restored when she submerges them in water, Lavinia will benefit from no such miracle, making Chiron's taunt after the attack, "Go home, call for sweet water, wash thy hands," all the more cruel (2.3.6). Lavinia lives to tell her story, through the external object of the book *Metamorphoses*, just as the folktale heroines often tell their stories in the third person, externalizing them, as Philomela did when she wove her tragedy into a tapestry. Lavinia also participates in the rough justice meted out to Chiron and Demetrius, whereas the folktale heroines either intercede for mercy against their wrongdoers, as in "The Envious Sisters" and "Olive," or stand discreetly aside while others exact gory revenge, as in "The Cruel Stepmother" and "The Armless Maiden."

"O handle not the theme, to talk of hands," Titus says to Marcus in a moment of black humor, "Lest we remember still that we have none" (3.2.29–30). Shakespeare handled the theme of handlessness he found in both Ovid's story of Philomela and in "The Maiden without Hands," and he added it handily to his "Revenge of the Castrated Man" plot. The loss of Titus's hand, as opposed to his nose or testicles, seems overdetermined by both Philomela's and the folktale maiden's mutilation. Aaron the Moor, the Goths, and the Romans all know the story of Philomela, but it is the Gothic party that sets in motion the plots that resemble the "Revenge" and "Hands" folktales. These are indeed Gothic tales that become "incorporate in Rome" (1.1.467), and the Andronici repudiate them violently as they slay Chiron, Demetrius, Tamora, and Aaron. At the very end of the play, however, the banished Lucius Andronicus returns to Rome at the head of a Gothic army, suggesting that Goths will ultimately become incorporated into Rome, just as Shakespeare has incorporated folktales into his Ovidian play.

THE REVENGE OF THE CASTRATED MAN

Mas'udi
Revenge*

The same Ibn Da'b relates that one day Hadi† received the following report:

"An inhabitant of the city of Mansura in Sind, one of the noblest and most important men in the government of the town, a member of the family of Muhallab ibn Abi Sufra, had brought up an Indian—or Sindi—slave. This young man conceived a passion for the wife of his owner and attempted to seduce her; she reciprocated. The master entered and found them together. He castrated the slave and made a eunuch of him, but looked after him until his wounds healed.

The slave was patient for a long time. His master had two sons, one still a child and the other an adolescent. One day, the master left the house, and the Sindi slave took the two children up to the top of the wall that encircled the house and there awaited the owner's return. When the man came home and, looking up,

---

*Mas'udi, *The Meadows of Gold: The Abbasids*, trans. and ed. Paul Lunde and Caroline Stone (London: Kegan Paul, 1989), 54. Mas'udi, a Muslim historian, was born in Baghdad around 896 CE and died in Egypt around 956 CE (11).

† Hadi was a caliph of the Abbasid Caliphate in the eighth century CE, and Isa ibn Da'b was a historian in his court (Mas'udi 51, 53).

saw his two sons and the slave balanced on the edge of the wall, he cried:

'Wretch! You are risking their lives!'

'Never mind that!' shouted the Sindi. 'I swear that you are going to castrate yourself in front of me, now, this moment, or else I shall throw your children down!'

'O God, O God,' he said, 'have pity on me and upon my two sons!'

'Leave off!' answered the slave. 'I have nothing to lose but my life and I would give that away for a drink of water!'

He was just preparing himself to carry out his threat, when his master took out a knife and castrated himself. When the slave saw that he had done it, he threw the two children off the roof and they were smashed to bits on the ground.

'Your wounds,' he said, 'are in expiation of mine, and the killing of your two children is something in addition.' "

Hadi then wrote to the governor of Sind ordering him to have this slave put to death with the most appalling tortures, and, furthermore, he ordered all Sindis to be driven out of his domains, which explains why slaves from that country became cheap and glutted the markets at that period and were sold for such low prices.

Gerald of Wales
The Scene of Sorrows*

The overlord of [a region in France] held prisoner in his castle a man whose eyes he had put out. From his long familiarity with

---

* Gerald of Wales, *The Journey through Wales and The Description of Wales*, trans. Lewis Thorpe (London: Penguin, 1978), 142–43. Book 1, chapter 11. *The Journey through Wales* was written in 1191 CE (38). "It describes, almost in diary form, the mission to South and North Wales undertaken in 1188 by Baldwin, Archbishop of Canterbury, with Gerald, Archdeacon of Brecon, as his companion" (24). I have supplied the title for this story.

them, this prisoner had committed to memory all the passageways of the castle and even the steps that led up to the towers. One day, in a fit of anger and longing for vengeance, he seized the child of the castellan, his only son and heir, and dragged him up to the topmost crenellation of one of the towers. As he went up, he locked all the doors behind him, and there he stood outlined against the sky, threatening to throw the boy over. A great shout arose, and everyone screamed in anguish. The boy's father came running, and no one's distress was greater than his. He made every offer he could think of, in an attempt to obtain the release of his son. The prisoner replied that that he would not give up the boy until the father had first cut his own testicles off, which deprivation he himself had suffered. The castellan went on with his appeals, but all in vain. In the end he pretended to agree, and had himself hit a mighty blow in the lower part of the body, to give the impression that he had mutilated himself. All those present moaned lugubriously. The blind man asked the castellan where he felt most pain, and he replied, falsely, that it was in his loins. Thereupon the blind man stepped forward to throw the boy over. The father was struck a second blow, and this time he said the worst pain was in his heart. The blind man did not believe him, and he dragged the boy forward to the very edge of the parapet. The third time, to save his son, the father really did cut off his own testicles. He shouted that it was his teeth which hurt most. "This time I believe you," said the blind man, "and I know what I am talking about. Now I am avenged of the wrongs done to me, in part at least, and I go happily to meet my death. You will never beget another son, and you shall certainly have no joy in this one." As he said this, he hurled himself over the battlements and plunged into the abyss, taking the boy with him. When he hit the ground his legs and arms were broken in many places, and the two of them died together. To save his son's soul, the knight built a monastery on the spot. It is still there today. They call it the Scene of Sorrows.

Anonymous Ballad

The Lady and the Blackamoor*

A Lamentable ballad of the tragical end of a Gallant Lord, and a Virtuous Lady, with the untimely end of their two children, wickedly performed by a Heathenish Blackamoor their servant, the like never heard of before. To the tune of *The Lady's Fall.*

In Rome a noble man did wed
    a virgin of great fame.
A fairer creature never did
    Dame Nature ever frame.
By whom he had two children fair,
    whose beauty did excel.
They were their parents' only joy
    they loved them both so well.

This Lord he loved to hunt the buck
    the tiger and the bear,[†]

---

* University of Glasgow Library Euing Ballads 197, EBBA 31955 in *English Broadside Ballad Archive*, ed. Patricia Fumerton, http://ebba.english.ucsb.edu /ballad/31955/image (accessed April 24, 2017). I have modernized the spelling and punctuation. Date published: 1658–64? An apparently similar ballad was registered in 1569–70, and a ballad with the same first line as this one was registered in 1624. See Rollins, *Ballad-Entries*, no. 2542 (220) and no. 1234 (107). I would like to thank Patricia Fumerton for her generous response to my questions and for sending me a manuscript chapter of her forthcoming *Moving Media, Tactical Publics: The Broadside Ballad in Early Modern England*. She notes that this ballad was extremely popular.

† The rhyme leads us to expect "boar" here.

And still for swiftness always took
    with him a Blackamoor.
Which Blackamoor within the wood
    his Lord he did offend,
For which he did him then correct
    in hope he would amend.

The day it grew unto an end,
    then homeward he did haste,
Where with his Lady he did rest
    until the night was past.
Then in the morning he did rise,
    and did his servants call.
A-hunting he provides to go,
    straight they were ready all.

Cause of the toil his Lady did
    entreat him not to go,
"Alas good Lady," then quoth he;
    "why art thou grieved so?
Content thyself, I will return
    with speed to thee again,"
"Good Father," quoth the little babes,
    "with us here still remain."

"Farewell dear children, I will go
    a fine thing you to buy."
But they therewith nothing content
    aloud began to cry.
The mother takes them by the hand,
    saying, "Come go with me
Unto the highest tower where
    your Father you shall see."

The Blackamoor perceiving now
   who then did stay behind,
His Lord to be ahunting gone
   began to call to mind;
"My master he did me correct,
   my fault not being great;
Now of his wife I'll be revenged
   she shall not me entreat."

The place was moated round about;
   the bridge he up did draw.
The gates he bolted very fast
   of none [he] stood in awe.
He up into the tower went
   the Lady being there,
Who when she saw his countenance grim
   she straight began to fear.

But now my trembling heart it quakes
   to think what I must write;
My senses all begin to fail
   my soul it doth affright.
Yet must I make an end of this
   which here I have begun
Which will make sad the hardest heart
   before that I have done.

This wretch unto the Lady went
   and her with speed did will,
His lust forthwith to satisfy
   his mind for to fulfill.
The Lady she amazed was
   to hear the villain speak,

"Alas," quoth she, "What shall I do?
    With grief my heart will break."

With that he took her in his arms;
    she straight for help did cry.
"Content yourself, Lady," he said,
    "your husband is not nigh.
The bridge is drawn, the gates are shut;
    therefore come lie with me.
Or else I do protest and vow
    thy butcher I will be."

The crystal tears ran down her face,
    her children cried amain[*]
And sought to help their mother dear
    but all it was in vain.
For that egregious filthy rogue,
    her hands behind her bound,
And then perforce with all his might,
    he threw her on the ground.

With that she shrieked, her children cried
    and such a noise did make,
The towns-folks hearing her laments,
    did seek their parts to take.
But all in vain, no way they found,
    to help the Lady's need.
Who cried to them most piteously,
    "O help, O help with speed."

Some ran unto the forest wide,
    her Lord home for to call,

[*]With all their might.

And they that stood still did lament
    this gallant Lady's fall.
With speed her Lord came posting home
    he could not enter in,
His Lady's cries did pierce his heart,
    to call he did begin.

"O hold thy hand, thou savage Moor,
    to hurt her do forbear,
Or else be sure if I do live,
    wild horses shall thee tear."
With that the rogue ran to the wall,
    he having had his will.
And brought one child under his arm
    his dearest blood to spill.

The child seeing his father there
    to him for help did call,
"O Father, help my Mother dear,
    we shall be killed all."
Then fell the Lord upon his knee,
    and did the Moor entreat,
To save the life of his poor child,
    whose fear as then was great.

But this vile wretch the little child,
    by both the heels did take,
And dash the brains against the wall,
    whilst parent's heart did ache.
That being done straightway he ran
    the other child to fetch.
And plucked it from the mother's breast,
    most like a cruel wretch.

Within one hand a knife he brought
    the child within another,
And holding it over the wall,
    saying, "Thus die shall thy mother."
With that he cut the throat of it,
    then to the father did call,
To look how he the head had cut
    then down the head did fall.

This done, he threw it down the wall,
    into the moat so deep,
Which made his father wring his hands
    and grievously to weep.
Then to the Lady went this rogue,
    who was near dead with fear.
Yet this vile wretch most cruelly
    did drag her by the hair.

And drew her to the very wall
    which when her Lord did see
Then presently he cried out,
    and fell upon his knee.
Quoth he, "If thou wilt save her life
    whom I do love so dear,
I will forgive thee all is past,
    though they concern me near.

"O save her life I thee beseech,
    O save her I thee pray!
And I will give thee what thou wilt
    demand of me this day."
"Well," quoth the Moor, "I do regard
    the moan that thou dost make.

If thou wilt grant me what I ask
    I'll save her for thy sake."

"O save her life and then demand
    of me what thing thou wilt."
"Cut off thy nose and not one drop
    of her blood shall be spilt."
With that the Lord presently took
    a knife within his hand,
And then his nose he quite cut off
    in place where he did stand.

"Now have I bought my Lady's life,"
    then to the Moor did call.
"Then take her," quoth this wicked rogue
    and down he let her fall.
Which when her gallant Lord did see,
    his senses all did fail.
Yet many sought to save her life
    but nothing would prevail.

When as the Moor did see him dead,
    then did he laugh amain,
At them who for their gallant Lord
    and Lady did complain.
Quoth he, "I know you'll torture me
    if that you can me get.
But all your threats I do not fear
    nor yet regard one whit.

"Wild horses shall my body tear,
    I know it to be true.
But I'll prevent you of that pain,"
    and down himself he threw.

Too good a death for such a wretch
    a villain void of fear.
And thus doth end as sad a tale
    as ever man did hear.

THE MAIDEN
WITHOUT HANDS

Jacob and Wilhelm Grimm
The Maiden without Hands*

A miller had been falling little by little into poverty, and soon he had nothing left but his mill and a large apple tree behind it. One day, as he was on his way to chop wood in the forest, he met an old man whom he had never seen before.

"There's no reason you have to torture yourself by cutting wood," the old man said. "I'll make you rich if you promise to give me what's behind your mill."

What else can that be but my apple tree, thought the miller, and he gave the stranger his promise in writing.

"In three years I'll come and fetch what's mine," the stranger said with a snide laugh, and he went away.

When the miller returned home, his wife went out to meet him and said, "Tell me, miller, how did all this wealth suddenly get into our house? All at once I've discovered our chests and boxes are full. Nobody's brought anything, and I don't know how it's all happened."

---

*Jacob and Wilhelm Grimm, *The Complete Fairy Tales of the Brothers Grimm*, trans. Jack Zipes (New York: Bantam, 1992), 118–23. No. 31

"It's from a stranger I met in the forest," he said. "He promised me great wealth if I agreed in writing to give him what's behind our mill. We can certainly spare the large apple tree."

"Oh, husband!" his wife exclaimed in dread. "That was the devil! He didn't mean the apple tree but our daughter, who was behind the mill sweeping out the yard."

The miller's daughter was a beautiful and pious maiden who went through the next three years in fear of God and without sin. When the time was up and the day came for the devil to fetch her, she washed herself clean and drew a circle around her with chalk. The devil appeared quite early, but he could not get near her, and he said angrily to the miller, "I want you to take all the water from her so she can't wash herself anymore. Otherwise, I have no power over her."

Since the miller was afraid of the devil, he did as he was told. The next morning the devil came again, but she wept on her hands and made them completely clean. Once more he could not get near her and said furiously to the miller, "Chop off her hands. Otherwise, I can't touch her."

The miller was horrified and replied, "How can I chop off the hands of my own child!"

But the devil threatened him and said, "If you don't do it, you're mine, and I'll come and get you myself!"

The father was so scared of him that he promised to obey. He went to his daughter and said, "My child, if I don't chop off both your hands, the devil will take me away, and in my fear I promised I'd do it. Please help me out of my dilemma and forgive me for the injury I'm causing you."

"Dear Father," she answered, "do what you want with me. I'm your child."

Then she extended both her hands and let him chop them off. The devil came a third time, but she had wept so long and so much on the stumps that they too were all clean. Then he had to abandon his game and lost all claim to her.

Now the miller said to his daughter, "I've become so wealthy because of you that I shall see to it you'll live in splendor for the rest of your life."

But she answered, "No, I cannot stay here. I'm going away and shall depend on the kindness of people to provide me with whatever I need."

Then she had her maimed arms bound to her back, and at dawn she set out on her way and walked the entire day until it became dark. She was right outside a royal garden, and by the glimmer of the moon she could see trees full of beautiful fruit. She could not enter the garden, though, because it was surrounded by water. Since she had traveled the entire day without eating, she was very hungry. Oh, if only I could get in! she thought. I must eat some of that fruit or else I'll perish! Then she fell to her knees, called out to the Lord, and prayed. Suddenly an angel appeared who closed one of the locks in the stream so that the moat became dry and she could walk through it. Now she went into the beautiful garden accompanied by the angel. She caught sight of a beautiful tree full of pears, but the pears had all been counted. Nonetheless, she approached the tree and ate one of the pears with her mouth to satisfy her hunger, but only this one. The gardener was watching her, but since the angel was standing there, he was afraid, especially since he thought the maiden was a spirit. He kept still and did not dare to cry out or speak to her. After she had eaten the pear, and her hunger was stilled, she went and hid in the bushes.

The next morning the king who owned the garden came and counted the pears. When he saw one was missing, he asked the gardener what had happened to it, for the pear was not lying under the tree but had somehow vanished.

"Last night a spirit appeared," answered the gardener. "It had no hands and ate one of the pears with its mouth."

"How did the spirit get over the water?" asked the king. "And where did it go after it ate the pear?"

"Someone wearing a garment as white as snow came down from heaven, closed the lock, and dammed up the water so the spirit could walk through the moat. And, since it must have been an angel, I was afraid to ask any questions or to cry out. After the spirit had eaten the pear, it just went away."

"If it's as you say," said the king, "I shall spend the night with you and keep watch."

When it became dark, the king went into the garden and brought a priest with him to talk to the spirit. All three sat down beneath the tree and kept watch. At midnight the maiden came out of the bushes, walked over to the tree, and once again ate one of the pears with her mouth, while the angel in white stood next to her. The priest stepped forward and said to the maiden, "Have you come from heaven or from earth? Are you a spirit or a human being?"

"I'm not a spirit, but a poor creature forsaken by everyone except God."

"You may be forsaken by the whole world, but I shall not forsake you," said the king.

He took her with him to his royal palace, and since she was so beautiful and good, he loved her with all his heart, had silver hands made for her, and took her for his wife.

After a year had passed, the king had to go to war, and he placed the young queen under the care of his mother and said, "If she has a child, I want you to protect her and take good care of her, and write me right away."

Soon after, the young queen gave birth to a fine-looking boy. The king's mother wrote to him immediately to announce the joyful news. However, on the way the messenger stopped to rest near a brook, and since he was exhausted from the long journey, he fell asleep. Then the devil appeared. He was still trying to harm the pious queen, and so he exchanged the letter for another one that said the queen had given birth to a changeling. When the king read the letter, he was horrified and quite distressed, but he wrote his mother that she should protect the queen and take care of her until his return. The messenger started back with the letter, but he stopped to rest at the same spot and fell asleep. Once again the devil came and put a different letter in his pocket that said they should kill the queen and her child. The old mother was tremendously disturbed when she received the letter and could not believe it. She wrote the king again but received the same answer because the devil kept replacing the messenger's letters with false letters each time. The last letter ordered the king's mother to keep the tongue and eyes of the queen as proof that she had done his bidding.

But the old woman wept at the thought of shedding such innocent blood. During the night she had a doe fetched and cut out its tongue and eyes and put them away. Then she said to the queen, "I can't let you be killed as the king commands. However, you can't stay here any longer. Go out into the wide world with your child and never come back."

She tied the child to the queen's back, and the poor woman went off with tears in her eyes. When she came to a great wild forest, she fell down on her knees and prayed to God. The Lord's angel appeared before her and led her to a small cottage with a little sign saying "Free Lodging for Everyone." A maiden wearing a snow-white garment came out of the cottage and said, "Welcome, Your Highness," and took her inside. She untied the little boy from her back and offered him her breast so he could have something to drink. Then she laid him down in a beautifully made bed.

"How did you know that I'm a queen?" asked the poor woman.

"I'm an angel sent by God to take care of you and your child," replied the maiden in white.

So the queen stayed seven years in the cottage and was well cared for. By the grace of God and through her own piety, her hands that had been chopped off grew back again.

When the king finally returned from the wars, the first thing he wanted to do was to see his wife and child. However, his old mother began to weep and said, "You wicked man, why did you write and order me to kill two innocent souls?" She showed him the two letters that the devil had forged and resumed talking. "I did as you ordered," and she displayed the tongue and eyes.

At the sight of them the king burst into tears and wept bitterly over his poor wife and little son. His old mother was aroused and took pity on him.

"Console yourself," she said. "She's still alive. I secretly had a doe killed and kept its tongue and eyes as proof. Then I took the child and tied him to your wife's back and ordered her to go out into the wide world, and she had to promise me never to return here because you were so angry with her."

"I shall go as far as the sky is blue, without eating or drinking, until I find my dear wife and child," the king said. "That is, unless they have been killed or have died of hunger in the meantime."

The king wandered about for seven years and searched every rocky cliff and cave he came across. When he did not find her, he thought she had perished. During this time he neither ate nor drank, but God kept him alive. Eventually, he came to a great forest, where he discovered the little cottage with the sign, "Free Lodging for Everyone." Then the maiden in white came out, took him by the hand, and led him inside.

"Welcome, Your Majesty," she said, and asked him where he came from.

"I've been wandering about for almost seven years looking for my wife and child, but I can't find them."

The angel offered him food and drink, but he refused and said he only wanted to rest awhile. So he lay down to sleep and covered his face with a handkerchief. Then the angel went into the room where the queen was sitting with her son, whom she was accustomed to call Sorrowful, and said, "Go into the next room with your child. Your husband has come."

So the queen went to the room where he was lying, and the handkerchief fell from his face.

"Sorrowful," she said, "pick up your father's handkerchief and put it over his face again."

The child picked up the handkerchief and put it over his face. The king heard all this in his sleep and took pleasure in making the handkerchief drop on the floor again. The boy became impatient and said, "Dear Mother, how can I cover my father's face when I have no father on earth. I've learned to pray to 'our Father that art in heaven,' and you told me that my father was in heaven and that he was our good Lord. How am I supposed to recognize this wild man? He's not my father."

When the king heard this, he sat up and asked her who she was.

"I'm your wife," she replied, "and this is your son, Sorrowful."

When the king saw that she had real hands, he said, "My wife had silver hands."

"Our merciful Lord let my natural hands grow again," she answered.

The angel went back into the sitting room, fetched the silver hands, and showed them to him. Now he knew for certain that it was his dear wife and dear son, and he kissed them and was happy.

"A heavy load has been taken off my mind," he said.

After the Lord's angel ate one more meal with them, they went home to be with the king's old mother. There was rejoicing everywhere, and the king and queen had a second wedding and lived happily ever after.

Peter Buchan

The Cruel Stepmother[*]

About the year 800, there lived a rich nobleman in a sequestered place of Scotland, where he wished to conceal his name, birth, and parentage, as he had fled from the hands of justice to save his life for an action he had been guilty of committing in his early years. It was supposed, and not without some good show of reason, that his name was Malcolm, brother to Fingal, king of Morven. Be this as it may, it so happened that he had chosen a pious and godly woman for his consort; who, on giving birth to a daughter, soon after departed this life. Malcolm (as we shall call him, for the better understanding of his history) lived a widower for the space of sixteen years, when thinking that his daughter now became of such age as to leave him, if she got a good offer. With these thoughts full in his head, he went to a distant place of the country where the thane of Mull dwelt, and made love to one of his daughters, whom he afterward married and brought to his own domain.

The new-come bride had no sooner fixed her eyes on Beatrix (for that was his daughter's name) than she conceived the most deadly hatred imaginable; so much so, that it almost deprived her of her rest, meditating schemes how to get rid of her, as she envied her for her superior beauty. One day on her husband going ahunting, she took the young lady and bound her by an oath that whatever she saw or heard her do or say, she would conceal the same

[*]Peter Buchan, *Ancient Scottish Tales: An Unpublished Collection Made by Peter Buchan, with an Introduction by John A. Fairley* (Peterhead, Scotland, 1908), 25–28, https://babel.hathitrust.org/cgi/pt?id=nyp.33433086946278;view=1up;seq=33 (accessed April 20, 2017). Buchan was a printer and ballad collector who collected and recorded these tales from 1827–29 (1–2). I have added paragraph breaks.

from her father. The oath being extorted from her by threatening her with death and destruction, if she did not comply.

The first act of the stepmother was to go into the garden and cut down a favorite tree that was in full blossom, and so destroyed the root and beauty of the branches by burning the same. On Malcolm's return, he immediately discovered the want of his favorite tree, and getting into such a passion, few could approach the place where he was for a considerable length of time. When his passion had somewhat subsided, he asked his wife what had become of it, or how it had been destroyed, but she desired him to ask his daughter, as she knew nothing about it herself. Beatrix was then summoned before him, and interrogated with all the rigor of a passionate father, as to her knowledge of the destruction of his tree. Her only answer was that He who was above knew all about it. No more satisfaction would she give him.

A second time he went from home, and on his return found his favorite hound weltering in his blood. This again renewed his passion, but who was the guilty person he could never learn; on inquiring at his daughter, he received the same answer as formerly. A third time he went ahunting, and on his return found his favorite hawk lying dead; but the perpetrators of these horrid deeds he could not discover. On applying to his wife, he was requested to ask his daughter; and on consulting her, her answer was as at the first. His wife thereby seeing that all the stratagems that she had devised for her destruction had proved abortive; to gratify her mortal hatred, rather than suffer her to live, she would sacrifice everything she had in the world.

One year had scarcely passed in this disagreeable manner, when the lady was delivered of a fine boy, which soon became the darling of his father. This was too glaring not to be easily perceived by the mother; but rather than live the life that she had done since they had been married, with the envious venom rankling in her breast, she would destroy her own child and offspring. This being determined upon, one night when Beatrix was in bed soundly sleeping, dreading no harm, this bad woman, her stepmother, took a knife, bereaved the sweetly smiling young thing of its life, and laid it with the knife reeking in gore, into the arms of the innocent Beatrix. After having been in bed for some time with her husband, she started as from some frightful dream, crying, O, my child, what has become of my lovely child! This alarmed the father, who, on looking for the child, it was not to be found. The mother then said, she was much afraid that Beatrix had stole it away from them while they slept, and had murdered it. The father by no means could be made to believe this; but upon examining her bed, the child was discovered horribly mangled, and the knife beside it. He was now petrified with horror, and could ask nor answer anything.

It was in vain for the young lady to plead ignorance, or deny the guilty deed, the proofs were too strong, as certainly no one could have suspected the unnatural mother of such cruel barbarity; and no one else had access to the place where it lay but Beatrix. Her father then having determined to put her to the most cruel torture for the death of his beloved child; she was now charged with all the other bad deeds that had been committed for the space of the bygone twelve months in his house and premises, which caused him to take her to a wood, and after having cut off her right hand and arm, he next cut off her right leg. She still pleaded her innocence, but rather than perjure herself, she would suffer all that he choosed to inflict upon her; but as proof of her innocence, she told him on his way homeward, a thorn would so stick in his foot that none but herself could extract, and that only after her arm and leg had been reunited to her body as before. He paid no attention to this, but next cut out her tongue, and left her to perish, or to be destroyed by wild beasts in the wood.

She had not, however, lain long in this humiliating posture, till a knight came riding that way, when, on observing her, he alighted from his horse, and enquired the nature of her sufferings. As she could not speak, she made signs to him for pen, ink, and paper, when she wrote an account of the whole. He then took her on his horse behind him and carried her home to his mother, who being acquainted with the virtues of the water of a particular well nearby, she soon restored to her the full use of her amputated limbs; but her tongue still continued useless. The knight, notwithstanding the deficiency of the want of her tongue and speech, took such a liking to her that they were shortly after married, and lived in the greatest peace and pleasure, till one day that he was necessitated to leave his country on some very urgent business. Previously to his setting off, he had matters so arranged that by giving certain directions to his wife, she might write to him by her page. All things being prepared, the knight went away with a sorrowful heart.

He had not been long away till his wife became sick at heart (being pregnant), and longed to see her esteemed lord. A message was then sent to the place of his residence with a request that he would return immediately home. The messenger was her own page, who was enjoined to make every dispatch, and not to tarry on the way; but these instructions he soon forgot when out of sight and reach of his mistress. As he journeyed on his way, it so happened that he should take up his abode for the night in the very house of Beatrix's father. His lady, observing the stranger, was desirous of knowing his errand, and so prevailed upon him to give her a sight of the letter that he carried from Beatrix to her husband. By her fair speeches, she so won his heart, that he gave it to her. On opening it she soon discovered from whom it came, and tore it, and wrote in its place one, as if come from his mother, requesting him to put away or destroy the bad woman he had brought unto her. To this letter he made no reply, when a second one was written by his wife, not knowing the cause of his delay; but it shared the same fate as the former, and another of like tenor, breathing the bitterest enmity and hatred against his beloved and virtuous wife, put in its place.

On receiving this second menacing letter, he hurried home, and finding his wife in the house, without any provocation or inquiry, he immediately dragged her forth, and abused her very unmercifully, till having driven her into a ditch to get quit of her altogether, a powerful herb happened to get into her mouth in the course of her struggle, which at once restored to her the use of her speech. It now became her turn to interrogate him, and ask why he had used her so cruelly without a cause. He then showed her the letters that he had received purporting to be from his mother. She said they were not written by his mother, as they lived on the most friendly terms imaginable. It was then referred to his mother, who, on seeing them, was no less surprised than vexed at them, and at his maltreating his wife so basely. The page was then called and examined, when he confessed what he had done. The knight, without further inquiry into the matter, took his sword and cut off his head, and threw it away, as a warning to all others not to betray their trust, but behave in a more upright and honorable manner.

As it was at length discovered that the cruel stepmother had been the sole cause of the whole of Beatrix's misfortunes, she was adjudged to be put to an ignominious death by the most cruel torture, which was put into execution immediately after, as a just reward for her hatred and cruelty. Beatrix then relieved her father from the pain that he suffered in his foot by a thorn that stuck in it, and baffled all the medical skill of that part of the country. They afterward lived to a good old age and died in peace.

W. Henry Jones and Lewis L. Kropf
The Envious Sisters*

A king had three daughters whose names were Pride, Gentleness, and Kindness. The king was very fond of them all, but he loved the youngest one, Kindness, the most, as she knew best how to please him. Many clever young gentlemen came to visit Kindness, but no one ever came near the other two, and so they were very envious of her, and decided they would get rid of her somehow or other. One morning they asked their father's permission to go out into the fields, and from thence they went into the forest. Kindness was delighted at having liberty to roam about in such pretty places; the other two were pleased that they had at last got the bird into their hands. As the dew dried up, the two eldest sisters strolled about arm in arm, whilst the youngest chased butterflies and plucked the wild strawberries, with the intention of taking some home to her father; she spent her time in great glee, singing and listening to the songs of the birds, when suddenly she discovered that she had strolled into an immense wood. As she was considering what to do, her two sisters appeared by her side, and said spitefully, "Well, you good-for-nothing! You have never done anything but try to make our father love you most and to spoil our chances in every way, prepare yourself for your end, for you have eaten your last piece of bread." Kindness lifted up her hands, and besought them not to harm her, but they cut off her hands, and only spared her life under the condition that she would never go near her home again; they then took her beautiful precious mantle from her, and dressed her

---

*W. Henry Jones and Lewis L. Kropf, *The Folk-Tales of the Magyars* (London: Folklore Society, 1889), 49–54, https://babel.hathitrust.org/cgi/pt?id=nyp.3343 3068198112;view=1up;seq=129 (accessed April 20, 2017). The term "Magyar" refers both to a people primarily native to Hungary and to the Hungarian language.

in old rags; they then led her to the highest part of the forest, and showed her an unknown land, bidding her go there and earn her living by begging. The blood streamed from Kindness's arms, and her heart ached in an indescribable way, but she never uttered the slightest reproach against her sisters, but started off in the direction pointed out to her. Suddenly she came to a beautiful open plain, where there was a pretty little orchard full of trees, and their fruit was always ripening all the year round. She gave thanks to God that he had guided her there, then, entering the garden, she crouched down in a by-place. As she had no hands to pluck the fruit with, she lived upon what grew upon low boughs; thus she spent the whole summer unnoticed by any one.

But toward autumn, when every other fruit was gone save grapes, she lived on these, and then the gardener soon discovered that the bunches had been tampered with and that there must be someone about: he watched and caught her. Now it so happened that the garden belonged to a prince, who spent a great deal of his time there, as he was very fond of the place. The gardener did not like to tell him of what had happened, as he pitied the poor handless girl and was afraid his master would punish her severely. He decided therefore to let her go. Accidentally, however, the prince came past and asked who she was. "Your highness," replied the gardener, "I know no more of her than you do. I caught her in the garden, and to prevent her doing any more damage I was going to turn her out." "Don't lead her away," said the prince; "and who are you, unfortunate girl?" "You have called me right, my lord," said Kindness, "for I am unfortunate, but I am not bad; I am a beggar, but I am of royal blood. I was taken from my father because he loved me most; crippled because I was a good child. That is my story." To this the prince replied, "However dirtily and ragged you are dressed, still it is clear to me that you are not of low birth: your pretty face and polished speech prove it. Follow me; and whatever you have lost you will find in my house." "Your highness, in this nasty, dirty dress—how can I come into your presence? Send clothes to me that I can put on, and then I will do whatever you order." "Very well," said the prince; "stay here, and I will send to you." He went and sent her a lady-in-waiting with perfumed water to wash with, a gorgeous dress, and a carriage. Kindness washed and dressed herself, got into the carriage, and went to the prince. Quite changed in her appearance, not at all like as she was before, however much she suffered she was as pretty as a Lucretia; and the prince fell so much in love with her that he decided on the spot that he would marry her; and so they got married, with great splendor, and spent their time together in great happiness.

When the two elder sisters came home from the forest their father inquired where Kindness was. "Has she not come home?" said they; "we thought that she would have been home before us. As she was running after butterflies she got separated from us. We looked for her everywhere and called for her; as we got no answer we set off home before the darkness set in."

The king gave orders that Kindness was to be looked for everywhere; they searched for days but could not find her; then the king got so angry in his sorrow that he drove the two elder girls away because they had not taken proper care of their sister. They set out into the world in quite another direction, but by accident arrived in the country where Kindness was queen; here they lived a retired life in a small town unknown to all. Kindness at this time was enceinte;* and as war broke out with a neighboring nation her royal husband was obliged to go to the field of battle. The war lasted a long time, and in the meantime Kindness gave birth to twins, two handsome sons; on the forehead of one was the sign of the blessed sun, on the other the sign of the blessed moon; in great joy the

---

*Pregnant.

queen's guardian sent a letter containing the good news to the king by a messenger to the camp. The messenger had to pass through the small town where the envious sisters dwelt; it was quite dark when he arrived, and as he did not see a light anywhere but in their window he went and asked for a night's lodging; while he stayed there he told them all about the object of his journey; you may imagine how well he was received, and with what pleasure they offered him lodging, these envious brutes! When the messenger fell asleep they immediately took possession of the letter, tore it open, read it, and burnt it, and put in its place another to the king, saying that the queen had given birth to two monsters that looked more like puppies than babes; in the morning they gave meat and drink to the messenger, and pressed him to call and see them on his way back, as they would be delighted to see him. He accepted their kind invitation, and promised that he would come to them, and to no one else, on his return. The messenger arrived at the camp and delivered his letter to the king, who was very downcast as he read it; but still he wrote back and said that his wife was not to be blamed: "If it has happened thus how can I help it? Don't show her the slightest discourtesy," wrote he. As the messenger went back he slept again in the house of the two old serpent-sisters; they stole the king's letter and wrote in its place: "I want neither children nor mother; see that by the time I come home those monsters be out of my way, so that not even so much as their name remain." When this letter was read every one was very sorry for the poor queen, and couldn't make out why the king was so angry, but there was nothing for it but for the king's orders to be carried out, and so the two pretty babes were put in a sheet and hung round Kindness's neck, and she was sent away. For days and days poor Kindness walked about suffering hunger and thirst, till at last she came to a pretty wood; passing through this she traveled through a valley covered with trees; passing through this at last she saw the great alpine fir-trees at the end of the vale; there she found a clear spring; in her parching thirst she stooped to drink, but in her hurry she lost her balance and fell into the water; as she tried to drag herself out with her two stumps, to her intense astonishment she found that by immersion her two hands had grown again as they were before; she wept for joy. Although she was hiding in an unknown place with no husband, no father, no friend, no help whatever, with two starving children in this great wilderness, still she wasn't sorrowful, because she was so delighted to have her hands again. She stood there, and could not make up her mind in which direction to go; as she stood looking all round she suddenly caught sight of an old man coming toward her. "Who are you?" said the old man. "Who am I?" she replied, sighing deeply; "I'm an unfortunate queen." She then told him all she had suffered, and how she had recovered her hands that very minute by washing in the spring. "My poor good daughter," said the old man, bitterly, "then we are both afflicted ones; it's quite enough that you are alive, and that I have found you. Listen to me: your husband was warring against me, he drove me from my country, and hiding from him I came this way; not very far from here with one of my faithful servants I have built a hut and we will live together there." The old man, in order to prove the miraculous curing power of the spring, dipped his maimed finger into it, which was shot off in the last war; as he took it out, lo! it was all right once more.

When the war was over, Kindness's husband returned home and inquired after his wife. They told him all that had happened, and he was deeply grieved, and went in search of her with a great number of his people, and they found her at last with her two pretty babes, living with her old father. On inquiry it was also found out where the messenger with the letters had slept and how the letters were changed. Pride and Gentleness were summoned and sentenced to death; but Kindness forgave them all their misdeeds, and was so kind to them that she obtained their pardon, and also persuaded her father to forgive them.

There is no more of this speech to which you need listen, as I have told it to the very end and I have not missed a word out of it. Those of whom I have spoken may they be your guests, every one of them, tomorrow!

Italo Calvino
Olive[*]

Once upon a time a rich Jew lost his wife in childbirth and had to leave his newborn daughter to be raised by a farmer who was a Christian.

In the beginning, the farmer was reluctant to take on the burden. "I have children of my own," he explained, "and can't bring up your little girl in the Hebrew faith. She'd always be with my children and become accustomed to our Christian ways."

"It doesn't matter," replied the Jew. "Please do me a favor and keep her, and you will be repaid. If I've not come back for her by the time she's ten, then you are free to do as you please, for that will mean I'll never return and the child will be with you for good."

The Jew and the farmer came to an agreement, and the Jew left on a journey to distant lands to look after his business. The baby was nursed by the farmer's wife who, finding her so gentle and pretty, became as attached to her as if she'd been her own daughter. The child learned to walk in no time, played with the other children, and did everything children of her age do; but no one ever

[*] Italo Calvino, *Italian Folktales*, trans. George Martin (San Diego: Harcourt Brace, 1980), 255–61. No. 71. Calvino's source for the story is an 1880 collection of folktales by Gherardo Nerucci. It was "told by the widow Luisa Ginanni" in Montale Pistoiese, Tuscany (730).

spoke to her about the Christian commandments. She heard everybody else saying their prayers, but she didn't know what religion was and remained in ignorance of it up to her tenth year.

When she reached ten, the farmer and his wife looked for the Jew to show up any day and reclaim her. But her eleventh year also passed, then the twelfth, thirteenth, and fourteenth, without any sign of the Jew. So they concluded he had died. "We've now waited long enough," they said. "It's high time to have this daughter baptized."

They had her instructed in the faith, then baptized in pomp, with the whole town looking on. They named her Olive and sent her to school to learn women's skills as well as reading and writing. So by the time she was eighteen, Olive was truly a fine girl, well-mannered, loving, beautiful, and cherished by all.

The farmer and his family were now happy and their minds at rest, when one morning a knock was heard on the door. They opened up. It was the Jew. "I've come for my daughter."

"What!" exclaimed the mother. "You said if you'd not returned by the time she was ten for us to do as we pleased, since she'd then be our daughter. Eighteen years have passed. What right can you possibly have to her? We had her baptized, and now Olive is a Christian girl."

"I don't care," replied the Jew. "I didn't show up sooner, because I couldn't. But the girl is my daughter, and I'm taking her back."

"We're not giving her to you, that's for sure!" screamed the whole family in unison.

A bitter quarrel ensued. The Jew took the matter to court, and the court granted him custody of the girl, since she was his own daughter. The poor farmer and his family therefore had no choice but comply with the law. They all wept, the most heartbroken of all being Olive herself, as her father was a total stranger to her. With tears streaming down her face, she broke away from those good people who'd been her mother and father for so long.

Bidding her goodbye, the woman slipped Olive a copy of the Office of the Blessed Virgin and urged her never to forget she was a Christian. With that, those two gentle souls separated.

When they got home, the first thing the Jew said to Olive was, "Here, we are Jews, and you are too. You will believe what we believe. Heaven help you if I ever catch you reading the book the woman gave you. The first time I'll throw it into the fire and beat you, and the next time I'll cut off your hands and turn you out of the house. Watch your step, because I mean what I say."

Under those threats, poor Olive had no choice but publicly pretend she was Jewish. Locked in her room, though, she said the Office and Litanies of the Blessed Virgin while her faithful maid kept watch, in case her father should unexpectedly appear. All precaution was useless in the end, for the Jew caught her by surprise one day kneeling and reading from the book. Seized with rage, he flung the book into the fire and beat her unmercifully.

That did not discourage Olive. She had her maid buy her a second book like the first and continued to read in it. But the Jew was suspicious and, without seeming to, watched her constantly. Finally he burst into her room and caught her again. This time, without a word, he led her to a workbench, motioned for her to stretch out her hands, and, with a sharp knife, cut them clean off. Then he ordered her taken into the woods and abandoned.

The unfortunate girl remained there more dead than alive, and with no hands what could she do now? She set out and walked and walked until she came to a large palace. She thought of going in and asking for alms, but the palace was surrounded by a high doorless wall, which enclosed a beautiful garden. Jutting out over the top of the wall were branches of a pear tree laden with ripe, yellow pears.

"Oh, if only I had one of those pears!" exclaimed Olive. "Is there any way of reaching them?"

The words were no sooner out of her mouth than the wall opened and the pear tree bent down its branches, so that Olive, who had no hands, could reach the pears with her teeth and eat them while they were still on the tree. When she had eaten her fill, the tree raised its branches once more, the wall closed back together, and Olive returned to the woods. She now knew the secret and went and stood under the pear tree every day at eleven o'clock and made a meal off the fruit. Then she would return to the densest part of the woods and get through the night the best she could.

These were very fine pears, and one morning the king who lived in the palace decided to sample them, so he sent his servant out to pick a few. The servant came back quite dismayed. "Majesty, some animal has been climbing the tree and gnawing the pears down to the core!"

"We'll catch him," said the king. He built a hut out of branches and lay in wait every night, but he lost sleep that way while the pears continued to be nibbled. He therefore decided to watch in the daytime; at eleven o'clock he saw the wall open, the pear tree bend down its branches, and Olive bite into first one pear and then another. The king, who had been ready to shoot, dropped his gun in amazement. All he could do was stare at the beautiful maiden as she ate and then disappeared through the wall, which closed behind her.

He called his servant at once, and they scoured the woods for the thief. Suddenly they came upon her sleeping under a bush.

"Who are you? What are you doing here?" asked the king. "How dare you steal my pears? I was about to shoot you down with my shotgun!"

By way of reply, Olive showed him her stumps.

"You poor girl!" exclaimed the king. "What villain mutilated you so cruelly?" After hearing her story, he said, "I don't care about the pears. Come and live in my palace. My mother the queen will indeed keep you with her and look after you."

So Olive was presented to the queen, but the son mentioned neither the pear tree's bending down nor the wall's opening by itself, lest his mother think the girl a witch and detest her. The queen did not actually refuse to take Olive in, but she had no love for her and gave her little to eat, for the simple reason that the king was too charmed by the handless maiden's beauty. To rid him of any idea he might have, she said, "My son, it's time you looked about for a wife. Any number of princesses could be yours for the asking. Take servants, horses, and money, and travel around until you have found her."

The king obediently departed and was away visiting courts in many lands. But six months later he came home and said, "Don't be angry with me, Mamma. There's no shortage of princesses in this world. But I met none so kind and beautiful as Olive. So I've decided Olive is the maiden I'll marry."

"What!" exclaimed the queen. "A handless girl from the woods? You know nothing about her! Would you disgrace yourself like that?"

But the queen mother's words fell on deaf ears, and the king married Olive without further delay.

Having a daughter-in-law of unknown origins was more than the old queen could bear, and she lost no opportunity to be rude and mean to Olive, taking care on the other hand not to displease the king. Wisely, Olive never made any protest.

In the meantime Olive expected a baby, to the great joy of the king; but certain neighboring kings declared war on him, obliging him to lead his soldiers to the defense of the kingdom.

Before leaving, he wanted to entrust Olive to his mother, but the old queen said, "No, I can't assume such responsibility. I too am leaving the palace and shutting myself up in a convent."

So Olive had to stay at the palace by herself, and the king urged her to write him a letter every day. Thus the king left for the battle-field and the old queen for the convent, while Olive remained at the court with all the servants. Every day a messenger left the court with a letter from Olive to the king, but at the same time an aunt of the old queen plied between court and convent to inform her of everything that went on. Upon learning that Olive had given birth to two fine babies, the old queen left the convent and re-turned to the palace under the pretext of coming home to help her daughter-in-law. She called the guards, forced Olive out of bed, thrust a baby under each of their mother's arms, and told the guards to take the young queen back to the woods where the king had found her.

"Leave her there to starve to death," she said to the guards. "Your heads will roll if you disobey my orders and if you ever breathe a word of this!"

Then the old queen wrote to her son that his wife had died in childbirth along with her babies; so that he would believe the lie, she had three wax figures made, then held a grand funeral and burial in the royal chapel. For the ceremony she wore mourning and wept many tears.

Off at war, the king couldn't get over the unfortunate event, nor did he suspect foul play on the part of his mother.

But let's go back to Olive, handless in the middle of the woods and dying of hunger and thirst, with those two babies in her arms. She walked onward until she came to a pool of water where a little old woman was washing clothes.

"My good woman," said Olive, "please squeeze the water out of one of your cloths into my mouth. I'm dying of thirst."

"No," replied the old woman, "do as I say: kneel down and drink right from the pool."

"But can't you see I have no hands and must hold my babies in my arms?"

"That doesn't matter. Go on and try."

Olive knelt down, but as she bent over the pool, both babies slipped out of her arms, one after the other, and disappeared under the water. "Oh, my babies! My babies! Help! They're drowning! Help me!"

The old woman didn't budge.

"Don't be afraid, they won't drown. Fish them out."

"How can I? Don't you see I have no hands?"

"Plunge in your stumps."

Oliver immersed her stumps in the water and felt her hands growing back. With her hands she then grabbed hold of the babies and pulled them up safe and sound.

"Be on your way now," said the old woman. "You no longer lack hands to do for yourself. Farewell." She was out of sight before Olive could even thank her for her fine deed.

Wandering about the woods in search of a refuge, Olive came to a brand-new villa with the door wide open. She went in to ask for shelter, but no one was there. A kettle of porridge was boiling on the hearth next to some heavier foods. Olive fed her children, ate something herself, then went into a room where there was a bed and two cradles; she put the two children to bed, then lay down herself. She thus lived in the villa without ever needing a thing or seeing a soul anywhere around the place.

But let's leave her and go back to the king, who went home when the war was over and found the town in mourning. His mother tried to comfort him, but he was more and more unhappy as time went on. In an effort to cheer up, he decided to go hunting. In the woods he was overtaken by a storm, and it looked as though the earth would yawn under all the thunder and lightning. "If only I might die!" said the king to himself. "What reason do I have to go on living without Olive?" Through the trees he spied a faint light and moved toward it in search of shelter. He knocked, and Olive opened. He did not recognize her, and she said nothing, but welcomed him cordially and invited him up to the fire to warm himself while she and the children bustled about to make him comfortable.

The king watched her, thinking how much like Olive she was; but noticing her perfectly normal hands, he shook his head. As the children jumped and played around him, he said, "I might have been blessed with children like that, but they died, alas, with their mother, and here I am all alone and miserable!"

Meanwhile Olive had gone to turn down the guest's bed and called her children to her. "Listen," she whispered to them, "when we go back in the other room, ask me to tell you a story. I'll refuse and even threaten to slap you, but you keep on begging me."

"Yes, Mamma, we'll do that."

So when they got back to the fireside, they began saying, "Mamma, tell us one of your stories!"

"What are you thinking of! It's late, and the gentleman is tired and doesn't want to hear any story!"

"Come on, Mamma, please!"

"If you're not quiet, I'll slap you!"

"Poor little things!" said the king. "How could you slap them? Go on and make them happy. I'm not at all sleepy and would like to hear a story too."

With that encouragement, Olive sat down and began her tale. The king gradually became serious, listened more and more anxiously, asking repeatedly, "And then? And then?" because it was the life story exactly of his poor wife. But he didn't dare get his hopes up, for the mystery of the hands was still unexplained. Finally he broke down and asked, "And about her hands that were cut off, how did that turn out in the end?" Olive therefore told him about the old washerwoman.

"Then it's you!" cried the king, and they hugged and kissed. But after they had given vent to their joy, the king's face darkened. "I must return to the palace at once and punish my mother as she deserves!"

"No, not that!" said Olive. "If you really love me, you must promise not to lay a hand on your mother. She will be sorry enough as it is. The poor old soul believed she was acting in the interest of the kingdom. Spare her life, since I forgive her for all she has done to me."

So the king returned to the palace and said nothing to his mother.

"I was uneasy about you," she said to him. "How did you get through the night out in that storm?"

"I passed a good night, Mamma."

"What!" said the queen, growing suspicious.

"Yes, at the home of kind-hearted people who kept my spirits up. It was the first time since Olive's death I've felt cheerful. By the way, Mamma, is Olive really dead?"

"What do you mean? The whole town was at the funeral."

"I'd like to put some flowers on her grave, and see with my own eyes . . ."

"Why all the suspicion?" asked the queen, flushed with anger. "Is that any attitude for a son to have toward his mother, doubting her word?"

"Go on, Mamma, enough of these lies! Olive, come in!"

In walked Olive leading their children. The queen, who had been crimson with rage, now turned white with fear. But Olive said, "Don't be afraid, we'll do you no harm. Our joy in finding one another again is too great to feel anything else."

The queen returned to the convent, and the king and Olive lived in peace for the rest of their life.

Aleksandr Afanas'ev

The Armless Maiden*

In a certain kingdom, not in our land, there lived a wealthy merchant; he had two children, a son and a daughter. The father and mother died. The brother said to the sister: "Let us leave this town, little sister; I will rent a shop and trade, and find lodgings for you; we will live together." They went to another province. When they came there, the brother inscribed himself in the merchant's guild, and rented a shop of woven cloths. The brother decided to marry and took a sorceress to wife. One day he went to trade in his shop and said to his sister: "Keep order in the house, sister." The wife felt offended because he said this to his sister. To revenge herself she broke all the furniture and when her husband came back she met him and said: "See what a sister you have; she has broken all the furniture in the house." "Too bad, but we can get some new things," said the husband.

The next day when leaving for his shop he said farewell to his wife and his sister and said to his sister: "Please, little sister, see to it that everything in the house is kept as well as possible." The wife bided her time, went to the stables, and cut off the head of her husband's favorite horse with a saber. She awaited him on the porch. "See what a sister you have," she said. "She has cut off the head of your favorite horse." "Ah, let the dogs eat what is theirs," answered the husband.

On the third day the husband again went to his shop, said farewell, and said to his sister: "Please look after my wife, so that she does not hurt herself or the baby, if by chance she gives birth to one." When the wife gave birth to her child, she cut off his head.

* Aleksandr Afanas'ev, *Russian Fairy Tales*, trans. Norbert Guterman (New York: Random House, 1973), 294–99.

When her husband came home he found her sitting and lamenting over her baby. "See what a sister you have! No sooner had I given birth to my baby than she cut off his head with a saber." The husband did not say anything; he wept bitter tears and turned away.

Night came. At the stroke of midnight he rose and said: "Little sister, make ready; we are going to mass." She said, "My beloved brother, I do not think it is a holiday today." "Yes, my sister, it is a holiday; let us go." "It is still too early to go, brother," she said. "No," he answered, "young maidens always take a long time to get ready." The sister began to dress; she was very slow and reluctant. Her brother said, "Hurry, little sister, get dressed." "Please," she said, "it is still early." "No, little sister, it is not early, it is high time to be gone."

When the sister was ready they sat in a carriage and set out for mass. They drove for a long time or a short time. Finally they came to a wood. The sister said: "What wood is this?" He answered: "This is the hedge around the church." The carriage caught in a bush. The brother said: "Get out, little sister, disentangle the carriage." "Ah, my beloved brother, I cannot do that, I will dirty my dress." "I will buy you a new dress, sister, a better one than this." She got down from the carriage, began to disentangle it, and her brother cut off her arms to the elbows, struck his horse with the whip, and drove away.

The little sister was left alone; she burst into tears and began to walk in the woods. She walked and walked, a long time or a short time; she was all scratched, but could not find a path leading out of the woods. Finally, after several years, she found a path. She came to a market town and stood beneath the window of the wealthiest merchant to beg for alms. This merchant had a son, an only one, who was the apple of his father's eye. He fell in love with the beggar woman and said: "Dear father and mother, marry me." "To whom shall we marry you?" "To this beggar woman." "Ah, my dear child, do not the merchants of our town have lovely daughters?" "Please marry me to her," he said. "If you do not, I will do something to myself." They were distressed, because he was their only son, their life's treasure. They gathered all the merchants and clerics and asked them to judge the matter: should they marry their son to the beggar woman or not? The priest said: "Such must be his fate, and God gives your son his sanction to marry the beggar woman."

So the son lived with her for a year and then another year. At the end of that time he went to another province, where her brother had his shop. When taking his leave he said: "Dear father and mother, do not abandon my wife; as soon as she gives birth to a child, write to me that very hour." Two or three months after the son left, his wife gave birth to a child; his arms were golden up to the elbow, his sides were studded with stars, there was a bright moon on his forehead and a radiant sun near his heart. The grandparents were overjoyed and at once wrote their beloved son a letter. They dispatched an old man with this note in all haste. Meanwhile the wicked sister-in-law had learned all about this and invited the old messenger into her house. "Come in, little father," she said, "and take a rest." "No, I have no time, I am bringing an urgent message." "Come in, little father, take a rest, have something to eat."

She sat him down to dinner, took his bag, found the letter in it, read it, tore it into little pieces, and wrote another letter instead: "Your wife," it said, "has given birth to a half dog and half bear that she conceived with beasts in the woods." The old messenger came to the merchant's son and handed him the letter; he read it and burst into tears. He wrote in answer, asking that his son not be molested till he returned. "When I come back," he said, "I will see what kind of baby it is." The sorceress again invited the old messenger into her house. "Come in, sit down, take a rest," she said. Again she charmed him with talk, stole the letter he carried, read it, tore it up, and instead ordered that her sister-in-law be driven out the moment the letter was received. The old messenger brought this letter; the father and mother read it and were grieved. "Why does he cause us so much trouble?" they said. "We married him to the girl, and now he does not want his wife!" They pitied not so much the wife as the babe. So they gave their blessing to her and the babe, tied the babe to her breast, and sent her away.

She went, shedding bitter tears. She walked, for a long time or a short time, all in the open field, and there was no wood or village anywhere. She came to a dale and was very thirsty. She looked to the right and saw a well. She wanted to drink from it but was afraid to stoop, lest she drop her baby. Then she fancied that the water came closer. She stooped to drink and her baby fell into the well. She began to walk around the well, weeping, and wondering how to get her child out of the well. An old man came up to her and said: "Why are you weeping, you slave of God?" "How can I help weeping? I stooped over the well to drink water and my baby fell into it." "Bend down and take him out." "No, little father, I cannot; I have no hands, only stumps." "Do as I tell you. Take your baby." She went to the well, stretched out her arms, and God helped, for suddenly she had her hands, all whole. She bent down, pulled her baby out, and began to give thanks to God, bowing to all four sides.

She said her prayers, went on farther, and came to the house where her brother and husband were staying, and asked for shelter. Her husband said: "Brother, let the beggar woman in; beggar women can tell stories and recount real happenings." The wicked sister-in-law said: "We have no room for visitors, we are overcrowded." "Please, brother, let her come; there is nothing I like better than to hear beggar women tell tales." They let her in. She sat on the stove with her baby. Her husband said: "Now, little dove, tell us a tale—any kind of story."

She said: "I do not know any tales or stories, but I can tell you the truth. Listen, here is a true happening that I can recount to you." And she began: "In a certain kingdom, not in our land, lived a wealthy merchant; he had two children, a son and a daughter. The father and mother died. The brother said to the sister: 'Let us leave this town, little sister.' And they came to another province. The brother inscribed himself in the merchant's guild and took a shop of woven cloth. He decided to marry and took a sorceress to wife." At this point the sister-in-law muttered: "Why does she bore us with her stories, that hag?" But the husband said, "Go on, go on, little mother, I love such stories more than anything!"

"And so," the beggar woman went on, "the brother went to trade in his shop and said to his sister: 'Keep order in the house, sister.' The wife felt offended because he had said this to his sister and out of spite broke all the furniture." And then she went on to tell how her brother took her to mass and cut off her hands, how she gave birth to a baby, how her sister-in-law lured the old messenger—and again the sister-in-law interrupted her, crying "What gibberish she is telling!" But the husband said: "Brother, order your wife to keep quiet; it is a wonderful story, is it not?"

She came to the point when her husband wrote to his parents ordering that the baby be left in peace until his return, and the sister-in-law mumbled: "What nonsense!" Then she reached the point when she came to their house as a beggar woman, and the sister-in-law mumbled: "What is this old bitch talking about!" And the husband said: "Brother, order her to keep quiet; why does she interrupt all the time?" Finally she came to the point in the story when she was let in and began to tell the truth instead of a story. And then she pointed at them and said: "This is my husband, this is my brother, and this is my sister-in-law."

Then her husband jumped up to her on the stove and said: "Now, my dear, show me the baby. Let me see whether my father and mother wrote me the truth." They took the baby, removed its swaddling clothes—and the whole room was illuminated! "So it is true that she did not just tell us a tale; here is my wife, and here is my son—golden up to the elbows—his sides studded with stars, a bright moon on his forehead, and a radiant sun near his heart!"

The brother took the best mare from his stable, tied his wife to its tail, and let it run in the open field. The mare dragged her on the ground until she brought back only her braid; the rest was strewn on the field. Then they harnessed three horses and went home to the young husband's father and mother; they began to live happily and to prosper. I was there and drank mead and wine; it ran down my mustache, but did not go into my mouth.

IV. THE MERCHANT OF VENICE

"A Pound of Flesh" folktales revolve around the same strange contract that Shylock proposes to Antonio in *The Merchant of Venice*, and its even stranger negotiation.* In the folktale, a man agrees that if he defaults on a loan, his lender can cut a specific amount of flesh from the man's body. Ultimately, this contract is voided by the argument that the creditor must cut the exact amount, no more and no less, and/or that he must not spill any of the man's blood, to which the contract gives him no claim. Just so in Shakespeare's play: the merchant Antonio asks his inveterate enemy Shylock for a loan. The money is for Antonio's friend Bassanio, who needs it to woo the beautiful heiress Portia. Shylock proposes a "merry sport," that if Antonio fails to pay back the loan in three months, Shylock may cut off a pound of Antonio's flesh (1.3.140–47). When three of Antonio's cargo ships are lost at sea and he is unable to repay the loan on time, Shylock has Antonio arrested and prepares to repossess his collateral, whetting his knife in the courtroom, but is thwarted by Portia, disguised as a lawyer. She demands the requisite impossibilities, that Shylock cut an exact pound and that he shed no blood. The duke of Venice enforces this sentence: Shylock must pay a devastating fine and convert to Christianity.

Despite this narrative core shared by the "Pound of Flesh" stories and the Shylock plot of *The Merchant of Venice*, the folktale characters often differ startlingly from Shakespeare's dramatis

---

* "A Pound of Flesh" is ATU 890. The central motif is J1161.2 *"Pound of flesh. Literal pleading frees man from pound of flesh contract. Contract does not give the right to shed blood. Impossible, therefore, to carry out."*

personae. In three of the tales that follow, the hero's wife, disguised as a man, successfully saves her husband the debtor, just as Portia saves Antonio in the judgment scene. Generations of Shakespeare's readers and audiences have seen Portia as an emblem of wise justice and Christian mercy. These folktale heroines, however, are tricksters and femmes fatales who lure men variously into bed, salvation, or doom. In the oldest known version of the story, from the twelfth-century story collection *Dolopathos* (reprinted here as "The Creditor"), the heroine is a sorceress.

In the Persian "Pound of Flesh" tale included here, "Fareed and the Kázi," it is not the wife but rather a judge who cleverly releases the debtor from his bond. This tale is an example of how "A Pound of Flesh" sometimes combines with another folktale type, "Series of Clever Unjust Decisions" (ATU 1534). In these stories, the judgment on the flesh contract is just one of several absurd pronouncements by a compromised, biased, or simply whimsical judge. This folktale context does not reflect well on Portia's tricky resolution of Shylock's lawsuit. A seventeenth-century adaptation of *The Merchant of Venice*, performed by the English Comedians theater company in Germany, alludes to these "Clever Unjust Decision" folktales, which suggests that they were known in Renaissance Europe.*

The nominal hero of the "Pound of Flesh" folktales, the borrower, is often feckless: irresponsible, gullible, unbelievably forgetful, and in the Moroccan version here, weepy. While in Shakespeare's play, the hero Bassanio's friend Antonio takes out the loan on Bassanio's behalf, in the folktales the hero himself nearly always borrows the money. The exception is a fourteenth-century Italian "Pound of Flesh" story, in which the hero's foster father takes out the loan to finance the young man's adventures. This story, from

---

* Brennecke, *Shakespeare in Germany*, 114–17.

Giovanni Fiorentino's *The Dunce* (*Il Pecorone*), was all but certainly known to Shakespeare, and is usually considered his source for the Shylock plot.* Interestingly, the English Comedians' 1611 adaptation of *Merchant* reverts to the simpler and arguably more dramatic folktale structure, in which the hero himself enters into the ill-advised contract with the villain.

Shylock seems defined by his Jewishness, but the folktale villains are not always Jews. In the Chilean folktale "White Onion," the cruel creditor is not an outsider, but the debtor's own godfather. The villain in *Dolopathos* has ample reason for his animosity against the hero: the young man borrows money from a rich serf whose foot the young man had cut off in a fit of rage sometime earlier. We might be reminded of Shylock's understandable hatred for his anti-Semitic persecutor, Antonio, even though the medieval story does not involve sectarian strife. Even in the folktales in which the lender is Jewish, the conflict is not always between a Jew and a Christian. The adversary is a Jew in the Persian story here, but his victim is a Muslim. "A Pound of Flesh" folktales circulated in Jewish communities, as the Moroccan tale "The Cruel Creditor" demonstrates. All of the characters in this story presumably are Jewish.

The Merchant of Venice includes a folktale motif distinct from the "Pound of Flesh" tradition, a test requiring a choice among gold, silver, and lead caskets in order to gain a spouse.† Portia's dead father left instructions in his will that his daughter could marry only the man who correctly chooses the lead casket over the more opulent gold and silver ones, as Bassanio does. Bassanio, it seems, is subjected to a test to win Portia that is often the lot of girls in folktales. Shakespeare apparently found this motif in a story from a

---

*Bullough, *Narrative and Dramatic Sources*, 1.463–76.

† The relevant motifs are L211: "*Modest choice: three caskets type*" and H511.1: "*Three caskets.* Princess offered to the man who chooses correctly from three caskets."

medieval collection of pulpit anecdotes, the *Gesta Romanorum*, in which a princess must prove her identity as the true bride through the casket trial. She correctly picks the lead casket and earns her husband.[*] The motif sometimes occurs in the folktale type "The Kind and Unkind Girls" (ATU 480),[†] represented here by the Irish folktale "The Maid in the Country Underground." In this story, the heroine's selection of the lead casket leads indirectly to her marriage to the king. Portia plays a song for Bassanio when he makes his choice that subtly suggests the correct answer, through its rhymes with "lead"—"Tell me where is fancy bred, / Or in the heart or in the head, / How begot, how nourished?" (3.2.63–65)—and its message that eyes cannot be trusted. Similarly, little birds chirp to the heroine of the Irish folktale that she should pick the lead casket.

A POUND OF FLESH

Johannes de Alta Silva

The Creditor[‡]

There was once a certain powerful nobleman who had a strong castle and many other possessions. After his wife died his only heir was a daughter whom he decided to educate in the liberal arts, thinking that training in the arts and the books of the philosophers would give her the wisdom (which is better than strength)

---

[*] Bullough, *Narrative and Dramatic Sources*, 1.511–14.

[†] Roberts, *Kind and Unkind Girls*, 4.

[‡] Johnannes de Alta Silva, *Dolopathos, or The King and the Seven Wise Men*, trans. Brady B. Gilleland (Binghamton, NY: Center for Medieval and Early Renaissance Studies, 1981), 55–58. *Dolopathos* dates from 1184–1212 and was written in Latin.

to protect her inheritance. A woman is physically weak and unable to bear arms. Nor was he wrong. She obtained such knowledge and cleverness from her studies that she even learned the art of magic without a teacher. Sometime after this her father took to his bed with a high fever. He realized that he could not recover and made a will in which he left everything to his daughter. When his affairs were in order he died. The girl, now mistress of the inheritance, decided that she would marry no man except one equal to her in wisdom and noble birth. Many young noblemen, attracted by her beauty or wealth, came to seek her hand in marriage. They wooed her with prayers, enticed her with gifts, gave much and promised more. She, however, wisely spurned and scorned no one, but offered to marry anyone on one condition. The suitor had to pay a hundred marks of silver on the first night and then might enjoy her and her charms. On the next morning, if they were both satisfied with the deed, they would hold a proper marriage in public. When this condition was made known many youths and many men of more advanced age came to offer her the twenty pounds of marks, but they always returned without enjoying her embraces and without their money. With her magic art she had cast a spell on the feather of a night owl, and when she put this under the head of the one lying with her, he immediately fell into a deep sleep and did not move until the dawn of the next day, or until she removed the feather. In this way she stripped many men of their money and stored up great treasure for herself, increasing her fortune by others' losses.

Among those who poured money down this bottomless pit was a certain noble youth sufficient in nobility of birth but poor. Finding the hundred marks beyond his means, he borrowed the money and accepted the maid's condition. When she had received the money, she spent the day feasting and drinking a great deal with the youth. At night both of them lay naked together on the soft bed covering, but first she placed the owl's feather under the youth's pillow. He had not even found a comfortable place in the bed when he fell asleep and forgot the maiden beside him. At dawn she arose and took away the feather. When he awoke, terribly upset, she sent him about his own business.

The young man, however, angry that he had been fooled, asked a certain rich serf to lend him another hundred marks of silver, since he wished either to lose the money again or take the girl's virginity. Now once in a fit of rage the young man had cut off the serf's foot, and with this in mind the serf promised him the money on the condition that he must repay it within a year. If he failed to repay, the serf could cut from the flesh and bones of the youth a weight equal to a hundred marks. The youth carelessly agreed, and in addition he gave him a contract sealed and signed in his own handwriting.

When he had received the money, he returned to the girl and offered it to her. She accepted and they spent the day happily until evening. Later, when the bedroom had been made ready and the feather placed under the pillow as usual, the girl sent him in first. As he approached the bed where he had lain before, the thought occurred to him that the stupor had come upon him because the bed was soft and comfortable. He picked up the pillow and removed it. By a lucky chance this dislodged the owl's feather. Then he lay down on the bed, kept his eyes open, and fought sleep with all his strength. She believed that the youth had fallen asleep again because of her magic and carelessly lay naked next to him. After he had pretended that he was sleeping heavily for a little while, he drew the maiden to him and demanded his due. Confused and astonished, she had to fulfill her promise. But why go on? The whole night was spent in pleasure. In the morning both were in complete agreement and they were properly married before their friends and relatives, although many were surprised and even envious.

In these happy circumstances, the young man forgot his creditor and did not repay the money within the allotted time. The cripple was overjoyed at the chance to gain vengeance for his injury and went to the king who was then ruling the country. He brought a complaint against the young man, showed the handwriting as witness of the agreement, and demanded that justice be done. The king was horrified at the cruel contract; nevertheless, because he was a very just man, he ordered the youth to come to reply to his accuser's complaints. Only then did he remember the debt. Terrified by the king's authority he went with a group of his friends, taking a great amount of gold and silver to the court. His enemy showed him the handwriting, which he admitted to be his, and the king ordered his nobles to pass sentence. They decreed that the cripple could do what the contract stipulated or instead he could receive as much money as he wished in payment. The king then asked if he would take double the amount and spare the youth. He refused and the king spent many days trying to convince him.

One day, the wife of the young man, in men's clothing, dismounted from her horse before the palace of the king. She had changed her features and voice by her magic power. She approached the king and greeted him reverently. When asked who she was and where she came from, she replied that she was a knight who had just come from the farthest parts of the world and was an expert interpreter of justice, the laws, and trials. The king was overjoyed and ordered her (whom he thought to be a knight) to sit in judgment and conclude the case between the cripple and the young man. When both parties were summoned, she said, "Cripple, according to the sentence of the king and the nobles you are permitted to carve from the flesh of the young man a weight equivalent to a hundred marks. But what will you gain except possibly death if you kill him? It is better that you receive your money seven times or even ten times over."

He said that he would not accept even ten thousand marks. Then she ordered a gleaming white cloth to be stretched on the floor and the youth, naked and bound, laid on it. When this was done, she said to the cripple, "Cut off a weight of flesh equivalent to your marks with any instrument you wish. But if you cut away a needle's point more or less than the just weight or if one drop of blood stains the cloth, since blood is the substance of the young man, you will immediately die a thousand deaths. You will be torn into a thousand pieces and thrown to the beasts and the birds, your whole family will undergo the same punishment, and your estate will be confiscated."

He began to quake at this horrible sentence and said, "There is no man, only God, who could control his hand so as to take neither more nor less. I shall not take the chance. I free the youth, I dismiss the debt, and I shall give him a thousand marks for reconciliation."

So the youth was freed by the wisdom of his wife and joyfully went his way.

Yolando Pino-Saavedra

White Onion*

A long, long time ago, White Onion lived on an island in the center of the sea. She vowed one day that she would give a ship full of gold and silver to whoever could go to bed with her and turn toward her side of the bed. He who turned was to marry her, and he who didn't was to pay her the treasure ship. There were many millionaires who thought about this and concluded, "Being in bed with her, how would it be possible not to turn over to her side?"

*Yolando Pino-Saavedra, *Folktales of Chile* (Chicago: University of Chicago Press, 1967), 194–98. "Collected in January 1951 in Ignao, Valdivia, from Francisco Coronado" (273).

One morning a very rich man arrived with his loaded ship to take up the bet. As they were tucking themselves in together, White Onion gave him a little glass of refreshment. Immediately he fell into a deep sleep until the next day, when she awoke him. The millionaire remembered with a fright that he had lost his fortune. After taking breakfast with the girl, he delivered her the ship and, penniless, took his leave. Very soon after, he told another millionaire about his encounter with White Onion. His friend was sure that he could certainly turn over in her bed, and loaded his treasure ship to set sail for the island.

"Do you come for the bet, my good gentleman?" she asked as he docked.

"For the bet, White Onion," he said confidently.

When they had agreed on the terms, she invited him to supper and bed. Just as they were getting under the covers, she gave him also the little bedtime nip. He took the drink in one swig and fell into the bed in a profound sleep. When she shook him awake the next morning, the poor man was greatly shocked at having lost all his riches. After breakfast, he headed home as poor as a church mouse.

Eventually he told a third millionaire of his misadventure with the famous White Onion. This one too set out confidently on the voyage. She invited him in for lunch and afterward took him for a stroll in the garden. The afternoon flew by agreeably and it was soon time for supper and bed. She gave him the same little glass just before bedtime, whereupon he too fell into a groggy slumber and didn't awake the whole night through. The girl roused him for breakfast in the morning, and of course he was heavily burdened with the loss of his fortune. In sheer dejection he nibbled at his breakfast and went trudging home, his pockets turned inside out. He told the tale to yet another millionaire, who tried and failed as the rest had done. She now had four victims to her credit.

Now it so happened that there was a very rich man who had one son. When this man was on his deathbed, he warned the boy never to fall in love with White Onion, for he would be left in the street with nothing. After this, the lad used to pass by many vendors selling onions, but he never bought a single one, for he wished to heed his father's advice. One day he passed a scabby old man with two baskets of onions.

"Will you buy some onions, young sir?" asked the vendor.

"I will if they're colored," he answered, "but not any white ones."

"Why on earth not?"

Then the boy told him how his father had warned him never to fall in love with White Onion. The grubby old fellow burst out laughing and said, "Young gentleman, it's not that at all. What your father said was never to fall in love with the princess White Onion who lives on the sea island and has a bet with all young men who will sleep with her that they can't turn over to her side of the bed."

The boy bought two baskets of onions from the seedy old fellow, and all the way home he wondered how it could possibly be that one could sleep with the princess without turning over. Right away he began to sell all his possessions and load a ship with gold and silver, after which he sailed away to the sea island. As he was getting into bed with White Onion, she gave him the glass of refreshment, and sure enough, he collapsed into a deep sleep until the next morning. He was greatly startled when she awoke him and cheerily served him breakfast. But immediately he asked her to lend him a boat so he could go for another shipload of gold and silver. The boy went straight to his godfather, who was twice as rich as White Onion. The old man knew that his godson had a great deal of wealth and decided that it was safe to lend him the ship for three days' time, on the condition that he would claim a pound of flesh from his godson's rump if the boat wasn't returned in time. As the boy was approaching White Onion's island for the second time he chanced through the garden near her house. Just at this moment a mangy, ragged old woman under the trees spoke up. "There goes that poor boy to lose another boatload. If only someone could tell him what it is that White Onion gives him."

"Listen, dirty one," said the boy, overhearing the woman's mumbling, "what makes me fall so sound asleep with her? If you'll tell me, I'll make you rich and powerful."

"Then heed me," she croaked. "Take the drink she gives you at bedtime and throw it away secretly under your cape. That way you won't fall asleep."

The boy went inside and undressed to go to bed with White Onion. She passed him the regular glass of refreshment, which he tossed away under his cape, tucking himself snugly under the covers. About midnight, he rolled over to her side of the bed, whereupon White Onion exclaimed, "This man is going to be my husband." The next morning, she sent for priests and bishops to wed the two of them. There was a great celebration, and in the midst of his joy, the young groom completely forgot about returning the boat to his godfather. When he remembered, he thought, "It doesn't really matter anyway. If he gets angry, I'll return two ships instead of one."

Once the celebrations were over, he sailed the ship back to hand it over to the old man. But his godfather refused to receive it, saying that he would demand his pound of flesh from the young man's rump. The boy refused and was immediately thrown in jail. As he still had a coin in his pocket, he sent for some paper and wrote a letter to White Onion. Upon receiving the news, she dressed herself as a viceroy and headed for the godfather's house, notifying him beforehand to expect a viceregal visit. White Onion sailed in her boat and went ashore with all the pomp of a true viceroy. She went directly to the jail and began to take declarations from the prisoners. One by one she set them free, until she came to the very last cell and spotted her husband. White Onion recognized him at once, but he had no idea who she was. She asked him for his declaration and got the whole story of his godfather's cruel greed.

"Is this so?" the viceroy asked the godfather sternly.

"It is," he answered.

"Very well, my dear sir. In that case, you shall take your pound of flesh, but all and exactly in one slice. If you cut either too much or too little, you'll have to pay."

The godfather protested that he wanted to take it in little pieces, and when the viceroy insisted on one single chunk, he shouted, "Then let everything be lost! To hell with it!"

With that, the viceroy took the prisoner aboard her boat and set sail. Since her husband was unshaven and disheveled after his days in jail, she dispatched him to clean up and change into some fresh clothes. When he was properly cleaned, he was the very mirror of fashion. The viceroy went to her cabin to change as well, and appeared dressed as a lovely woman.

"Look at me," she commanded her husband. "Do you know your woman now?"

"Maybe so and maybe not," he answered hesitantly, for they had been together only a short time before he was jailed.

"I'm your true wife," she announced joyously.

"No!" he gasped incredulously.

"What marks did your wife have?"

"Why, there were three golden hairs on the left side of her waist."

At that, the woman lifted her skirt. "Are these the ones?"

"By God, so they are!" he cried, opening his arms and hugging his wife to him.

They arrived home in great joy and began the celebrations again without any danger. The young husband was so happy that he went to see the grubby old woman and gave her a furnished house and a shipload of gold and silver. She became rich and powerful, and

White Onion and her husband lived happily together on the island.

Dov Noy

The Cruel Creditor*

In Casablanca there lived a very rich and highly respected Jewish merchant, who had an only son. One day the merchant fell ill. He called to his son and said: "I wish to talk to you, for it may well be that within a few days I shall die. What will you do, my son, with all the property that will remain in your hands, with all the houses and all the stores? I should like to know this before I die."

The son replied: "What do you mean 'What shall I do with it?' He who wishes for money and will ask me for it, I shall give it to him. When I see a great rejoicing, I will go there, I will take part in it and will rejoice in it, for I love rejoicing. When I see a beautiful girl, I will take her and I will give her much wealth."

"Woe to me!" said the father and wept on his bed. "Where shall all my money go, for which I have striven so long, all my life?"

The father died and there was no man to take care of the money and the many stores. Before the year was out, of all the goods that the merchant had left behind the widow and the son had not a single penny. The son had no choice and he began to beg for alms for himself and for his mother.

One day the poor mother revealed to her son that there was nothing in the house to eat. The son said to his mother: "I shall leave this town, for everybody knows me here. They know that I

---

*Dov Noy, *Moroccan Jewish Folktales* (New York: Herzl, 1966), 44–47. I have shortened the original title of this story, "The Cruel Creditor and the Judge's Wise Daughter," because there is no judge's daughter in the story. The title suggests a variant with a different heroine.

have been rich and that I have lost my money and property. For very shame I cannot stay here any longer."

And so he did. He left Casablanca and settled in Marrakesh. Who knows me there? he asked himself. But in Marrakesh there were many rich people, who in the past had done much business with his father and they knew his only son. "Why have you come here?" they asked him.

"I have come to buy goods!" he told them. "But the money that I took with me I spent on the road. If you will lend me money, I will return it to you."

One of the rich men said to him: "I can lend you any sum you ask for, but on one condition—you can do whatever you wish with the money and whatever profit you make will be yours. But if at year's end you do not pay up, you must give me one kilogram of the flesh of your body."

The unfortunate young man had no choice. He agreed to the condition and signed an agreement to that effect.

Throughout the year the young man engaged in business, but he was unlucky. He lost all the money that he had borrowed. Two months before the year's end he stopped taking food because of his anxiety about returning the money on the due date. He was especially worried by the condition that a kilogram of flesh would be cut from his body if he did not return the money.

What did the poor young man do? On the seashore there lived a king who had forbidden anyone to enter his palace. Only those who wished to die went there. The young man made his way to this palace, for he could see no other way out. He had not the courage to take his life with his own hands, but he said to himself: "I will go to the palace and there they will kill me."

The unlucky young man wished to enter the palace but, behold, it was shut and bolted. What did he do? He went straight to the window of the room of the king's daughter, and sat there weeping bitterly. The king's daughter looked out of the window to see who was weeping, but she could not make out who it was below.

Three days passed. All the time the young man sat beneath the princess's window weeping. On the fourth day the king's daughter called him:

"Come forth, man! If you are a man and not a spirit, show yourself and I will do all that you ask, for your tears have touched my heart. But if you are a spirit, I cannot be of any help to you."

Three times the princess called out to the young man until he replied. Before he showed himself, he asked her to promise that she would not kill him or do him any harm.

The princess promised and the young man emerged from his hiding place. Then the princes saw that the young man was very handsome. She asked him: "Tell me, young man, why do you weep? Perhaps I can help you?"

The unfortunate young man told her who he was, and the princess told him that she had known his dead father.

"I was wicked. I wasted all my father's money and my life. My poor mother has remained at home and who knows whether she has not died already of starvation. I wished to change my fortune and so I changed my place of residence. Then I met a rich man who had known my father . . ." And he continued to tell the king's daughter the tale of his life and of his agreement with the rich man. "Now the time has come for me to return the money, else I must give him a kilogram of my flesh."

"Go back to the town of that rich man to whom you owe the money," the princess advised him, "and tell me where you will live. I wish to send you a lawyer in order to help you." The young man remained in the palace and he and the princess loved each other without the king knowing anything of it. Before the year was out the young man returned to Marrakesh. All those who met him asked: "Where have you been all of this time?"

And he told them: "I went to such and such a city and there I married the beauty queen."

"And what about your lawsuit?"

"A lawyer will come and plead the case for me."

The time of the lawsuit came. The princess disguised as a lawyer entered the court together with the judge. The judge asked the rich man: "What does the young man owe you? What do you want of the young man?"

The rich man took the agreement out of his pocket and showed it to the judge. The judge read the agreement and asked the young man: "Do you agree that you signed this document?"

"Your Honor! What can I say? You see my signature here. But one thing you must know. I entered into this agreement with the rich man because I had no other choice."

Then the princess rose from her place, dressed in the robes of a lawyer. She addressed the judge: "Your Honor! I agree, on behalf of my client, to give a kilogram of flesh to the rich man but I insist that he cut off exactly one kilogram. If he cuts off too little then he must make up the difference himself, and if he cuts off too much, he will restore the extra amount from his own flesh to the young man."

The rich man rose and said: "I cannot cut exactly one kilogram of flesh in a single stroke. I am prepared to waive both the flesh and the money."

When the lawsuit was over, everybody went home. The princess changed her clothes and sought out her husband. "What sort of a lawyer was he that I sent you? Was he an able man?"

"He was very able," the young man replied. "I did not think that I would win the case."

"I will tell you something," she said to him. "I was the lawyer."

The young couple, accompanied by the young man's mother, left Marrakesh where everybody knew him and went to the king's palace. There a brilliant wedding was held, and the young couple lived a life of wealth and happiness.

Meherjibhai Nosherwanji Kuka

Fareed and the Kázi[*]

A person named Fareed had a beautiful wife, whom a Jew was in love with. The husband being poor and without any occupation, remained for the most part in his house, and the Jew could not get any opportunity of laying siege to the affections of his wife. So the Jew began to devise means of getting the husband away from the city, and accordingly one day said to him, "My friend, why do you remain idle here? Why do you not travel in order to become a successful trader? The little money that I have acquired was by traveling from place to place, bartering the commodity of one place for that of another, and so on." The husband replied, "It is all very well to say so, but you know trading requires money. And who is going to lend me the money necessary for the purpose?" The Jew, hereupon, good-naturedly (!) offered to accommodate him, saying, "I will lend you gold weighing one hundred *miscals*, on the condition that you return it to me on the very first day of your return to town from your journey." "But what security can I give to you?" asked Fareed. "None whatsoever do I need, but for form's sake, what say you to a hundred *miscals* of your flesh, which, on your failing to make the payment, I should be at liberty to cut off from your body?"

The condition was agreed upon, and Fareed, with the money in his pocket, left the town with the view of seeing the different com-

[*]Mehrjibhai Nosherwanji Kuka, *The Wit and Humour of the Persians* (Bombay: 1894), 229–32, https://babel.hathitrust.org/cgi/pt?id=njp.32101077700795;view =1up;seq=243 (accessed April 20, 2017). No. 188. I have supplied the title for this story

mercial centers. On the road he was attacked by robbers, who stripped him of everything valuable that he possessed, and so he was obliged to return, almost naked, to the town. The Jew was very much vexed on seeing him back in so short a time, and demanded back his money. As Fareed had absolutely nothing and could not comply with the demand, he said, "Let us go to the Kázi, and let him decide on this matter." So the two took their way toward the Court of the Kázi.*

On the road, they heard a donkey-driver asking for help, as his ass had fallen into a pit, whence he was not able to take him out without the help of others. Fareed good-naturedly offered to help him, and while the owner took hold of the head of the ass, Fareed took hold of the tail, and the two began to pull, when suddenly the tail of the animal came off in the hands of Fareed. The owner of the ass thereupon began to quarrel with him, and said, "Come with me to the Kázi. You must pay me damages." So the three now took their way to the Court of the Kázi.

But as the Kázi's Court was situated at some distance, and as it was already night-fall, they determined to put up in a mosque for the night. Fareed was locked up in the mosque, and the other two kept guard outside the gate. When it was near dawn, Fareed got up, and going to the terrace on the hind part of the building, jumped down, and came plump on the head of a Fakeer† who was sleeping at the foot of the walls. The Fakeer was killed. His son got up and laying hold of Fareed, charged him with the murder. The noise brought the other two persons who were near the gate, and so the four now took their way to the Court of the Kázi.

During the walk Fareed said to himself, "I wish the Court were soon reached; for I am afraid, the longer I am on the road the more

---

*A kázi (also spelled "kadi" or "cadi") is a civil judge, usually of a town or village.

† A fakir: a religious mendicant.

will be the mishaps befalling me. I had better move on with a quicker pace." And with this determination he walked faster, followed by his prosecutors. But on taking a turning at the end of a lane, he collided with a pregnant woman, who fell down with the shock, and miscarried. The husband of the woman caught hold of him, and accused him of killing the child, and the five now took their way to the Court of the Kázi.

The Court was at last reached. The Kázi was in his private chambers, and so they all had to wait outside the room, but after a time Fareed getting afraid of another mishap entered the room alone. He found the Kázi drinking *wine*, and so he stood quiet for some time, and then coughed to attract the attention of the Kázi. The latter turned with a start, and asked him what he wanted, saying "How long have you been here and what did you notice?" Fareed discreetly replied that he had merely seen the Kázi drinking *sherbet* (emphasizing the last word), and then related to him his adventures. "Well, well," said the Kázi, "we shall see justice done to you." They then came into the Court, and the Kázi after taking his seat, asked the men what were their complaints.

First came the Jew who claimed his 100 *miscals* of flesh. The Kázi told him to cut it off, but neither more nor less than the 100 *miscals*, otherwise he would have to undergo the penalty of being bled to death. The Jew on hearing this decision of the Kázi wanted to withdraw his complaint, but this the Kázi would not allow, saying "You ought to have thought of that beforehand. You have needlessly put this man to a deal of trouble, and as a penalty you must lay down here one hundred dinars. Only then I can allow you to go." So the Jew laid down his one hundred dinars and departed.

Next came the son of the Fakeer who charged Fareed with the death of his father. The Kázi said: "You must take his life in return. Kill him in the same way that he killed your father,—by jumping down on him from the terrace." "But I might get killed myself, jumping down from such a height!" urged the young Fakeer. "I can't help that!" said the Kázi. The Fakeer then wanted to withdraw his complaint, but he was not allowed to do so till he had laid down one hundred dinars.

The husband of the woman now laid his complaint, and charged the accused with the death of his child. The Kázi said to him, "It is but proper that the man should restore to you the young life that he has taken. I therefore order that you should divorce your wife, and give her to this man in marriage. When she is again with child, he shall then divorce her, and you can take her back." So the husband too withdrew his complaint, laying down one hundred dinars.

The owner of the donkey had meanwhile slunk away unperceived, saying, as he went, to the attendants in the antechamber, that as he had not the sum necessary for withdrawing his complaint, he was going to bring witnesses to prove that his ass had never a tail!

When the Kázi saw that there was no further complaint against Fareed, he released him, giving him as a compensation for his trouble, one hundred dinars out of the sums received.

THREE CASKETS

Patrick Kennedy

The Maid in the Country Underground[*]

There was once a man that was left a widower with a good and handsome daughter; but he thought fit to marry a widow, a very

[*] Patrick Kennedy, *The Fireside Stories of Ireland* (Dublin, 1870), 33–37, https://babel.hathitrust.org/cgi/ pt?id=hvd.32044014273197;view=1up;seq=49 (accessed April 20, 2017).

bad woman, who had a daughter as wicked as herself. They did all they could, by telling lies on her, to persuade her father to turn her away, but he would not. So one day that she was sent to the draw-well her stepmother came behind her, and threw her head foremost into it. She gave herself up for dead; but wasn't she surprised, after her breath was stopped for awhile, to find herself lying in a green meadow, with a bright sun and blue sky over her? Well, she walked on till she came to a hedge, that was so old it was not able to bear up a bird. "I'm old and worn, fair maid," said the hedge; "step lightly over me." "That I will do with pleasure, poor hedge," said she. So she stepped so gently and lightly over, that not a twig was stirred. "I'll do you a good turn another time," said the hedge.

She went on a while till she came to where an oven stood with a hot fire under it, and all at once the loaves spoke. "Take us out, take us out, fair maiden. We're baking for seven years, and now we'll be all burned if you don't release us." So she took the shovel, opened the door, and laid them nicely side by side on the grass. "Now take one of us with you," said the loaves, "and good luck be in your road." She went on, and found a poor woman sitting on a stone, and crying with the hunger. She gave her the greater part of her loaf, and went on till she met a flight of sparrows sitting on a block, and they all chattered out, "Some crumbs, fair maid; some crumbs, fair maid, or we'll all be dead with the hunger. It's seven years since we got a good meal." So she crumbled the rest of the bread, and they all cried, "Some day, fair maid, this good will be surely repaid."

She next passed by an apple tree, and the branches were bent down to the ground with the fruit. "Shake me, shake me, fair maid; it's seven years since I was shaken before." So she gently shook the tree and the boughs, and gathered all into a nice heap round the trunk. "Take some in your hand and eat them," said the tree; "I'll remember this deed some day." The next she met was a ram, with his wool all trailing on the ground behind him. "Shear me, fair maid," said he, "for I wasn't shorn for seven long years." So she laid his head on her knee, and clipped him so nice that he cried out when she was walking away, "Fair maid, I'll do you a good turn for this some day." The next she met was a cow, with her poor *elder* (udder) so full that it was trailing on the ground. "Milk me, fair maid," said she; "I wasn't milked these seven long years." So she did, and the cow licked her, and mooed after her, "Fair maid, I'll do you a good turn for this some day."

Well, the day was spent, and she got lodging at a lonely house, where there was no one but a woman with hair on her chin, and very long teeth, and her daughter that had the same sort of teeth, but no beard as yet. They gave her some moldy bread and some small beer for supper, and next day when she was going off, they said there was no one else living in that underground country, and so she might as well live with themselves. "I'll give you food and clothes," said the old woman, "and your choice of three caskets when you are leaving me, and one of them contains more gold and silver and precious stones than the king of England has in his court."

The first task she gave her was to go milk the cows, but when she went into the byre where they stood, they *lued*, and they kicked, and they horned, so that she was afraid to come near them. But a flight of sparrows came in, and lighted on their heads, and took hold of their ears, and they stood as quiet as lambs till they were milked. Then they all chirruped, "This is what we do for rewarding of you, fair maiden, fair maiden, for giving us crumbs, for giving us crumbs." Then they all flew off, and very sour looks she got from the two women inside for getting away with her life from the cows. "It was not from your own breast you sucked your knowledge," said the young one.

The next morning said the old witch, "Take this short black hank of thread and this long white hank to the stream, and bring the black one back to me white, and the white one black, or you'll sup sorrow." The poor girl took the hanks with a heavy heart and went to the spring, and washed and cried till she was weary, and then sat down on a stone, and wrung her hands. Who should come up at the moment but the poor woman she fed the day she cleared the oven, and she did no more than swale the white hank with the stream, and the black hank against the stream, and the colors were changed in a moment. "This is the good turn I promised you, fair maiden," said she, and she vanished.

As vexed as the witches were before, they were twice as much vexed now, and their faces were fiery and vinegary enough to frighten a horse from his fodder. "Wait till tomorrow!" said they to themselves.

When the breakfast of moldy bread and small beer was over, said the old hag, "Take that sieve to the stream, and bring it back full of water; there mustn't be a drop wanting." So she went and tried to fill it, and it was no sooner full than it was empty, and she began to cry. "Oh, where are my sparrows and my fairy now?" said she. "Here we are," said the birds.

"Stuff with moss,
  Plaster with clay,
And carry it full
  Of water away."

She did so, and took home the sieve full to the brim. "Oh, ho," said the angry old witch, "you're too clever for us, I see. Go up to that loft, and take your choice of three caskets you'll find on the table." She went up, and there were three caskets—one of gold, one of silver, and one of lead. She was in doubt which to select, till she heard the sparrows twittering on the roof at the skylight, "Pass by the gold, pass by the silver, but take up the lead, fair maiden." So she did, but as she was quitting the house the old witch was so vexed at her choice, that she snapped up a burning log, and flung it after her.

She ran away very swiftly and as swift came the witches after her, till she came up to where the cow was standing. "Come under me," says the cow; "I'll hide you behind my *elder*, and I'll put a charm on their eyes." "Did you see a young girl pass this way?" said they. "Yes," said the cow, "she turned into that wood on the left." Off they ran that way, and the cow licked the maiden, and off she ran. Well, when she came near the ram, she heard the clatter of their feet behind her. "Get under that heap of wool," says he, "and they won't see you." "Ram, ram, did you see a young girl run by?" "Yes, I did. She ran into that wood on the right." Off with them again, and the maiden thanked the ram, and ran on. Just as she was near the apple tree, she heard the clatter of their feet again. "Get under the heap of apples," said the tree, and so she did. "Apple tree, apple tree, did you see a young maid run this way?" "Yes, I did. She is hiding in my branches." Up they both climbed, and off ran the maid. They thought to get down and pursue her, but the branches twisted round them and held them fast, and it wasn't till the maid was near the hedge that they were again on land. Just as she was at the hedge, she heard the clatter of their feet, but the fence opened a gap for her, and she was soon in the green meadow where she first opened her eyes in the underground world. When the hags attempted to cross the hedge, it pricked them with thorns and brambles, and just as they were over, it tumbled on them, and it took them half a day to get clear again.

A heaviness came over the maid as she sat down to rest on a green ridge, and when she woke she found herself sitting by the well in the upper world. Her father was glad to see her again, but the wicked women of the family drove her to an out-house to take her meals and sleep. Well, she swept it out, and brushed the cobwebs off the walls, and then she sat down at a little table they gave her, and opened her box to see what was inside. All the silk, and gold, and silver, and jewels that were in it were enough to dazzle anyone's eyes, and she began to hang the walls with the silk curtains, and cover the floor with the fine carpets, that grew in size according as they were wanted, and then she was like a queen in her bower, with as much gold, and silver, and jewels in her casket as she chose.

Oh, weren't the stepmother and her daughter in a bad way when they came by chance into the room! They asked how she got all the fine things, and when she told them, the daughter popped herself head foremost into the well, and there she met all the same adventures as her sister, but she was cross and impudent with every one, and she had no one to help her milking the wicked cows, nor dyeing the hanks, nor filling the sieve, and at last she chose the gold casket, and when the hags sent her away after half starving her, the ram and the cow pucked her with their horns, and the apple tree had like to kill her with the load of fruit it let fall on her, and the hedge wounded her with its thorny boughs, and when she found herself by the well in the upper world she was more dead than alive. It was worse when she came home, and the gold casket was opened, for out there swarmed toads, and frogs, and snakes, that crept under the beds, and filled every corner of the house; and day after day new ones were coming out, and making a purgatory on earth for herself and her mother. The father was glad enough to be let live with his daughter, and there was so much talk about it in the country that the young king came to see the maiden. To make a long story short, they were married, and if they didn't live happy ever after, it surely wasn't the fault of the young queen.

V. All's Well That Ends Well

ℰ

A ll's Well That Ends Well is a so-called problem play, one of the comedies Shakespeare wrote as he was transitioning into his major tragic period. All's Well centers on the wedding of its young principals, Helena and Bertram, but it's a sour sort of wedding. Bertram is forced to marry Helena against his will, and he flees from her. Helena retrieves him and, in doing so, reveals the depths of his character flaws. Much of the problem in this problem play can be traced to its folktale source, "The Man Who Deserted His Wife" (ATU 891).

"The Man Who Deserted His Wife" has a long literary history. The earliest known version is in the eleventh-century Indian collection of tales, Ocean of the Streams of Story. The folktale appears in Icelandic saga and a medieval French romance, as well as in medieval and early modern Italian story collections. Shakespeare patterned All's Well quite closely on Boccaccio's version of the "Deserted Wife" folktale in his Decameron (the ninth story of the third day), which is readily available. I've included here Giovanni Francesco Straparola's sixteenth-century story, a less familiar Italian novella version of "The Man Who Deserted His Wife."

In these "Deserted Wife" stories, a clever young woman marries a man who leaves her shortly after their wedding without consummating the marriage. In two of the four stories included here, the man marries the woman because she is clever, either as a reward, as in "The Sultan's Camp Follower," or because she has made him look foolish and he wants to gain the power to humble her, as in "Catherine the Wise." In some versions, such as Indian tale "The Talisman of Chastity" here, the husband orders her to perform tasks he believes to be impossible, among them to bear his child although he intends never to sleep with her.* Sometimes the woman performs these tasks by her own inspiration, and not at his insistence. The wife bears her husband's child by disguising herself as another woman whom he desires. Later, the heroine confronts her husband with his baby (or babies) and usually some lover's token he gave to her, proving that he is in fact the father. The husband, tricked by his wife, now accepts her as his spouse and the mother of his heir.

The folktale is sour enough in itself—an intelligent woman uses her husband's infidelity to bring him to heel—yet it seems even more so in Shakespeare's adaptation. Helena, a "poor physician's daughter" (2.3.115), is besotted with Bertram, the young count of Rossillion. When she cures the desperately ill king of France, she demands as her payment the husband of her choice—Bertram, of course. But he angrily and publicly rejects her as his social inferior. In two of the following stories, "Catherine the Wise" and "The Sultan's Camp Follower," the wife is beneath her husband in rank, but it is he who proposes marriage. The difference in rank is not much of an impediment, and the bride shows no signs of being besotted. Helena seems much at a disadvantage compared to her folktale counterparts—she is a despised pursuer. Even in Boccaccio's story, the heroine is not of noble birth but is rich, which is a compensation for her lower-class status that Helena lacks.

Helena's cleverness in restoring the king from a deadly illness leads directly to her marriage. The *Decameron* story seems to be the only version of "The Deserted Wife" in which the heroine cures a king and thereby gains the husband of her choice. In the Iraqi folktale "The Sultan's Camp Follower," the heroine's skill with riddles

---

* This story combines "The Man Who Deserted His Wife" with another folktale type, "The Wager on the Wife's Chastity," one of the folktale sources of *Cymbeline* included in chapter 7.

leads the sultan to marry her. Catherine the Wise opens a school, which the prince attends. After she punishes him for being a dunce, he marries her in order to get revenge. In "The Talisman of Chastity," the heroine's devotion to her studies, and to one teacher in particular, causes her bridegroom to suspect her of unchastity and to torment her.

In all of these cases, the heroine then uses her wits again to regain her husband. Bertram, after abandoning Helena immediately after their wedding to go to war, sends her a letter: "When thou canst get the ring upon my finger, which never shall come off, and show me a child begotten of thy body that I am father to, then call me husband; but in such a 'then' I write a 'never'" (3.2.56–59). Helena then announces that she will go on pilgrimage to St. Jacques's shrine in the hopes that her husband will come home from the war to safety if she is not there. The next time we see her, however, she is in Florence, exactly where Bertram and the other troops are parading themselves. Earlier, Helena had told Bertram's mother, the countess, of her plan to go to Paris to cure the king, but under the shrewd countess's cross-examination, admits that her first idea was to go to see Bertram there. Helena twice covers her pursuit of Bertram by claiming more rarefied motives, medical aid and religious devotion. Isabella, in Straparola's story, more shockingly claims that an angel transported her to her wayward husband's side, when really it was a demon summoned by a witch she had hired.

In Florence, Helena learns that Bertram has been pursuing a young woman, Diana, who has steadfastly refused him. Helena persuades Diana to agree to a midnight rendezvous with Bertram and then takes Diana's place, sleeps with Bertram, and conceives his child. Diana also, at Helena's instruction, demands the ring that Bertram swore he would never take off, and gives it to Helena. Later, in the hectic final scene of the play, Bertram accuses Diana of being a prostitute, a camp follower—a disguise that the deserted wives often take on in the folktales. Helena meanwhile fakes her own death, whereas Catherine the Wise is declared dead by her husband, who proceeds to engage himself to an English princess. The sultan in the Iraqi folktale also decides to marry another woman. In these two folktales, the wedding festivities are interrupted by the return of the deserted wives with their children, which causes the perfidious husbands to break off their second engagements. Bertram is forming an engagement to yet another woman when Diana disrupts the proceedings, insisting that he promised marriage to her, before the pregnant Helena appears, whom everyone had believed dead.

Folktales generally do not have much to say about the inner workings of their characters. It seems safe to assume, though, that the men who have deserted their wives gain an appreciation for their tenacity and bravery at the end of the tales, after seeing how hard they have worked to secure their marriages. We can imagine a happily ever after for these couples. Bertram, however, seems to have been shamed and cornered into respecting his marriage vows, and Helena appears disenchanted with the man whose child she is carrying:

> HELENA: . . . There is your ring,
>   And look you, here's your letter. This it says:
>   When from my finger you can get this ring
>   And is by me with child, &c. This is done;
>   Will you be mine now you are doubly won?
> BERTRAM: If she, my liege, can make me know this clearly
>   I'll love her dearly, ever, ever dearly.
> HELENA: If it appear not plain and prove untrue
>   Deadly divorce step between me and you!
>   O my dear mother, do I see you living? (5.3.304–13)

Bertram addresses his declaration of love not to Helena, but to the king, and uses the conditional "if." The lame second line of his couplet, "I'll love her dearly, ever, ever dearly," is padded with repetition to the point of inanity. Helena responds with the menacing threat of "deadly divorce," and then immediately turns to Bertram's mother, greeting her with more affection than she had Bertram. While Shakespeare's ending is grimmer than the folktales', it does seem more psychologically plausible. How might a man respond when he finds himself tricked by a woman who had already proven herself cleverer than he? How could a wife remain devoted to a husband who had slept with her in the belief she was another woman, paradoxically cheating on her with her? "The Man Who Deserted His Wife" has a trickster heroine, as does "A Pound of Flesh." The heroine in the latter tale, however, connives against the hero before he is her husband, and then she connives on his behalf. The deserted wives, however, remain their husbands' adversaries until they finally have defeated them. Adapting this story into a romantic comedy turns it into a problem play.

THE MAN WHO DESERTED HIS WIFE

Giovanni Francesco Straparola

Ortodosio, Isabella, Argentina[*]

There lived once upon a time, gracious ladies, a merchant called Ortodosio Simeoni, a man holding noble rank in the city of Flor-

---

[*] Giovanni Francesco Straparola, *The Nights*, trans. W. G. Waters, 2 vols. (London: Lawrence and Bullen, 1894), 2.44–50, https://babel.hathitrust.org/cgi/pt?id =njp.32101013253115;view=1up;seq=64 (accessed April 20, 2017). The First Fable of the Seventh Night. Straparola's *Le Piacevoli Notti* (1550–53)—the title has been translated as *The Delectable* (or *Facetious*) *Nights*—has a framework in which ladies and gentlemen tell each other tales. I have supplied the title of this story.

ence, and having to wife a lady called Isabella, who was fair to see, of gentle manners, and holy and saintly in her life. Ortodosio, being strongly moved to embark in traffic, took leave of his kinsmen and of his wife, lamenting sore as he bade them farewell, and, having set forth from Florence, betook himself with his goods to Flanders. Having arrived in that country, it happened that Ortodosio, moved by fate, which seemed at first propitious, but proved evil in the end, hired a house opposite to that of a courtesan called Argentina, and he, being inflamed with an ardent passion for her, lost all thought of Isabella his wife and of his former life in guilty dalliance with her.

Five years had passed away since Isabella had received any news of her husband. She knew not whether he was alive or dead, or in what land he was abiding. For this reason she was smitten with the greatest sorrow that a woman could feel, and it seemed to her continually as if the very life were being torn from out her breast. The unhappy Isabella, who was very devout and exceedingly reverent of all the ordinances of religion, went to the Church of the Annunciata every day, and there falling on her knees would pray to God with scalding tears and piteous sighs that He would grant her the speedy return of her husband. But her humble prayers, her long fasts, and her many charities availed her nothing. Wherefore the poor lady, seeing that neither for her fastings, nor for her prayers, nor for her almsgivings, nor for the many acts that she did for the welfare of others, did she obtain a favorable hearing, resolved to change her manner of living and to fix upon some other course. So, in the same measure as she had formerly been devout and fervent in her orisons, she henceforth gave herself up entirely to the practice of incantations and witchcraft, hoping that by these means her affairs might be brought to a more prosperous issue. She went therefore one morning early in search of a certain witch, Gabrina Fureta, and entreated her kind offices. She forthwith laid bare all her troubles to the wise woman, who was very old, and had greater experience in the arts of magic than any other person in the city; indeed, she could bring to pass things that were quite out of the ordinary course of nature, so that it was an amazement to see and hear them.

Gabrina, when she heard of Isabella's troubles, was moved to pity on her account, and having spoken divers comforting words, promised to help her, telling her to be of good cheer, for she should soon see her husband and rejoice over her reunion with him. Isabella, who was mightily gratified at this favorable answer, opened her purse and gave Gabrina ten florins; these the witch joyfully took, and, after having murmured certain mysterious words, she bade Isabella return to her at nightfall. When the appointed hour for the meeting had come, the witch took her little book in hand and drew a small circle on the ground; then, having surrounded the same with certain magic signs and figures, she poured out some subtle liquor from a flask and drank a drop of it and gave as much to Isabella. And when the lady had drunk it, Gabrina spake thus to her: "Isabella, you know that we have met here to work an incantation in order that we may discover the place of your husband's present abode, wherefore it is absolutely necessary that you should be firm and not flinch at anything you may see or feel, however terrible. And do not let it enter into your mind to invoke the assistance of God or of the saints, or to make the sign of the cross; for if you do this you will never be able to recall what you have done, and at the same time you will be in the greatest danger of death."

To this Isabella answered: "Do not doubt my constancy in any way, Gabrina, but be sure that if you were to conjure up before me all the demons which live in the center of the earth, they would not affright me." "Undress yourself, then," said the witch, "and enter the circle." Isabella, therefore, having stripped herself, stood naked as on the day when she was born, and boldly entered the circle, whereupon Gabrina opened her book and likewise entered the circle, and thus spake: "Powers of hell, by the authority which I hold over you, I conjure you that you instantly appear before me!" Astaroth, Fafarello, and the other demon princes, compelled by the conjurations of Gabrina, immediately presented themselves before her with loud shrieks, and cried, "Command us to do thy will." Gabrina then said, "I conjure and command you that, without any delay, you truthfully disclose to me where Ortodosio Simeoni, the husband of Isabella, now abides, and whether he be living or dead."

"Know, Gabrina," said Astaroth, "that Ortodosio lives, and is in Flanders, and that he is consumed by so fierce a passion for a certain woman called Argentina that he no longer remembers his own wife." When the witch heard this, she commanded Fafarello that he should change himself into a horse and transport Isabella to the spot where Ortodosio was abiding. The demon, who was straightway changed into a horse, caught up Isabella and flew with her into the air, she in the meantime feeling neither hurt nor fear, and when the sun appeared he set her down unscathed in Argentina's palace. This done, Fafarello put upon Isabella the form of Argentina, and so complete was the resemblance that she no longer seemed to be Isabella but Argentina herself, and at the same time he transformed Argentina into the shape of an old woman who was invisible, neither could she hear or see anybody herself.

When the hour for supper had come, Isabella in her new guise supped with Ortodosio her husband, and then, having withdrawn together into a rich bedchamber in which there was a bedstead with a downy bed thereon, she placed herself by Ortodosio's side, and he, while he thought he was in bed with Argentina, really lay with his own wife. And so ardent and impassioned were the tender caresses and kisses he bestowed upon her, and so close their embraces and kisses when they took their pleasure one with another, that in the course of that very night Isabella became with child. Fafarello, in the meantime, contrived to steal from the chamber a rich gown, all embroidered with pearls, and a beautiful necklace that Ortodosio had formerly given to Argentina, and when the following night had come Fafarello made Isabella and Argentina resume their own natural shapes, and at daybreak, having once more transformed himself into a horse and taken Isabella on the saddle, he transported her back to Gabrina's house, at the same time handing over the gown and the necklace he had stolen to the old woman. The witch, when she had received the gown and the necklace from the hands of the demon, gave them to Isabella with these words: "My daughter, guard these things with care, for at the right time and place they will be real proofs of your loyalty." Isabella took the garment and the fair necklace, and, having thanked the witch, she returned to her home.

After four months had passed Isabella began to show signs of pregnancy, and her kinsfolk, when they remarked this, marveled greatly, as they had always held her to be a virtuous and saintly dame. Wherefore they often asked her if she were with child, and by whom; to which question she, with a cheerful face, would always reply that she was with child by Ortodosio her husband. But her kinsfolk declared this to be false, for they knew well enough that her husband had been absent from her for a long time, and was at the present moment in a distant country, and that, with matters standing as they did, it was impossible she could be with child by him. For this reason her kindred were greatly grieved, and began to fear the shame that should befall them, often taking counsel together whether they should not kill her. But the fear of God, the dread of the loss of the child's soul and of the murmurs of the world, and their care for the husband's honor, restrained them from committing this crime, so they determined to await the birth of the little creature.

When the time of her lying-in had come, Isabella gave birth to a beautiful boy, but when they heard of it, her kinsfolk were overwhelmed with grief, and without hesitation wrote to Ortodosio in the following words: "It is not with the design to give you annoyance, dearest brother, but in order to tell you the truth, that we write to inform you that Isabella, your wife and our kinswoman, has to our great shame and dishonor given birth to a son. Who his father may be we know not, but we would assuredly judge him to have been begotten by you had you not been away from her for so long a time. The child and his brazen-faced mother would have been before now deprived of life by us, had not the reverence that we bear to God stayed our hands on their behalf, for it pleaseth not God that we should stain our hands with our own blood. Set therefore your own affairs in order, and save your honor, and do not suffer this crime to remain unpunished."

When Ortodosio had received these letters and the sad news therein written, he lamented greatly, and having summoned Argentina into his presence, he said to her: "Argentina, it is absolutely necessary that I should return to Florence in order that I may dispatch certain affairs of mine that are of no small weight. After a few days, when I shall have them set in order, I will come back to you forthwith. You, in the meantime, take good care of yourself and of my affairs, treating them in the same manner as if they were your own, and live merrily and always remember me."

Ortodosio thereupon left Flanders, and with a prosperous wind sailed for Florence. Having come to his own house he was joyfully received by his wife; but as the days went on he was many a time seized with a diabolical inclination to kill her, and to leave Florence secretly, but when he considered the danger and the dishonor he would incur thereby, he determined to postpone his revenge to a more convenient season. So without delay he made known his return to her kinsmen, and after a while he sent out an invitation begging them to come and dine with him on the following day. When his wife's kinsmen, in response to the invitation given to them, arrived at Ortodosio's house, they were well received by him, and after their gracious welcome they all dined merrily together. When the dinner had come to an end, and the table cleared, Ortodosio began to speak as follows: "Kind brothers and sisters, I think that the cause of our meeting here together must be plainly manifest to you all; wherefore it is not necessary that I should spend many words over the matter, but I will at once come to the subject that concerns all of us." And raising his eyes toward his wife, who sat opposite to him, he said: "Isabella, who is the father of the child that you keep in this house?" and Isabella answered, "You are his father." "I? I, his father?" said Ortodosio; "I have now been away these five years, and from the hour on which I departed you have not seen me, so how can you say that I am his father?" "Still I declare that the child is your son," replied Isabella, "and that he was begotten by you in Flanders." Then Ortodosio, waxing very wroth, cried out, "Ah, woman, lying and brazen that you are! when were you ever in Flanders?" "When I lay in bed with you," answered Isabella. And then she told him everything from beginning to end—the place, the time, and the very words that had passed between them on that night. Ortodosio and her brothers, when they heard this thing, were filled with astonishment, but still they refused to believe her words. Wherefore Isabella, seeing the stubborn pertinacity of her husband, and knowing well that he did not believe what she said, rose from her seat, and having withdrawn into her chamber, she took the embroidered robe and the beautiful necklace and went back to the room where the company sat, and spake thus: "My lord, do you know this robe that is so cunningly embroidered?"

Ortodosio, quite bewildered and almost beside himself at the sight, thus answered: "It is true that I have missed a similar robe, and I could never discover what had become of it." "Know, then," said Isabella, "that this is the self-same robe that you lost." Then she put her hand into her bosom and drew forth the rich necklace, and said, "Do you also know this necklace?" And her husband, who could not deny that he knew it, said that it also had been stolen from him at the same time as the robe. "But, so that my fidelity may be made clearly manifest to you, I will show you that I am worthy of your trust," said Isabella. And having spoken thus, she caused the nurse to bring the child, which she carried in her arms to her, and when she had stripped off its white garments she said, "Ortodosio, do you know this child?" And with these words she showed him how one of its feet was faulty, for the little toe was missing, and this afforded a true indication and absolute proof of her wifely fidelity, since Ortodosio's foot was in like manner naturally wanting of a toe. When Ortodosio saw this, he was so completely silenced that he could not say a word in contradiction; so he took the child in his arms and kissed him and acknowledged him as his son. Then Isabella took greater courage and said, "You must know, Ortodosio, my beloved, that the fastings, the prayers, and the other good works that I performed in order that I might have news of you, brought me fulfilment of my wishes, as you will presently hear. For one morning, when I was kneeling in the holy Church of the Annunciata, and praying that I might have news of you, my prayer was granted, and an angel carried me invisibly into Flanders and placed me by your side in bed, and so close and loving were the caresses that you bestowed on me that night that I then and there became with child. And on the following night I found myself in my own house in Florence again, together with the things I have just laid before your eyes." When Ortodosio and the brothers had seen these trustworthy signs, and heard the words that Isabella spake with such great show of good faith, they all embraced and kissed one another, and in this wise, with all good feeling, they restored their affectionate relationship one with another.

And after some days had passed Ortodosio returned to Flanders, where he procured honorable marriage for Argentina, and, having laden his goods on a great ship, he returned to Florence, in which city he lived a long time in tranquil peace and happiness with Isabella and his child.

Italo Calvino

Catherine the Wise[*]

Here in Palermo they tell, ladies and gentlemen, that once upon a time there was a very important shopkeeper in the city. He had a daughter who, from the time she was weaned, proved so wise that she was given her say on every single matter in the household. Recognizing the talent of his daughter, her father called her Catherine the Wise. When it came to studying all sorts of languages and reading every kind of book, no one could hold a candle to her.

When the girl was sixteen, her mother died. Catherine was so grief-stricken that she shut herself up in her room and refused to come out. There she ate and slept, shunning all thought of strolls, theaters, and entertainment of any kind.

Her father, whose life centered on this only child of his, thought it advisable to hold a council on the matter. He called together all the lords (for, even though he was a shopkeeper, he was on familiar terms with the best people) and said, "Gentlemen, you are aware I have a daughter who is the apple of my eye. But ever since her mother's death, she's been keeping to the house like a cat and won't for the life of her stick her head outside."

[*] Italo Calvino, *Italian Folktales*, trans. George Martin (San Diego: Harcourt Brace, 1980), 540–46. No. 151. Calvino's source for this story was an 1875 collection of Sicilian folktales by Giuseppe Pitrè. It was told in Palermo by Agatuzza Messia (747).

The council replied, "Your daughter is known the world over for her vast wisdom. Open up a big school for her, so that she directs others in their studies, and she will get this grief out of her system."

"That's a splendid idea," said the father, and called his daughter. "Listen, my daughter, since you refuse every diversion, I have decided to open a school and put you in charge of it. How does that suit you?"

Catherine was instantly charmed. She took charge of the teachers herself, and they got the school all ready. Outside they put up a sign: WHOEVER WISHES TO STUDY AT CATHERINE THE WISE'S IS WELCOME, FREE OF CHARGE.

Numbers of children, both boys and girls, flocked in at once, and she seated them at the desks, side by side, without distinction. Someone piped up, "But that boy is the son of a coal merchant!" "That makes no difference: the coal merchant's son must sit beside the prince's daughter. First come, first served." And school began. Catherine had a cat-o'-nine-tails. She taught everyone alike, but woe to those that didn't do their lessons! The reputation of this school even reached the palace, and the prince himself decided to attend. He dressed up in his regal clothes, came in, found an empty place, and Catherine invited him to sit down. When it was his turn, Catherine asked him a question. The prince didn't know the answer. She dealt him a back-handed blow, from which his cheek still smarts.

Crimson with rage, the prince rose, ran back to the palace, and sought out his father. "A favor I beg, Majesty: I wish to get married! For a wife, I want Catherine the Wise."

The king sent for Catherine's father, who went at once, saying, "Your humble servant, Majesty!"

"Rise! My son has taken a fancy to your daughter. What are we to do but join them in matrimony?"

"As you will, Majesty. But I am a shopkeeper, whereas your son is of royal blood."

"That makes no difference. My son himself wants her."

The shopkeeper returned home. "Catherine, the prince wants to wed you. What do you have to say about that?"

"I accept."

The wool for the mattresses was not wanting, no more than the chests of drawers; in a week's time everything needed had been prepared. The prince assembled a retinue of twelve bridesmaids. The royal chapel was opened, and the couple got married.

Following the ceremony, the queen told the bridesmaids to go and undress the princess for bed. But the prince said, "There's no need of people to undress her, or of guards at the door." Once he was alone with his bride, he said, "Catherine, do you remember the slap you gave me? Are you sorry for it?"

"Sorry for it? If you ask for it, I'll do it again!"

"What! You're not sorry?"

"Not in the least."

"And you don't intend to be?"

"Who would?"

"So that's your attitude? Well, I'll now teach *you* a thing or two." He started unwinding a rope with which to lower her through a trapdoor into a pit. "Catherine," he said when the rope was ready, "either you repent, or I'll let you down into the pit!"

"I'll be cooler there," replied Catherine.

So the prince tied the rope around her and lowered her into the pit, where all she found was a little table, a chair, a pitcher of water, and a piece of bread.

The next morning, according to custom, the father and mother came to greet the new wife.

"You can't come in," said the prince. "Catherine isn't feeling well."

Then he went and opened the trapdoor. "What kind of night did you spend?"

"Pleasant and refreshing," replied Catherine.

"Are you considering the slap you gave me?"

"I'm thinking of the one I owe you now."

Two days went by, and hunger began to gnaw at her stomach. Not knowing what else to do, she pulled a stay out of her corset and started making a hole in the wall. She dug and dug, and twenty-four hours later saw a tiny ray of daylight, at which she took heart. She made the hole bigger and peered through it. Who should be passing at that moment but her father's clerk. "Don Tommaso! Don Tommaso!" Don Tommaso couldn't imagine what this voice was, coming out of the wall like that. "It's me, Catherine the Wise. Tell my father I have to talk to him right away."

Don Tommaso returned with Catherine's father, showing him the tiny opening in the wall. "Father, as luck would have it, I'm at the bottom of a pit. You must have a passageway dug underground from our palace all the way here, with an arch and a light every twenty feet. Leave everything else to me."

The shopkeeper agreed to that and in the meantime he brought her food regularly—roast chicken and nourishing dishes—and passed it through the opening in the wall.

Three times a day the prince peered through the trapdoor. "Are you sorry yet, Catherine, for the slap you gave me?"

"Sorry for what? Just imagine the slap you are going to get from me now!"

The workers finally got the underground passage dug, with an arch and a lantern every twenty feet. Catherine would pass through it to her father's house after the prince had looked in on her and reclosed the trap door.

It wasn't long before the prince was fed up with trying to get

Catherine to apologize. "Catherine, I'm going to Naples. Have you nothing to tell me?"

"Have a good time, enjoy yourself, and write me upon your arrival in Naples."

"So I should go?"

"What? Are you still there?"

So the prince departed.

As soon as he shut the trapdoor, Catherine ran off to her father. "Papa, now is the time to help me. Get me a brigantine ready to sail, with housekeeper, servants, festive gowns—all to go to Naples. There let them rent me a palace across from the royal palace and await my arrival."

The shopkeeper sent the brigantine off. Meanwhile the prince had a frigate readied, and he too set sail. She stood on her father's balcony and watched him leave, then she went aboard another brigantine and was in Naples ahead of him. Little vessels, you know, make better time than big ones.

In Naples Catherine would come out on the balcony of her palace each day in a lovelier gown than the day before. The prince saw her and exclaimed, "How much like Catherine the Wise she is!" He fell in love with her and sent a messenger to her palace. "My lady, the prince would like very much to pay you a visit, if that won't inconvenience you."

"By all means!" she replied.

The king came regally dressed, made a big fuss over her, then sat down to talk. "Tell me, my lady, are you married?"

"Not yet. Are you?"

"Neither am I, isn't it obvious? You resemble a maiden, my lady, who captured my fancy in Palermo. I should like you to be my wife."

"With pleasure, Prince." And a week later they got married.

At the end of nine months, Catherine gave birth to a baby boy that was a marvel to behold. "Princess," asked the prince, "what shall we call him?"

"Naples," said Catherine. So they named him Naples.

Two years went by, and the prince decided to leave town. The princess didn't like it, but he had made up his mind and couldn't be swayed. He drafted a document for Catherine saying the baby was his firstborn and in time would be king. Then he left for Genoa.

As soon as the prince had gone, Catherine wrote her father to send a brigantine to Genoa immediately with furniture, housekeeper, servants, and all the rest, and have them rent a palace opposite the royal palace of Genoa and await her arrival. The shopkeeper loaded a ship and sent it off to Genoa.

Catherine also took a brigantine and reached Genoa before the prince. She settled down in her new palace, and when the prince saw this beautiful young lady with her royal coiffure, jewels, and wealth, he exclaimed, "How much like Catherine the Wise she is, and also my wife in Naples!" He dispatched a messenger to her, and she sent back word she would be happy to receive the prince.

They began talking. "Are you single?" asked the prince.

"A widow," answered Catherine. "And you?"

"I'm a widower, with one son. By the way, you look just like a lady I used to know in Palermo, not to mention one I knew in Naples."

"Really? We all have seven doubles in the world, so they say."

Thus, to make a long story short, they became man and wife in one week's time.

Nine months later, Catherine gave birth to another boy, even handsomer than the first. The prince was happy. "Princess, what shall we call him?"

"Genoa!" And so they named him Genoa.

Two years went by, and the king grew restless once more.

"You're going off like that and leaving me with a child on my hands?" asked the princess.

"I am drawing up a document for you," the prince reassured her, "stating that this is my son and little prince." While he made preparations to leave for Venice, Catherine wrote her father in Palermo for another brigantine with servants, housekeeper, furniture, new clothes and all. The brigantine sailed off to Venice. The prince departed on the frigate. The princess left on another brigantine and arrived before he did.

"Heavens!" exclaimed the prince when he beheld the beautiful lady at her casement. "She looks exactly like my wife in Genoa, who looked exactly like my wife in Naples, who looked exactly like Catherine the Wise! But how can this be? Catherine is in Palermo shut up in the pit, the Neapolitan is in Naples, the Genoese in Genoa, while this one is in Venice!" He sent a messenger to her and then went to meet her.

"Would you believe, my lady, that you look like several other ladies I know—one in Palermo, one in Naples, one in Genoa—"

"Indeed! We are supposed to have seven doubles in this life."

And thus they continued their customary talk. "Are you married?" "No, I'm a widow. And you?" "I'm a widower, with two sons." In a week's time they were married.

This time Catherine had a little girl, radiant like the sun and moon. "What shall we call her?" asked the prince.

"Venice." So they baptized her Venice.

Two more years went by. "Listen, princess, I have to go back to Palermo. But first, I'm drawing up a document that spells out that this is my daughter and royal princess."

He departed, but Catherine reached Palermo first. She went to her father's house, walked through the underground passage and back into the pit. As soon as the prince arrived, he ran and pulled up the trapdoor. "Catherine, how are you?"

"Me? I'm fine!"

"Are you sorry for the slap you gave me?"

"Have you thought about the slap I owe you?"

"Come, Catherine, say you're sorry! Otherwise I'll take another wife."

"Go right ahead! No one is stopping you!"

"But if you say you're sorry, I'll take you back."

"No."

The prince then formally declared that his wife was dead and that he intended to remarry. He wrote all the kings for portraits of their daughters. The portraits arrived, and the most striking was of the king of England's daughter. The prince summoned mother and daughter to conclude the marriage.

The entire royal family of England arrived in Palermo, and the wedding was set for the morrow. What did Catherine do in the meantime but have three fine royal outfits readied for her three children—Naples, Genoa, Venice. She dressed up like the queen she actually was, took the hand of Naples, clothed as crown prince, climbed into a ceremonial carriage, followed by Prince Genoa and Princess Venice, and they drove off to the palace.

The wedding procession with the prince and the daughter of the king of England was approaching, and Catherine said to her children, "Naples, Genoa, Venice, go and kiss your father's hand!" And the children ran up to kiss the prince's hand.

At the sight of them, the prince could only admit defeat. "This is the slap you were to give me!" he exclaimed, and embraced the children. The princess of England was dumbfounded; she turned her back on everybody and stalked off.

Catherine explained all the mystery to her husband about the ladies who looked so much alike, and the prince couldn't apologize enough for what he had done.

They lived happily ever after,
While here we sit grinding our teeth.

Inea Bushnaq
The Sultan's Camp Follower*

In one of the furthest provinces of the land there lived a saddle-
maker with his three daughters. He owned his house and his shop
and lived off what he earned through his skill. In time he saved one
hundred gold coins. When he thought about where to hide them,
he decided to sew them into the saddle that he was stitching.

One day a mountain herdsman came to buy a saddle. Only after
the man had left did the saddler realize that he had given him the
saddle with the gold in it. What could he do? Nothing. So he kept
his grief in his heart and said not a word to anyone. However, from
that time, as he worked and tooled his leather, he hummed these
words:

It has gone and I'm to blame.
What it is I cannot name.

A year later the same herdsman brought the saddle back to the
saddler's shop and said, "It is worn in some places. Can you patch
it for me?" The saddler was overjoyed and promised to have it ready
the next day. Without losing a moment, he cut the seams, shook
out his hundred pieces of gold, and began to sing:

Long ago it left me,
What it is I'll not betray.
Now again it's found me,
What it is I'll never say.

*Inea Bushnaq, *Arab Folk-tales* (New York: Pantheon, 1986), 339–43.

And thereafter, this became the saddler's song while he worked. One day when the sultan rode through that part of the *suq*,* he heard the tune and puzzled over it. So he called the saddler and asked him its meaning. The saddler's only answer was to sing, "I'll never say!" The sultan questioned him once, twice, and a third time, and received the same reply. Then the ruler grew angry. "How many daughters do you have?" he inquired. "Three, *maulana*,"† said the saddler with proper respect. "Then I wish to see them pregnant before the palace gates tomorrow morning," ordered the sultan. "They are virgins, *maulana*," said the saddler, "How can virgins be pregnant?" "If I don't see them pregnant tomorrow morning, I shall cut off your head," said the sultan, and rode away.

Sunk in care, the saddler walked slowly to his house. His youngest daughter noticed how dejected he was and asked the cause. "My child, the sultan has commanded me to bring you and your sisters to him, pregnant, or he will have my head!" said her father. "That is a simple request, Father. Buy me three earthenware jars, and I shall show the sultan how virgins can be pregnant." When he did as she said, she tied one jar round her own waist under her gown and bade her sisters do the same. And in this guise the three girls filed past the palace gate the next day.

"How many months are you with child?" the sultan asked the eldest girl. "Three, *maulana*," she told him. "And what do you crave?" "Cucumbers steeped in brine," said the girl. Then he put his question to the middle sister, and she said, "Six months, and what I crave is eggplant pickled in vinegar." When it was the turn of the youngest daughter, she told the sultan, "This month is my month, and I have a longing for fish roasted under the seven seas." "How

---

*Souk: a marketplace.

†A Muslim man revered for his religious learning or piety.

can the fish be roasted under the sea?" protested the sultan. "In the same way that a virgin can be pregnant!" replied the girl.

The sultan said nothing and sent the girls home. But on the following day he summoned an old woman who served as a marriage broker and handed her a purse of one hundred gold liras. "Go the saddler's house and ask for the hand of his youngest daughter," he commanded.

The old woman slipped two of the gold coins into her own pocket and set off on her mission. It was the youngest daughter who opened the door when she knocked. "I want to speak to your mother," said the old woman. "My mother has gone to change one into two," said the girl. "Then let me have two words with your oldest sister," the old woman said. "She has gone to change black into white." "And your middle sister?" "She is plucking roses." "At this time of year there are no flowers," said the old woman, "but here is a purse that the sultan has sent you; take it." When the youngest daughter had examined the contents, she said, "Ask the sultan this: when a man makes a present of a lamb, does he cut off its tail?"

The old woman returned to the sultan and reported everything that the girl had said, although she understood nothing of it. She added that the saddler's daughter was mad; but the sultan was wiser. "To change one into two," he said, "means that her mother is a midwife and went to assist at a birth. To change black into white means that the sister is a ladies' maid and has the skill of removing body hair. And to pluck roses in the winter means that the other sister is a needlewoman and embroiders roses in silk. This is no madwoman but a girl fit to be a sultan's wife! You may keep the gold pieces you stole from my purse, but do not steal again, for that was the meaning of cutting off the lamb's tail." The old woman slipped away in fear and shame, and the sultan did what was necessary to make the saddler's youngest daughter his wife.

But the sultan's bride became his wife only in name, for while she awaited him in the bridal chamber, he was off to war. He sent word that he must lead his armies to the land of Siin in far-off China. Before the wedding night he was gone.

The saddler's daughter did not mourn or wait for her husband's return. The next day she assembled an army of her own, changed her clothes to those of a man, and rode after the sultan. Setting up her tents not far from his camp, she faced him across a river as if she were an enemy. In the evening she sent a messenger challenging him to a game of chess. To while away the time he played, and she won his dagger off him. They played again, and this time the sultan won and asked for his dagger back. But she said, "I have a Kurdish girl in my camp, a virgin; let me send her to you this night instead." The sultan agreed, never suspecting who the chess player really was.

That night the girl put on her women's robes and let down her perfumed hair and took herself to the sultan's tent. At dawn she left him and in her man's disguise led her army home again. Nine months later she gave birth to a boy and called him Siin.

After two years the sultan rode back victorious from the wars, but he did not linger many days. He came to his wife's chamber only to say, "I must go beyond the land of Siin to Masiin. I promise that we shall be man and wife on my return."

Once again the girl, wearing the clothes of a man, followed her husband with an army of her own. And as before, she camped nearby and passed an evening with him at chess. This time she won his prayer beads of precious amber. And when he won the second game and asked for their return, she said, "I own a Kurdish slave who has only known a man once. She is beautiful, and I am ready to let her sleep with you tonight." The sultan was willing, and the girl spent the night in the sultan's tent as before and disappeared with her army next morning. This time when she gave birth to a son, she called him Masiin.

The sultan's army returned laden with spoils after more than a year, and still the sultan thirsted for further victories. Without resting he told his bride, "I have decided to travel west to the land of Gharb. This will be my last campaign and I shall be your husband when I return."

A few days later, the saddler's daughter prepared her army and set out for the land of Gharb. She camped opposite the sultan's tent and invited him to try and beat her at chess. She won the first game and took his headcloth, and he won the second game and accepted the favors of her slave. Once more she adorned herself in women's finery and shared the sultan's bed, then dressed herself as a man and guided her soldiers home. When her time came, she gave birth to a girl, to whom she gave the name of Gharb.

Three years passed, and then the sultan turned toward home. But this time he did not approach the bridal chamber, for he had decided to marry his father's brother's daughter, as is the custom, and abandon the saddler's daughter. Sheep were slaughtered for the banquet, and the notes of the horn and the throbbing of the drums began to sound in celebration of the coming wedding between the sultan and his cousin.

Now the saddler's daughter could not sit still. She called her three children and dressed them carefully. She gave the eldest the sultan's dagger to carry, slipped the amber prayer beads round the second son's neck, and tied the sultan's headcloth round her daughter's hair. Then she taught them to sing this song:

> We're going to the sultan's wedding
> To join the feast and laughter!
> Who in the palace will be guessing
> That we are his two sons and daughter?

Holding each other by the hand, the three children lisped the verse as they were brought into the sultan's presence. When he heard the words they were chanting and saw one boy carrying his own dagger, another wearing his precious amber prayer beads, and a little girl wrapped in the cloth he used to wear on his head, he asked, "Who is your mother?" They led him to the saddler's daughter, and the sultan immediately understood all that had happened in the long years while he was absent. He said,

> After all the eating and drinking,
> Even after the deed has been done,
> Draw a line both black and winking
> Of wedding *kohl* though the hour has gone.

And he sent his cousin back to her father and at last married the saddler's daughter, the mother of his three children.

> So there we left them, and home we came,
> And then we never saw them again.

Saṅgēndi Mahāliṅgam Naṭeṣa Ṣāstrī

The Talisman of Chastity*

In the land of Akhandakaveri there reigned a king, named Viradeva. He had an only daughter, named Ambika. She was his only hope, and so he brought her up very tenderly. Nor was her education neglected on that account, as is usually the case with spoilt children. She was put to school at a very tender age, and was very carefully educated. Every day she rose up early from her bed and devoted her whole time to her studies. It was a very hard routine that she had to undergo, attending upon various teachers and receiving instruction from them, for they were numerous. Indeed, there was

---

*Saṅgēndi Mahāliṅgam Naṭeṣa Ṣāstrī, *Indian Folk-Tales* (Madras: Guardian, 1908), 409–34, https://babel.hathitrust.org/cgi/pt?id=inu.39000005763854;view=1up;seq=425 (accessed April 20, 2017). No. 38.

a professor employed for each of the sixty-four departments of knowledge—*chatus shashtikalas*. So ardent was her desire to acquire knowledge,—so great was her thirst for it, that she drank deep at the fountain, and before she attained to mature age she became a great *pandita*.* Of all the sixty-four teachers presiding over her tuition, there was one whom she specially venerated, for he deserved it. To him she gave the best of her love. He had instructed her the most, and rightly deserved the extreme veneration in which he was held by his royal student.

When Ambika had almost completed her education, it was time for her to retire from the company of her much venerated masters, and shut herself up in the closely guarded rooms of her palace, as became a royal maiden. She, therefore, proceeded to the house of each of her teachers to take leave of them in person. Everywhere she found a ready welcome. The usual presents were exchanged; advice was freely given; and the parting was so joyous and pleasant. Then, after taking leave of her minor teachers, she reached the house of the great master whom she held in such veneration. When the usual presents were placed before him, he said:—

"My dear Ambika, it was not for these presents and flimsy nothings that I took so much care of you. My fee is an embrace from you, not now, but, on the first day of your nuptials with your lawful husband, whoever he may be. On that busy day, when the festivities are over, and when you are ready to enter your lord's rooms, you must take leave of him for a short time and visit me in this house with all your nuptial decorations and allow me to embrace you first. This is the fee I demand for all my trouble on account of your education, and no other fee will I accept."

Thus spoke the master, and Ambika nodded assent to his demand, for she was so mad in her veneration for his learning that she overlooked his moral character. She perceived his meanness and

* A learned or wise person.

depravity, as in reality she had strong ideas on morality and chastity; but her childish veneration for the man made her consent, and she promised to visit him on her wedding day as ordered. Without any ill-will toward him she returned home, and thence remained shut up according to the custom of the country, expecting her wedding.

A princess, so learned and so beautiful, could not have long to wait for marriage. The prince of the Pandiyas soon sought her hand, and, as usual, the marriage was celebrated in the capital of Akhandakaveri. Great were the preparations. Grand were the ceremonies. The busy day was drawing to a close. The night had set in. The preparations for ushering in the bride and bridegroom were gone through; but, as Ambika was just on the point of entering her lord's room, she made some signs to her mother, as if she wanted to retire for five or ten minutes for some urgent reason.

The princess thereupon disappeared in the twinkling of an eye, and vanished like lightning among the clouds. She had already planned a secret way for her escape, and for the faithful execution of her promise to her master. All this she had done for herself. No second soul knew anything about it. With the rapidity of lightning she flew to her master's house and knocked at his door, and he, knowing well that it was the day of the princess's marriage, was all agog to test Ambika's faithfulness. At the first knock he came out suddenly and opened the door, and, in reality to his amazement, found the princess standing in all her wedding attire before him. Now, this man was the noblest of human beings and had all along perceived that Ambika had the greatest regard for a promise. His indecent demand was merely a strong test to examine her. He bowed himself at her feet, and, instead of meeting a tutor come to ravish her and make her life a burden to her, she heard a voice from the ground:—

"My noble Ambika, never hereafter take me for a vile brute. My demand was only made to test your power of keeping a promise.

Return home at once, and repose happily by the side of your husband. Till now you were my daughter by the rules of tutorship. From this night you are my mother."

Thus said the master, and showering his blessings on her, requested her to return in haste to the palace. Ambika, overjoyed and extremely pleased at heart at her adventure and her unsullied reputation, returned as quickly as she had left. But for all that, the time had been longer than she had expected, and her beating heart and profuse perspiration roused the suspicions of her husband. And, as usual, with young princes, he suspected her chastity at once. At their very first meeting there was a quarrel.

"Where did you go for so long?" asked he.

"Only to the back of the palace," said Ambika.

"So!" said the husband. "Till I have more confidence in your chastity, I shall not sleep by your side. Sleep in a distant cot. Never approach me," roared the enraged prince.

"My lord! I am as chaste as pure milk. I have never known anyone till now. If it is my fate that I should be thus suspected, I shall bear it without any murmur and wait for your lordship's pleasure to regain your confidence. I agree to your lordship's hard condition," replied Ambika, and calmly waited upon her husband.

The prince was unbendable. His suspicion was very strong, and it was not easily to be overcome. All Ambika's explanations were in vain. But she did not utter a syllable about her promise to her tutor, dwelling only upon her purity of conduct. There was no other place to go to; so she had to sleep apart from her husband in the same room. Thus the first night passed away; and so the second, and third—a week—a month. Every night the prince and princess retired to their bedchamber and slept on different beds. To the outer world they seemed very loving and affectionate to each other; but in their hearts they knew their extreme misery.

When the first month was over, the prince requested his father-in-law to permit him to return to Pandiyadesa with his wife.

The lord of Akhandakaveri readily gave his consent, and sent off his son-in-law and Ambika with suitable presents and other things becoming to the occasion, and himself accompanied the prince and his daughter for three days on their journey to Pandiyadesa. Then the father-in-law took his leave, and bent his way back to his kingdom. The prince and Ambika, after a journey of a few more days, reached his home, and the old king gave them a suitable welcome, and all the usual festivities were conducted at Madura, the capital of the Pandiyas. Here, too, no one knew of the difference that existed between the prince and his newly married wife. Everyone took them to be the happiest of newly married pairs. They slept in the same room, though not in the same cot, regularly for two full months.

During this long interval of three months and more, the prince had been closely watching Ambika. The more he tested her, the more the force of his suspicions began to decline. Her patient conduct, her close application to her books, her profound learning and deep experience, her most correct behavior toward himself, notwithstanding his unkindness toward her, the unabated affection she showed him, and a thousand other little matters came before him to upbraid him for his brutal conduct toward her, till, one night, he spoke to her thus:—

"Ambika, will you, now at least, tell me the truth? Tell me plainly that you are not unchaste. Whatever may have been your previous course of life, I shall gladly excuse you. Be true now, and utter no lie."

Replied Ambika:—"My most noble lord, I have not till now known any person. It is very unkind of you to harbor such suspicions of me. I am as chaste as chastity itself."

Said the prince:—"You are chaste because I watch you so carefully. Who knows what you may be if you are left to yourself?"

Said Ambika:—"If this idea had been lingering in your mind, why did you not, my lord, mention it long ago to me? You may leave me here and disappear for any period of time you like. I shall never think of any being in this world but yourself. I shall ever continue to be your loyal wife, however hardly you may behave to me."

Said the prince:—"What guarantee is there to me that you will always continue chaste? Give me some proof by which I may know, wherever I may be, that you are chaste."

"Agreed," said the wife, and took out from her box a garland of lotuses. "This is the test of my chastity. This was given to me by my mother as soon as I came to understand. The moment the flowers fade you must know my chastity is lost, and that as long as these flowers retain their freshness I am chaste. You can take it with you, and roam over the whole world with a calm mind, never harboring any anxiety as to my conduct; for when you perceive the color and freshness of these flowers to fade, you will know that I will have lost my reputation."

The husband took the garland, for had his wife told an untruth and said that she was impure, he would have easily forgiven her. But her denial increased his suspicions and he intended to try his best to test her: to regain her with increased love if she withstood the trial: to banish her for all her assumed goodness if she was really bad. With these thoughts in his mind the prince said to her:

"You seem to be a more and more curious woman every time I examine you. Do you practice magic to deceive people? What! These are merely ordinary lotuses, and if they are fresh now, they will fade tomorrow."

"Keep them, my lord, for some days before you judge of them. As for your statement, I swear by everything that I hold sacred that I know of no magic, except the magic of being chaste and obedient to my husband, and I have confidence that that magic will one day remove all your doubts and make you love me all the more for your doubts now," said Ambika.

The husband knew not what to say; so he took the garland and locked it up in his box. He kept it with him for some days in

Madura, and every morning when he left his bed he examined it, and to his surprise, which daily increased, he found it unchanged in color and freshness. He now resolved upon a plan to put his wife under the severest conditions for testing her fidelity and thus spoke to her:

"My Ambika! you must leave this roof tomorrow. I intend sending you to the east end of this town to a ruined choultry,* with your maidservants to take care of you. They will bring you every morning from the palace two measures of rice with other necessaries to live upon. You must live there, while I go on a pilgrimage to Benares to wash away my sins for having married an unchaste wife. With your own money and I do not know how you will get it—you must build a Siva temple opposite to the choultry, must become pregnant of a son through me and unknown to myself, before my return to this city. I shall be absent for two years. Till you perform successfully all these conditions, I shall never call you my wife, nor imagine you to be chaste."

"Agreed," said Ambika. "I am sure that my chastity will successfully help me in all these undertakings. With the talisman of my chastity in your hands you can go wherever you like. I shall contrive to live in the humble house selected for me by my lord as happily as in this palace. It is the mind that makes the house happy."

Thus said Ambika, without in the least fearing her change of dwelling. Her husband admired her perseverance, but firmly made up his mind to put her to this most severe test. With his mind thus made up, he approached his father next morning, and disclosed to him the secret about his wife's conduct, which he had till then kept to himself. He never told the old man a word about the talisman, nor his conditions to his wife, but proposed a pilgrimage to Benares with the double object of forgetting his past miseries and of search-

*An inn for travelers.

ing for a better wife. The father tried his best to dissuade his son from his project.

"Remain at home, and I shall find you a better wife," said he.

But the son was already resolved. He sent Ambika that very morning to the choultry with four maidservants to attend upon her, and every morning one of them had to come to the palace to receive the dole of rice.

Ambika bravely faced her new life, hopeful of successfully performing all her husband's conditions; but for a time she was wholly at a loss as to how to do it. She was now very miserable,—an outcast of womankind, a suspected woman,—living on the charity of the prince. So the outer world took her to be. She had neither money, nor friends, nor influence and she feared that she might be closely watched without in the least knowing it.

As for the prince, the greater the distance he traveled the more his heart turned back to his wife, for the talisman, which he daily examined, indicated his wife's chastity. Now and then a strong desire came over him to turn back and embrace his loyal and faithful wife; but at other times a headstrong stupidity to see how his wife would execute his hard conditions impelled him on his course. Thus he traveled for a month and reached Vijayanagara.

The king of Vijayanagara was a bad man. His pride was in having many wives, and his motto was that no woman in the world was chaste. The Pandiyan prince reached the Court, and in a conversation about the chastity of the women of different parts of India, dwelt at length on the fidelity of his wife, and produced the talisman as a proof of it. The king of Vijayanagara called him a great fool for putting so much trust in womankind, and promised to send one of his ministers to Madura to ruin the woman he extolled so much, and whose talisman he possessed.

"Agreed," said the prince; and a minister was at once dispatched to Madura.

Now he was one of the most depraved of human beings, whose sole object of life was to gain the favor of his master by doing his dirty work for him. He attired himself like a vendor of pearls and precious stones, and with a good quantity of these articles proceeded to Madura, which he reached soon. He took up his abode in the eastern quarter, and in a small house he opened his shop for vending gems and pearls. Crowds began to collect, and these goods which are very valuable, were purchased now and then by a few rich people in the place. The news spread throughout the town that a merchant with a fine stock had arrived from the north, and that he was exposing good stuff for sale. Few bought, for the articles were of high value, but the whole town congregated there to see the fine goods.

About a month after the arrival of the merchant, the people ceased to pour into the shop to take a look at the goods, and only those who really wanted to purchase went there. So on a certain day, when there was no one there except Devi, a maidservant of Ambika, who had come out of curiosity, the pretended merchant thus spoke to her:—

"Good woman, may I know who you are?"

She replied:—"I am a poor woman, servant to the princess of Akhandakaveri, who is undergoing punishment."

"Who is this princess? What is her story? Why is she undergoing punishment?" the merchant asked, as if he knew nothing about her.

The maidservant related what little she knew, but all she knew was that Ambika was suspected, and that her husband, the prince, was punishing her for unfaithfulness. When he had heard all she had to say the merchant, as if a new thought had dawned upon his mind, thus replied:—

"Then it is already established that her character is bad. If you but aid me in seeing her for a night, I shall in return make over to you, or to her, my whole property. That may also relieve you from your present miseries. Nothing will be lost thereby. The reputation of the princess is already tainted."

The maidservant did not know what reply to make. But the merchant, by his winning conversation, soon made her agree to talk upon the subject to the princess; and with this mission she went away. At first she did not know what to do. How to open the subject was the great difficulty she felt but, she was somewhat emboldened by the thoughts that Ambika was already a suspected character. At last she told her everything.

Ambika listened to what the maidservant had to say very attentively, and, taking her into her confidence, related to her in detail every part of her miserable life—her pure unsullied character, the cruelty of her husband, the vow, and so on.

Ambika then continued:—"My kind Devi, from today you must lend me all your help to enable me to fulfil my vows, for today I make you the chief of my maidservants. To secure us funds for the raising of the Siva temple, the suggestion of the pearl merchant has provided us with means. He wants to sleep with a princess. Let him have his wish, and let my character still remain unimpaired. What if we decorate one of the maidservants in all my ornaments and pass her off for me for a night? I can easily wear her clothes for a night. By doing thus, the pearl merchant will be duped, the funds required will be secured, and my character will remain unsullied. So run you to the merchant and tell him that he shall have his desire fulfilled this very night."

Devi pitied Ambika for all she had related to her, and, resolving within herself to do her best to assist the poor princess, at once arranged everything with one of her co-servants and ran to the pearl merchant. He was delighted to hear that matters were settled so easily, and was full of hope that he would the next day carry the news to Vijayanagara as to how pure a princess Ambika was; so he hastened that very night to Ambika's quarters. He spent the night with a maidservant in the belief that the woman he slept with was the princess, and the next morning quite in keeping with his promise, he made over to Devi all the wealth he had with him, in return for her assistance, and left Madura. He journeyed for a fortnight, and reached Vijayanagara, informed his monarch that his mission was successfully accomplished, and the princess was no better than other women. In proof he showed one or two ornaments of the princess, which he had carefully brought with him. They were, no doubt, the ornaments of the princess, which the maidservant had worn on the night on which she slept with the emissary. These proofs were quite enough to convince the Pandiyan prince that his wife was of a bad character. He had all along entertained that kind of doubt about her, though now and then there were circumstances, which made him waver in his opinion. The minister's mission and the supposed successful execution of it, made the husband think that he was all along wrong in having now and then entertained a better and higher idea of the Akhandakaveri princess. He looked at his talisman, and not a petal had faded. The king of Vijayanagara called it magic, and the trophy, which the minister had brought with him, in the shape of the ornaments of the princess, in token of his having spent a night with her, made the enraged husband think that the talisman was magical, that his wife was a bad woman, and that there was no use in testing her conduct any longer.

"Shall I go back and have her killed for her crime?" thought he within himself. But he did not like to be so very hasty, and as the princess was his wife only in name, he did not much care what life she led.

"She is already proclaimed by me to be a bad woman, and deservingly has been placed in a disgraceful corner of the town. If she had established her conduct to be above suspicion, I would have her taken back to myself; but now she has forfeited all chance of ever returning to me as my wife. Why should I, therefore, care anymore for her? Why should I curtail my pleasures in traveling over several countries to visit Benares?"

Thus thought he within himself, and though the insinuating taunts of the Vijayanagara monarch and his minister pierced him to his heart, he heard them calmly and started toward the north. The talisman he still kept with him, though he no more cared to look at it and examine it every day. Thus was the husband of the most chaste Ambika poisoned in his judgment, and, after leaving Vijayanagara, he banished from his mind all thoughts of her.

The various countries he passed through, and their scenery, people's manners, and customs engaged his attention. After a seven months' journey, he reached Benares, and took up his abode in a fashionable quarter, generally occupied by well-to-do people.

He was still new to the place, and was spending the first month in making the acquaintance of several princes and noblemen's sons, who were staying in that sacred city, like himself. Almost opposite to his lodging there was sojourning the prince of Simhaladvipa, keeping a large establishment of servants and courtesans. The Pandiyan prince contrasted himself with the Simhala prince and thought he to himself:—

"How happy this prince of Simhala spends his stay here! What a large establishment he keeps! What a pity it is that I did not make as pleasant arrangements for myself!"

Thus thought he and wished to cultivate his acquaintance, but the Simhala prince seemed to care for nothing in the world except his own enjoyments. There was feasting, dancing, and music in his house every day almost, but he kept it all to himself, and invited none to it.

Now the Pandiyan prince was always unhappy. His wife's conduct since he had married her, the curious talisman that still preserved its color notwithstanding the months that had passed since he first received it from her hands, her goodness, sound learning, and then that she should so easily have received the Vijayanagara minister to her embrace, would come to his mind in his loneliness and make him extremely sad. At other times, he would entirely forget her, and even if he thought of her, would never bestow any thought upon her conduct, or how his reputation would be affected by it, as long as he did not regard her as his wife. But little by little he entirely gave up his ideas about his wife, and his great object was to cultivate the friendship of the prince of Simhaladvipa, and enjoy, in his company, all the festivities to which that prince was so addicted.

Meanwhile the fair name of Ambika had been spoilt by the minister of Vijayanagara. But she had no idea of how great the mischief was that has been done. All she had wanted were funds for the Siva temple, which her lord had ordered her to acquire for herself. The funds had been acquired in the manner directed. So when the merchant, after giving away all that he had to Devi, left Madura for the north, and when all this property was safely and secretly collected and kept in the choultry, Ambika said to Devi:—

"My dear friend, I mean to entrust the building of the Siva temple to you, for I must leave this place soon, if I am to execute the last hard condition of my lord. Meanwhile, you must daily go to the palace to receive the dole for our maintenance. Everything must go on, as if I remained here. Not a word, not a syllable, must escape from your lips about my absence. The building of the Siva temple, opposite to our choultry, must commence from tomorrow, and slowly must the work go on. You must keep a regular account of all the money that you spend upon it, and it must be built strictly from the funds that we have acquired from the merchant."

Devi listened eagerly to what all Ambika said, and put her a thousand questions, and promised to do all a maidservant could do in helping Ambika.

Now, as her lord left for Benares, the princess had determined to follow him there in disguise, for successfully accomplishing the last and the most severe of his conditions—that she should, through him and without his knowledge,—give birth to a son. But she now saw that unless she had strong help, the successful execution of her project would be an extremely difficult, nay, an impossible, task. So she wrote to her father secretly about her hard life, and why she had to go to Benares, and saying that for this journey she wanted a good retinue composed of men and women quite foreign to India, a very confidential man for superintending her affairs at Madura, and ample funds for her journey and stay at Benares. Her father had the greatest regard for his daughter, and so he at once sent men and money, and, as desired by his daughter, made the whole retinue wait at a day's journey from Madura. The men and women that composed this retinue were all persons from the Simhaladvipa, and the king made two of his confidential ministers assume the guise of common men of that island, and ordered them to obey the princess's orders.

One of these men was to superintend the work that Devi was to undertake for the Siva temple; and great was Ambika's delight when she saw him near her, disguised as a beggar. She came to know through him that a retinue of a hundred women, with another person, disguised like himself, was waiting for her at a day's journey from Madura. Her joy knew no bounds when she heard of this. She called Devi to her side, recommended her to the confidential friend in disguise, and made arrangements that the Siva temple should be built by him with funds supplied by Devi. She then took a box from the hands of the disguised friend, which contained something for her from her father, and went in to her own room.

After a *ghatika** she returned, and the persons found a strange prince standing before them, and no longer the princess Ambika, for the box that the princess received from her father contained a complete set of a male dress. The confidential friend accompanied the disguised Ambika to the spot where the retinue was waiting, and returned to Madura to attend to his duty. Thus did Ambika, disguised as a prince, begin her long, troublesome, and rapid pilgrimage to Benares. She reached the sacred city a day after her lord's arrival there, and took up her abode opposite to his house, calling herself, in her disguise, the prince of Simhaladvipa.

The several festivities, the music and the nautch† parties were purposely held in the house of the Simhaladvipa prince to attract the attention of the Pandiyara prince. But the latter never for a moment had any reason to suspect that these things were wholly done for his sake and he was for several days eagerly waiting for an opportunity to get himself introduced to one whom he considered to be the happiest prince in the world. In about a couple of months after his arrival in Benares, he was allowed to become the friend of the prince of Simhaladvipa, and little by little the friendship between the two princes grew thicker and thicker, till on a certain day the Simhaladvipa prince thus questioned his friend:

"O Pandiya, notwithstanding the several festivities, nautches, and music that I get up day after day on your account, I now and then find that you are absent-minded. There must be some cause for all this. Though we have become bosom friends now, you have not been free with me. Tell me now, please, what lurks in your mind, and let me try my best to console you."

The prince then related all about his wife, except her banishment to the choultry, and so his listener came to understand who

---

* Twenty-four minutes.

† A dance performance by one or more professional dancing girls.

the pearl merchant had been. The Simhaladvipa prince laughed freely over the story, and this want of politeness enraged the vexed husband very much.

"You laugh now, O Simhala! I do not know how you would have liked these things, if your wife behaved thus toward you," said the Pandiyan prince, to which the listener replied:—

"Thank God, O Pandiya, I have no wife. I shall never marry one."

Now that the topic had been once mooted, there were several occasions in the next succeeding days on which they had again to revert to it. Though Ambika, disguised as the Simhala prince, had laughed over the volley of abuse that her husband, without knowing who his listener was, had showered upon her, there was no sadder soul in the world than herself at the time.

"Thus," thought she, "has my lord been deceived by the Vijayanagara minister, and believes me to be a bad woman and disbelieves my talisman, and calls it a magic. It is my fate to undergo such hardship. Let things only go on as I wish them now, and I shall win over my lord to my side."

One evening, the Simhala prince thus consoled his friend:—

"From all that I can gather from your speech, you seem to envy my happy life in the midst of so many courtesans, while you look upon your stay opposite to me all alone as a great hardship. If you have no objection, I can easily send you one of these courtesans for company."

The Pandiyan prince accepted his friend's suggestion, and from that night, the Simhala prince assumed the disguise of a courtesan of Simhaladvipa during the nights, and spent them with her lord. The Pandiyan prince never suspected that the prince and the courtesan, who visited him every night, were one and the same person. Thus matters continued till Ambika became certain of her pregnancy, and the moment she was certain of this, her whole thoughts were on Madura. But before she thought of returning there, she secured the best of his ornaments from her lord of his finger and ear rings, garlands, and even the talisman of lotuses that she had given him. Having no more thought of his bad wife, and never suspecting the courtesan to be a princess or his wife, he gave her all that she asked and more. The object of the pilgrimage of the princess to Benares was now successfully accomplished, and four full months she had spent happily with her lord.

One day, the following letter was shown to the Pandiyan prince by the Simhala prince:—

"My dearest son! Your presence is urgently needed here. Start at once and come away. You have spent too long a time at the sacred city."

"Do you see, O Pandiya, this letter from my father? I cannot stay long. I must be off in a day or two. Though we may part now, we shall meet soon, I hope. Before I go, I want to advise you a bit, encouraged to do so by our long friendship. On your return to your country take care first to dive into the whole secret of your wife's conduct, before you think of punishing her. She may still be chaste, and the minister's story after all a lie. He might have purchased the ornaments easily from some maidservants."

The Pandiyan thanked the Simhala for his good advice. Now that a kind and good friend suggested it to him, this idea,—that the Vijayanagara minister's version of his wife's character might after all be a tale and that the ornaments might have been got by unfair means, occurred to him at once. But the original warmth of his true regard to his singular wife, which he had before he came to Vijayanagara, was gone. He promised to himself secretly that, on his return, he would sift the matter well before taking any harsh steps, and no sooner had this idea entered into his head than he also wanted to return to his country.

The Simhala prince, after intimating to his friend that he would be going down to the south in a few days, resolved within himself that his departure must be sudden, secret, and rapid. All arrangements necessary for this were secretly made, and executed the very next day. The third morning after the letter was seen by the Pandiyan prince, he saw the mansion opposite his house vacant and the inmates all gone. On asking the landlord, he was told of the abrupt departure of the inmates to their country on the previous night.

"What," thought the Pandiya. "Is friendship a mere name without any meaning attached to it, that my friend, the Simhala, should thus quit the place without one word, as to the time of his leaving? But let me not accuse him. I was advised by him only the other day not to be so hasty and foolish in believing the Vijayanagara minister's accusation against my wife."

Thus thought he, and made arrangements for going also to his country.

As soon as princess Ambika in her male disguise left Benares, she requested her confidential friend to hasten the journey as much as possible and reached Madura in four months' time. As might be expected, she sent away to her father all the men and women who had formed her retinue a day's journey from her choultry, and taking only two chosen and trustworthy friends with her, she reached her poor habitation safely in the middle of the night. She met her confidential friends and Devi. Great were their rejoicings at this happy meeting, and Ambika was delighted to find that the temple was almost approaching to completion. The other part of her promise, too, she expected to be fulfilled in a couple of months in the natural course of circumstances. No one ever doubted that the princess had not remained in the choultry, for the morning doles had been regularly received, and now Devi and the other servants were mightily pleased at all the steps Ambika had taken for successfully retrieving her character. She requested them all to keep everything to themselves till her lord's return.

Six months after her return to Madura, her lord, the prince of the Pandiya country, returned to his palace from his pilgrimage to the north. The first news that he heard, when entering his dominions, was a scandal about his banished wife. Births and deaths cannot be kept secret for long time, and it became known throughout the palace first, then throughout the city, that the banished princess had given birth to a son. Then the whole Pandiyan realm came to know of it. This event took place just four months before the return of the prince, who, after leaving Benares, traveled in haste for a few days to join the Simhala prince, but, being unable to catch him up and obtain news of his movements, had taken his own time for his return journey.

The prince's return was welcome to all in the capital except to himself, for though now and then he consoled himself with the thought that the character of a banished princess should not at all put him out of his usual peace of mind, the scandal, as it appeared to him, was in the mouths of every one, and made him hang his head. His father the old king gave the prince a very kind and hearty welcome, but at their first meeting it so happened that Devi also was waiting to receive her morning dole. All the anger which the prince was keeping to himself broke out at once at the sight of that maidservant:—

"Has your lady a baby with her?" asked the prince.

"Yes, my lord," replied she.

"Cannot the father of that child feed you all?" roared out the prince, his tone of speech having changed itself by anger to a high pitch.

Coolly the maidservant replied:—"Your Highness, my lord, is its father, and in keeping with Your Highness's orders, I come daily to the palace gates."

The prince, who had not the slightest reason to connect himself with its origin, thought himself doubly insulted by the cutting remarks of the maidservant. He would have rushed at her and plunged his dagger in her body, had not half a dozen friends near him held him back, fearing his attitude. He abused her, and several people had already rushed at her to push her away, when the old king restored order, and severely reprimanded Devi.

But she was glad at heart that unwillingly the matters had taken such a course.

"Let me be abused and thrashed," thought she. "I shall be proud of having brought this separation between the prince and his chaste wife the sooner to an end."

With this thought, she bowed very respectfully to the prince, and requested him to turn his mind back to the Simhala prince, and that she was not at all joking, but in earnest, when she said that he was the father of the beautiful baby. She even went out of her way, and remarked that in all the fourteen worlds there could not be found a better lady than the princess of Akhandakaveri.

The prince's face changed color when the name of the Simhala prince fell into his ears.

"What! Is it possible! What connection is there with that company in Benares and the baby's birth here? Let me inquire," thought he.

Devi was not that day permitted to return to the choultry. Immediately, the princess with her baby and the other maidservants were sent for. The prince, overcome by extreme anger, had forgotten all his hard conditions, which he had imposed on his wife before he started for the sacred city:—the raising of the Siva temple and the giving birth to a son by his own self without his knowledge.

Ever obedient to orders issued by her lord or his father, Ambika, with her little baby at her bosom, arrived at the Court like an ordinary woman without any reference to her position. But what did she, the gem of womankind, care for all the outward formalities?

Her face, which bore on every line of it, furrows of deep anxiety and misery, indicated for all her chaste innate character. Reaching the Court she bowed with grace to her father-in-law and then to her lord. When questioned by the former as to who was the father of the baby, she replied:—

"Respected father-in-law. Your noble son and my husband is its father. Let him kindly remember the Simhala prince, his friend at Benares, and the courtesan that visited him every night there. This is that courtesan, and the cause of all this is the imposition of two severe conditions that your own son will explain to you. If he is doubtful of the courtesan, let him please examine these ornaments, which he presented to me."

Here she placed before the old king all the jewels that her husband had given her in her disguise as a courtesan. She then explained her whole story, from the beginning of her wedding night to that moment. All the people concerned in the affair were called and examined. The further the examination went, the more the prince began to admire his chaste wife. What hardships, what renunciations she has undergone to please the whims of his own bad self? Even the Vijayanagara minister with his sovereign had to come in to give evidence, and on the former's saying that the princess he slept with for a night, as a pearl merchant, had a mole in her right cheek, the last lingering doubt in the minds of the most suspicious of men assembled there was removed. This on examination was proved to exist on the face of the maidservant who had put on the disguise of the princess for a night. The examination was thorough and extremely minute, and before it was over there was not a single soul in the Court who did not condemn the prince for his bad treatment of his excellent wife, nor praise Ambika for all her successful adventures and noble execution of her undertakings for unsullied fame.

The prince was more than sufficiently pleased. He took back with pleasure his virtuous wife, and many were the occasions when they recounted their Benares adventures. Once thus closely united by so many pleasant recollections and adventures they never became separated afterward in their life. Ambika, by her purity of conduct, soundness of learning, and kindness to everyone, became an object of respect to every person, and even to her husband. And they now lived together happily for a long time.

VI. KING LEAR

King Lear, perhaps Shakespeare's bleakest tragedy, shares a common ancestry with "Cinderella," perhaps the world's most beloved fairy tale. The opening scene of the play enacts the first episode of the folktale "Love Like Salt" (ATU 923), which often features a princess who serves as a menial but changes into beautiful clothes to go to a dance, where a prince falls in love with her. She flees the scene, and he is able to find her only by seeking the woman who fits the mystery lady's shoe or ring. In these "Love Like Salt" folktales, however, this familiar "Cinderella" plot is framed by an episode in which the heroine's father asks her and her sisters how much they love him. The two older sisters flatter him, but the youngest answers in heartfelt but unconventional terms. Her sisters may love their father better than anything in the world, or as much as they love sugar, but the youngest loves her father like she loves salt. Her enraged father banishes her, and so she must fend for herself and eventually finds work as a servant. The story moves through its "Cinderella" paces until the heroine's wedding day. Her father arrives as a guest, not realizing the bride is his daughter. When he cannot eat the insipid food he is served, which contains no salt, he finally understands his daughter's metaphor and bursts into tears, only to have the bride reveal her identity and embrace him.

The first three of the "Love Like Salt" stories in this chapter—"Cap o' Rushes," "The Turkey-Girl," and "Marie, the King's Daughter"—follow this pattern. The second two, "The Gift of God" and "The Goose Girl at the Spring," use the "Love Like Salt" love test in different ways, as does King Lear. In the Turkish folktale "The

Gift of God," the father demands that his daughters tell him whose gifts are more precious, God's or the king's. The eldest two daughters are willing to blaspheme to please their father, but the youngest is not. The king banishes her, but through a series of remarkable events, she becomes even wealthier than her father, proving that God's gifts to her far exceed the king's power to punish her. In the Grimms' tale "The Goose Girl at the Spring," the love contest is an inset episode that explains how a princess came to be separated from her parents for three years.

I've included two nineteenth-century French folktales, "The Turkey-Girl" and "Marie, the King's Daughter," because they share elements with *King Lear* that I have not yet seen in other versions of "Love Like Salt." In "The Turkey-Girl," the demanding king is blessed with a faithful servant who, like Kent in *King Lear*, protests the love test and the mistreatment of the honest youngest daughter but serves the king at his own expense when the two older princesses declare that their father cannot live with them. In "Marie," the king goes mad when his two eldest children mistreat him, and returns to health under Marie's care, just as Cordelia's return to her father's side restores his sanity after he is turned out of his other daughters' homes. In both of these versions, the heroine's husband lends his military aid to restore her father to the throne, just as Cordelia's husband, the king of France, sends troops to Britain. The similarities between these French folktales and the play are so striking that I wonder if the play might have exerted an influence on these stories, although in general their plots are Cinderellesque. If *King Lear* contributed some details to "Turkey-Girl" and "Marie," that itself is an interesting phenomenon. It suggests that some taleteller recognized the *Lear*–"Love Like Salt" connection and borrowed some touches from the play when retelling the tales.

The history of the British King Leir intertwined with the "Love Like Salt" story from its earliest days. Geoffrey of Monmouth's twelfth-century *History of the Kings of Britain* provides the earliest account of Leir, and includes the "Love Like Salt" tale to explain how Leir's foolishness leads to internal strife and full-blown war. Cordelia and Leir emerge victorious and Cordelia rules for several years after her father's death. Shakespeare's audience would thus have been expecting a happy ending whether they knew the history of Leir, which had already been metamorphosed into an anonymous play in 1594, or the "Love Like Salt" folktale. Shakespeare's horrific final scene, in which Lear howls over Cordelia's corpse and then dies of grief, would thus have been even more devastating to his original audience than to most of us.

Lear claims that he is more sinned against than sinning, and the love test may indeed seem like nothing more than an indulgence of his vanity, although the banishment of his youngest daughter is a more serious misdeed. The love test, however, is a serious trespass, as both the folktale and the play make clear. In the Turkish story "The Gift of God," the king rewards his daughters for saying, when he asks them, that he is more powerful than God, a blasphemous overreaching. In "Marie," the older daughter avers that she would willingly allow Christ to be crucified a second time, a startling and heretical answer to the prompt, "Tell me how much you love me." In these two stories, the love test violates the first commandment. It also can seem queasily incestuous for a father to demand from his grown daughters extravagant expressions of love. When the exiled Marie dons a donkeyskin so as not to attract anyone's desire, the connection to the French folktale "Donkeyskin" is clear. Best known in Charles Perrault's 1694 version, "Donkeyskin" (ATU 510B), like "Love Like Salt," is also part of the Cinderella cycle. In "Donkeyskin" stories, the heroine is cast out of her own home not because she answers moderately when her father asks how much she loves him, but rather because she resists when her father asks her to marry him. Cordelia makes the incestuousness of Lear's demand plain when she responds:

> Why have my sisters husbands, if they say
> They love you all? Haply when I shall wed,
> That lord whose hand must take my plight shall carry
> Half my love with him, half my care and duty.
> Sure I shall never marry like my sisters
> To love my father all. (1.1.99–104)

Lear's demand seems especially fraught because it is at that very moment when Cordelia's marriage will be settled, and the love test takes place with her two older sisters' husbands present. Jane Smiley's 1991 novel *A Thousand Acres*, an adaptation of *Lear* set in 1970s Iowa farmland, also makes the incestuous subtext manifest.

Both the explicit blasphemy and the more subterranean incest inherent in the love test make it apparent that the king asks for more love from his daughters than he should. One reason I have included the Grimms' tale "The Goose Girl at the Spring," and not their "Princess Mouseskin" (a more straightforward "Love Like Salt" tale*) is because "Goose Girl" includes two maternal figures, the queen who pleads with her husband not to banish their daughter and mourns her absence, and the old woman who takes in the girl and protects her, and later upbraids the king for his foolish behavior. Most "Love Like Salt" tales do not mention a wife for the king or a mother for the princesses, and nor does *King Lear*, except for a few remarks about the dead queen's saintliness. One imagines a wife and mother would exert a restraining influence, both against the king's excessive demands for love and against his severe punish-

---

*"Princess Mouseskin" appeared in the Grimms' first collection of folktales, published in 1812, but not in later editions.

ment for his youngest daughter. In *A Thousand Acres*, the Lear-figure's wife died while her daughters were children.

Both Geoffrey of Monmouth and Shakespeare diverge significantly from the folktale. Leir/Lear in anger banishes Cordelia, but she does not undergo a period as a kitchen drudge before marrying a prince. Rather, Cordelia marries the king of France right away. Geoffrey and Shakespeare rather follow Lear as *he* suffers banishment. Cordelia may not suffer as a servant, but she also does not get a happy ending. In *The History of the Kings of Britain*, two of her nephews rebel against her rule as queen. This time, she loses the war and kills herself in prison—a fate to which Shakespeare alludes when the villain Edmund plans to have Cordelia hanged and then claim it was a suicide. Cordelia's fate is so devastating that from 1681 to 1838, the version of *Lear* performed onstage was a revision of Shakespeare's play by Nahum Tate in which Cordelia does get her happily ever after, a timely rescue and marriage to Edmund's good brother Edgar. Shakespeare's masterpiece offers us no such comfort.

LOVE LIKE SALT

Joseph Jacobs
Cap o' Rushes*

Well, there was once a very rich gentleman, and he'd three daughters, and he thought he'd see how fond they were of him. So he says to the first, "How much do you love me, my dear?"

"Why," says she, "as I love my life."

*Joseph Jacobs, *English Fairy Tales*, illus. John Dixon Batten (London: David Nutt, 1890), 51–56, https://babel.hathitrust.org/cgi/pt?id=hvd.32044024186231 ; view=1up;seq=75 (accessed April 20, 2017).

"That's good," says he.

So he says to the second, "How much do *you* love me, my dear?"

"Why," says she, "better nor all the world."

"That's good," says he.

So he says to the third, "How much do *you* love me, my dear?"

"Why, I love you as fresh meat loves salt," says she.

Well, he was that angry. "You don't love me at all," says he, "and in my house you stay no more." So he drove her out there and then, and shut the door in her face.

Well, she went away on and on till she came to a fen, and there she gathered a lot of rushes and made them into a kind of a sort of a cloak with a hood, to cover her from head to foot, and to hide her fine clothes. And then she went on and on till she came to a great house.

"Do you want a maid?" says she.

"No, we don't," said they.

"I haven't nowhere to go," says she; "and I ask no wages, and do any sort of work," says she.

"Well," says they, "if you like to wash the pots and scrape the saucepans you may stay," said they.

So she stayed there and washed the pots and scraped the saucepans and did all the dirty work. And because she gave no name, they called her "Cap o' Rushes."

Well, one day there was to be a great dance a little way off, and the servants were allowed to go and look on at the grand people. Cap o' Rushes said she was too tired to go, so she stayed at home.

But when they were gone, she offed with her cap o' rushes, and cleaned herself, and went to the dance. And no one there was so finely dressed as her.

Well, who should be there but her master's son, and what should he do but fall in love with her the minute he set eyes on her. He wouldn't dance with anyone else.

But before the dance was done, Cap o' Rushes slipt off, and away she went home. And when the other maids came back, she was pretending to be asleep with her cap o' rushes on.

Well, next morning they said to her, "You did miss a sight, Cap o' Rushes!"

"What was that?" says she. "Why, the beautifulest lady you ever see, dressed right gay and ga'. The young master, he never took his eyes off her."

"Well, I should have liked to have seen her," says Cap o' Rushes.

"Well, there's to be another dance this evening, and perhaps she'll be there."

But, come the evening, Cap o' Rushes said she was too tired to go with them. Howsoever, when they were gone, she offed with her cap o' rushes and cleaned herself, and away she went to the dance.

The master's son had been reckoning on seeing her, and he danced with no one else, and never took his eyes off her. But, before the dance was over, she slipt off, and home she went, and when the maids came back, she pretended to be asleep with her cap o' rushes on.

Next day they said to her again, "Well, Cap o' Rushes, you should ha' been there to see the lady. There she was again, gay and ga', and the young master he never took his eyes off her."

"Well, there," says she, "I should ha' liked to ha' seen her."

"Well," says they, "there's a dance again this evening, and you must go with us, for she's sure to be there."

Well, come this evening, Cap o' Rushes said she was too tired to go, and do what they would she stayed at home. But when they were gone, she offed with her cap o' rushes and cleaned herself, and away she went to the dance.

The master's son was rarely glad when he saw her. He danced with none but her and never took his eyes off her. When she wouldn't tell him her name, nor where she came from, he gave her a ring and told her if he didn't see her again, he should die.

Well, before the dance was over, off she slipped, and home she went, and when the maids came home, she was pretending to be asleep with her cap o' rushes on.

Well, next day they says to her, "There, Cap o' Rushes, you didn't come last night, and now you won't see the lady, for there's no more dances."

"Well I should have rarely liked to have seen her," says she. The master's son he tried every way to find out where the lady was gone, but go where he might, and ask whom he might, he never heard anything about her. And he got worse and worse for the love of her till he had to keep his bed.

"Make some gruel for the young master," they said to the cook. "He's dying for the love of the lady." The cook she set about making it when Cap o' Rushes came in.

"What are you a-doing of?" says she.

"I'm going to make some gruel for the young master," says the cook, "for he's dying for love of the lady."

"Let me make it," says Cap o' Rushes.

Well, the cook wouldn't at first, but at last she said yes, and Cap o' Rushes made the gruel. And when she had made it, she slipped the ring into it on the sly before the cook took it upstairs.

The young man he drank it and then he saw the ring at the bottom.

"Send for the cook," says he.

So up she comes.

"Who made this gruel here?" says he.

"I did," says the cook, for she was frightened.

And he looked at her.

"No, you didn't," says he. "Say who did it, and you shan't be harmed."

"Well, then, 'twas Cap o' Rushes," says she.

"Send Cap o' Rushes here," says he.

So Cap o' Rushes came.

"Did you make my gruel?" says he.

"Yes, I did," says she.

"Where did you get this ring?" says he.

"From him that gave it me," says she.

"Who are you, then?" says the young man.

"I'll show you," says she. And she offed with her cap o' rushes, and there she was in her beautiful clothes.

Well, the master's son he got well very soon, and they were to be married in a little time. It was to be a very grand wedding, and everyone was asked far and near. And Cap o' Rushes's father was asked. But she never told anybody who she was.

But before the wedding she went to the cook, and says she:

"I want you to dress every dish without a mite o' salt."

"That'll be rare nasty," says the cook.

"That doesn't signify," says she.

"Very well," says the cook.

Well, the wedding-day came, and they were married. And after they were married, all the company sat down to the dinner. When they began to eat the meat, that was so tasteless they couldn't eat it. But Cap o' Rushes's father he tried first one dish and then another, and then he burst out crying.

"What is the matter?" said the master's son to him.

"Oh!" says he, "I had a daughter. And I asked her how much she loved me. And she said, 'As much as fresh meat loves salt.' And I turned her from my door, for I thought she didn't love me. And now I see she loved me best of all. And she may be dead for aught I know."

"No, father, here she is!" says Cap o' Rushes. And she goes up to him and puts her arms round him.

And so they were happy ever after.

*Jean-François Bladé**

The Turkey-Girl

Once there was a king who loved salt. This king was a widower, and he had three marriageable daughters. He also had a servant who was wiser than just about anyone. One day when this servant was busy kneading in the bake-house, the king went to find him and said, "Servant, you are a sensible man, and I would like to consult you about a very secret matter."

"Master, I don't like secrets. If you must tell anyone else about this matter, don't say a word of it to me. You would think I was the one who had betrayed you, and you would drive me away."

"I won't speak of it to anyone but you."

"I'm listening."

"Servant, I have three marriageable daughters; I am old, and I no longer want to be king. When you have finished your kneading, go and find a lawyer. I will divide my property among my three daughters, reserving a pension for myself."

"Master, in your place I wouldn't do that."

"Why, servant?"

"Master, a man without property is soon despised. In your place, I would keep my land, and give my daughters reasonable dowries on their wedding days."

"Servant, my daughters love me; I have nothing to fear."

"Master, put them to the test before you decide."

The king went back up to his room, and had his three daughters summoned.

"Do you love me?" he asked the oldest.

*Jean-François Bladé, *Contes Populaires Recueillis en Agenais* (Paris, 1874), 31–41, https://babel.hathitrust.org/cgi/pt?id=pst.000012502325;view=1up;seq=43 (accessed April 20, 2017). No. 8. "Written from the dictation of Marianne Bense" (31). My translation.

"Father, I love you more than anything in the world."

"Good. And you, my younger daughter, do you love me?"

"Father, I love you more than anything in the world."

"Good. And you, my last child, do you love me?

"Father, I love you as much as you love salt."

"A wicked tongue! You insult your father. Return to your room, and wait there until I decide what to do with you."

The youngest daughter returned to her room; then her two older sisters said to their father, "Our sister insulted you: she deserves death."

"She will die; but you two love me, and you will soon receive your reward. Wait here for me."

The king went back down to the bake-house, where the servant was still kneading, and told him what had happened. "Now, servant, the test is done. Go find me a lawyer to divide my kingdom between my two older daughters, and the executioner to kill my youngest."

"Master, words are female; but actions are male. Your test is no good, and in your place I would judge my daughters by what they do, not by what they say."

"Silence, servant: you don't know what you're talking about. Be quiet, or I'll cudgel you."

When the servant saw the king brandish his cudgel, he pretended to change his mind. "Very well, master, I am wrong, and your word is law. Do as you will. I'll go find the lawyer, and I myself will be your youngest daughter's executioner. I will take her to the woods, kill her, and bring you her tongue."

"You see clearly, servant, when you are of my mind. Go first to seek the lawyer."

The servant went to fetch the lawyer, and the king married his eldest daughters at once, and gave each of them half of his realm.

"Lawyer," he said, "I reserve the right, for the rest of my life, to live six months of each year with my oldest daughter, and six months with my younger daughter. Don't forget to write that in your document."

The lawyer was a great blackguard who was sentenced that very year to the galleys for the rest of his life. He had secretly received payment from the two older daughters, and he did not put the king's stipulation in the deed.

"Master," said the servant, "May God grant that what is done is well done. Now I must take your daughter to the woods, to kill her and bring you her tongue."

"Go ahead, servant; when you return, I will reward you."

The servant found a chain and put it around the poor girl's neck. That done, he took his sword and whistled for his dog. "Come on, you insolent, miserable girl! You don't have long to live. Commend your soul to God, and to the Holy Virgin and the saints."

The servant called this out for the king's ears; but in the woods it was another story. "Lady, don't be afraid. I've done all this to save you from the executioner. Your dresses and your most beautiful clothes are in my pack. I have also brought peasant's clothing, which you must change into at once. Before I worked for your father, I served in another king's castle. His wife won't refuse me if I ask her to take you on as a turkey-herd, and there you will be well hidden."

Indeed, the servant brought the princess to this castle. The queen took her into service as a turkey-girl, and lodged her in a little room under the stairs. This done, the servant returned to his master; but while he was passing through the woods, he took his sword, killed his dog, and pulled out her tongue.

"Master, I have killed your daughter and brought you her tongue."

"Servant, I am pleased with you. Here are a hundred *louis d'or* for your pains."

"A hundred *louis d'or*, master, is not enough for this work."

"Well, here are a hundred more."

"And you, ladies, will you give me nothing for killing your sister and bringing you her tongue?"

"Servant, we will each give you as much as our father has."

"Thank you, master. Thank you, ladies."

The next day, the two older daughters each went with her husband to find the king. "Father, this is no longer your home. The right half of this castle belongs to the younger daughter, and the left to the older daughter. Go wherever you please."

"Wicked girls, you repay me ill for all the good I did for you. I don't want to go. The lawyer's deed gave me the right, for the rest of my life, to live six months with my oldest daughter, and six months with my younger."

"Let the document speak, and shut your mouth. The lawyer didn't write that."

"The lawyer is as much a villain as you are."

"Go! Quickly! Get out, or beware the dogs."

The poor king left the castle. On the doorstep he met the servant. "Where are you going, master?"

"I am going where God wills. This castle is no longer mine, and my daughters and my sons-in-law have chased me away. Why did you counsel me so badly when I wanted to divide my kingdom among my daughters?"

"Master, I said to you, 'Test them.' You believed in words, which are female, whereas actions are male, and you acted on your own notions. But what is done is done, and regret is useless. Wait for me a moment; we will leave together. I want to be your servant always."

"Stay here, for your own good. I'm no longer able to pay or feed you."

"I will serve you for nothing, and I have enough for us both to live on."

"As you wish."

The servant went back into the castle, and retuned a moment later with a full pack on his back. "Come on, let's go."

At the end of seven days of walking they arrived at a country where they found a little farm for sale, with a farmhouse. The servant bought it, and paid with the money that they had given him in the belief that he had killed the youngest princess. "Master, this little farm is yours. Drink, eat, and walk about, while I work in the fields and vineyards."

"Thank you, servant. Even a powerful master doesn't deserve you."

While all this was happening, the youngest daughter, whose father thought she was dead, was still a turkey-herd in the castle where the servant had found her a position. The king of this castle had a son so strong, so brave, and so handsome, that all the ladies in that country fell in love with him. The turkey-girl fell in love like the others; but he never paid her the least attention. "You lout," she often thought, "I will make you notice me."

Carnival began, and every evening after supper, the prince dressed up and rode off on his horse to go dancing until morning in the neighboring castles. What did the turkey-girl do? In the evening she said she was sick, and pretended to go to bed. But she secretly went down to the stables, saddled and bridled a horse, and gave it a double portion of oats. Then she went back up to her room and opened the pack with the clothes she had brought from her father's house. That done, she combed her hair with a golden comb, pulled on white stockings and little red morocco shoes from Flanders, put on a beautiful dress the color of the sky, returned to the stable, leapt on the horse and galloped away to the castle where the king's son had gone to dance.

When she entered the ball, the musicians stopped playing their hurdy-gurdies and fiddles, the dancers stopped dancing, and all the guests said, "Who is that beautiful lady?"

Finally, the hurdy-gurdy players and fiddlers began to play again, and the prince took the young lady by the hand to lead her in the dance. But at the first stroke of midnight, she left her dance partner, leapt on her horse, and galloped away. The next day she tended the turkeys as usual, and when the prince came upon her while he was out hunting, he thought, "It's astonishing how much this young peasant looks like the beautiful lady I saw at the ball last night."

The same evening, after supper, he dressed, mounted his horse, and left again for the ball. So what did the turkey-girl do? In the evening she said she was sick, and pretended to go to bed. But she secretly went down to the stables, saddled and bridled a horse, and gave it a double portion of oats. Then she went back up to her room and opened the pack with the clothes she had brought from her father's house. That done, she combed her hair with a golden comb, pulled on white stockings and little red morocco shoes from Flanders, put on a beautiful dress the color of the moon, returned to the stable, leapt on the horse and galloped away to the castle where the prince had gone to dance.

When she entered the ball, the musicians stopped playing their hurdy-gurdies and fiddles, the dancers stopped dancing, and all the guests said, "Who is that beautiful lady?"

Finally, the hurdy-gurdy players and fiddlers began to play again, and the king's son took the young lady by the hand to lead her in the dance. But at the first stroke of midnight, she left her dance partner, leapt on her horse, and galloped away. The next day she tended the turkeys as usual, and when the prince came upon her while he was out hunting, he thought, "It's astonishing how much this young peasant looks like the beautiful lady I saw at the ball last night."

The same evening, after supper, he dressed, mounted his horse, and left again for the ball. What did the turkey-girl do? In the evening she said she was sick, and pretended to go to bed. But she secretly went down to the stables, saddled and bridled a horse, and gave it a double portion of oats. Then she went back up to her room and opened the pack with the clothes she had brought from her father's house. That done, she combed her hair with a golden comb, pulled on white stockings and little red morocco shoes from Flanders, put on a beautiful dress the color of the sun, returned to the stable, leapt on the horse and galloped away to the castle where the prince had gone to dance.

When she entered the ball, the musicians stopped playing their hurdy-gurdies and fiddles, the dancers stopped dancing, and all the guests said, "Who is that beautiful lady?"

Finally, the hurdy-gurdy players and fiddlers began to play again, and the king's son took the young lady by the hand to lead her in the dance. But at the first stroke of midnight, she left her dance partner, leapt on her horse, and galloped away. But this time, as she escaped, she lost her little red shoe, the right one, at the ball.

Since the young lady had first appeared at the ball, the prince had fallen deeply in love, and he was unable to eat or drink. He picked up the little red shoe and tried it on all of the ladies at the ball; but all of their feet were too big for it. So he put the shoe in his pocket and returned to his father's castle.

"Father, I have fallen in love with the young lady who lost this little red shoe at the ball. If you do not give her to me in marriage, you will cause great misery. I will go far, far away and become a monk in a country from which I will never return."

"My son, I don't want you to become a monk. Tell me where this young lady dwells, and we will both go on horseback to ask her father for her hand in marriage."

"Father, I do not know where she dwells."

"Well then! Go fetch me the town drummer." The prince left and returned with the drummer. "Drummer, here are a hundred *pistoles.* Go and proclaim everywhere that the lady whom this shoe fits will become my son's wife."

The drummer left, and made the proclamation everywhere as he had been told. For three days, the king's castle was full of ladies who came to try on the little red shoe, but none of them could put it on. The turkey-girl watched what they were doing and laughed with all her heart.

"Your turn, turkey-girl," said the prince.

"Don't think of it, sir. I'm nothing but a poor little peasant. How would you like it if I did what none of these beautiful ladies could?"

"Come on, come on," cried the ladies, "make the insolent little thing who mocks us all the time come here, and if she cannot put on the red shoe, let her be whipped bloody."

The turkey-girl approached, pretending to cry and be afraid. Instantly, she slipped on the shoe. "Now," she said, "everyone wait for me here."

She went and shut herself in her room, and returned a moment later, wearing the red shoes on both feet, and dressed in her sky-colored dress.

"My dear," said the king, "you must marry my son."

"I will marry him when I have my father's consent. Until then, I would like to continue watching over the turkeys."

The king and his son found themselves at a loss.

Meanwhile, the other king, driven out by his two daughters, still remained with his servant at the little farm, and he frequently said, "My two daughters are rotten, and my two sons-in-law are a bad lot. If I had my youngest daughter with me, I would not be so unhappy. She would keep me company while making my shirts and patching my clothes. Servant, why did you kill her and bring me her tongue?"

"Master, it was you who commanded me to do so."

"Yet, servant, I was wrong to give you that order, and you were wrong to obey me."

"I was not wrong, because I did not obey you. Your youngest daughter isn't dead. I found a position for her in the castle of another king, as a turkey-herd, and the tongue you thought was hers was my dog's."

"Good, servant. Let us set off for the countryside to bring the poor thing back here."

They both left for the countryside, and seven days later, they arrived at the other king's castle.

"Good day, king."

"Good day, my friends. How can I help you?"

"King, I am a king myself, and I have a castle as beautiful as your own. My two older daughters drove me out, and my youngest is here working as a turkey-girl. You must return her to me."

"My friend, I cannot. My son has fallen in love with your daughter, to the point that he is unable to eat or drink. I ask you to marry her to him."

"King, bring my daughter to me so she can speak freely. I don't want to force her to marry."

Someone went and found the turkey-girl. "Hello, papa, and everyone."

"Hello, my girl. Speak freely. Do you wish to marry this young man?" The poor young man was as white as flour, and trembled like a cow's tail. "Speak freely, daughter."

"Papa, I would rather marry this man than any other. But first I would like him and his father to help you regain the castle my older sisters took from you."

So the king and his son immediately assembled all the men of that country, and armed them with swords and guns. They all got on the road during the night and took control of the castle from the two older sisters, who had expected nothing of the sort. These two women and their husbands were hanged, and their bodies were not buried on sacred ground. The corpses were abandoned in a field, where dogs, crows, and magpies gnawed them down to the bones.

Now that was done, the king said to the turkey-girl's father, "My friend, take your castle again, and become again the king you once were. Now we must think about the wedding of my son and your daughter."

Never had the people of this country seen such a beautiful wedding. A hundred casks of old wine were tapped; I don't know how many calves and sheep were slaughtered, and for three days and three nights, a hundred women plucked turkeys, capons, and ducks. All that wanted to could eat and drink. The servant, wearing new clothes and shining like a chalice, stood behind the bride's chair and did not let her lack for anything.

"Servant," his master said to him, "this is the last time you will serve at table. I want to marry you off today as well."

"Master, that's very decent of you."

"Servant, we don't lack for pretty girls here for you to marry."

The servant chose a girl as pretty as the day and as good as gold. "Master, here is my wife."

"Servant, let me embrace you. Now come to the table with us, both of you, and lack for nothing. The priest will marry you tomorrow morning. My daughter and I will be your sponsors."

*Jean-Baptiste Frédéric Ortoli**

Marie, the King's Daughter

A king had two daughters and one son. Feeling that he was growing old, he called his children and said to them, "Today I would like to

---

*Jean-Baptiste Frédéric Ortoli, *Les Contes Populaires de l'Ile de Corse* (Paris, 1883), 48–56, https://babel.hathitrust.org/cgi/pt?id=mdp.39015035828089;view =1up;seq=72 (accessed April 20, 2017). "Told in 1881 by Mademoiselle Adelaide de Alma, of Porto-Vecchio" (56). My translation.

divide among you my kingdom and all my possessions; but first, tell me how you love me."

The first daughter stepped forward and said, "I love you more than my life and soul; for you I would let Jesus Christ be crucified a second time."

"Very good, my girl, come and embrace me."

The young man said in his turn, "I love you, father, more than the kingdom you would give me; if it gave you a single moment of pleasure, I would throw myself into a blazing fire."

"You also, my child, come and embrace me; your father will not forget you."

The youngest, whose name was Marie, went at last before her father and said to him, "Me, father, I love you as a submissive and dutiful daughter should love a father such as you."

At these words, the old king went pale. He believed that his daughter didn't love him and was furious. "Get out! Get out! Ungrateful girl who loves no-one!"

And the unfortunate girl was obliged to obey, because her father would have killed her if she did not. Before leaving, Marie went to her room and wept. But as time was passing, she gathered all of her beautiful gowns embroidered with gold and silver and bundled them in a large cloth. She left at once, taking the first road she found before her.

After traveling through the night, the poor girl came to a farm; but the moment she knocked on the door, she feared that the boys there might find her too beautiful, and she retraced her steps, wandering in a vast forest.

There, the poor child ate nothing but wild fruits and drank nothing but water from streams. After wandering for many weeks, she made her way out of the forest at last. At the side of the road she found a dead donkey. The princess skinned it with her knife, let the hide dry, and then put it on so that everyone would take her for a simple servant. Dressed like this, the young lady traveled yet further, but always carrying with her the cloth containing her beautiful gold-embroidered gowns.

At last, she arrived at a beautiful castle. "Do you need a servant?"

"Yes, we need a shepherdess to watch the goats." And so the king's daughter became a nobleman's servant.

Every morning, Marie went and led the goats into the mountains, but the donkeyskin that covered her made her so ugly that no-one dared look at her. She still remained very tidy, the poor little thing. You might well think that Marie was hardly pleased, fallen as she was into such a sad position. The memory of her father, whom she loved very much even though he had driven her from his presence, and also that of her brother and sister, whom she might never see again, filled her heart with sadness.

One day the young shepherdess dreamed of her country, of her father, of the lovely days of her childhood, and she wanted to put on her beautiful dresses embroidered with gold and silver once again.

She led her goats over to a little stream that she had found in the mountains, and there she smoothed her hair, washed her hands and feet well, and then dressed as she had in her father's house. Never had the sad Marie found herself so beautiful. The desire came over her to sing a song from her homeland, and she did so with such sweetness that the goats stopped grazing and drinking. Night was coming on, however, and the girl put on her donkeyskin again.

But then a young man appeared who had become lost while hunting, and who was none other than the prince of that country. He had seen and heard everything; how, after that, could he not love such a charming child? Seeing that she had been observed, the gentle shepherdess began to tremble all over; thinking nothing of her goats, she fled toward her master's castle. Unfortunately, Marie had forgotten, in her haste, a beautiful little shoe. It was so little, so little, that its like had never been seen.

After that day, the prince fell hopelessly in love with the shepherdess he had found so beautiful and who sang with such a sweet voice. He searched everywhere for her, but it was useless; she was not to be found. So, throughout the kingdom, it was trumpeted that the prince would marry whoever could wear the shoe he had found.

Imagine the hordes of women! All believed their feet were so little that they were guaranteed to marry the prince, but not one could get even her toe-tips in.

The prince was in despair; he was dying of love, when someone mentioned to him that the little shepherdess at the castle nearby had not come. Someone ran right away to fetch Marie, who still wore the donkeyskin over her head, and brought her before the prince. What a surprise! Her foot fit the shoe exactly.

"Long live the queen!" cried the courtiers, but they said that to mock her. When the young prince's parents learned what kind of a person their child had chosen, they went into a rage and swore they would never allow their son to marry such an ugly shepherdess.

But Marie, who was royal herself, said to them, "Even if I tend goats at this time, do not believe that I have done this job since childhood, for my father is the king of a great people."

All the courtiers began to laugh to hear her say such things. However, the young lady asked to dress herself as she once had, and soon they saw her appear in her beautiful dresses embroidered with gold and silver. Everyone was amazed. They could not stop crying, "Oh! How beautiful she is! Oh! How beautiful she is!"

Transported with joy, the young prince wanted to marry her that same day; but Marie told him, "I will not marry you until my father casts aside his mistake about me and attends my wedding."

They sent messengers to the old king; but alas, they returned quickly, as mournful as death. "Why are you so sad, good messengers?" Marie asked them.

"Great princess, the king your father is mad. His son and daughter, after having despoiled him of all he possessed, not even sparing him basic necessities, locked him away in a frightful dungeon, where no one can enter."

Marie, who was kind and loving, began to cry at this sad news. "Calm down," said her fiancé. "I swear to you that he will be revenged." And he tried to console her.

"I will not marry you," the poor girl said again, "until my father is reestablished on his throne and, healthy in body and spirit, he is able to attend our wedding."

Upon learning of this decision, the young prince's parents declared war on the ungrateful children who had so abused their old father. These children were quickly defeated, and the unhappy old man restored to his throne. Unfortunately, Marie's father was quite mad, and only after an entire year of boundless care and devotion did his loving daughter succeed in restoring his reason.

Finally, nothing obstructed the marriage of the prince and the charming princess, and it was celebrated with truly extraordinary pomp. From all around, people came to attend the wedding and the feast that followed. Music played in the town squares, and the bells rang a full peal. As for myself, who am neither princess nor marquise, I had a place at the table, and it was there that I had right under my nose many of the bones from the feast.

Naki Tezel

The Gift of God[*]

Many years ago there lived a king who had three daughters. One day he sent for his eldest daughter and said:

[*]Naki Tezel, *Fairy Tales from Turkey*, trans. Margery Kent (London: Routledge, 1946), 74–78.

"My daughter, I am going to ask you a question. Answer me truthfully: which is the more precious—God's gift or the king's?"

Without hesitation she answered:

"Dear father, God's gift is precious, but the king's gift is precious above all."

This greatly pleased the king.

"Well said, my daughter. I will give you in marriage to the son of my Grand Vizier," said he. "Go now, and prepare for your betrothal."

After a while he sent for his second daughter, and to her too he said:

"Let us see what you have to say: which is the more precious—God's gift or the king's?"

And she too said, without a thought:

"In truth, father, the king's gift."

The king rejoiced and said:

"You have answered well. I will give you in marriage to the son of my Vizier of the second rank. Go and prepare for your betrothal."

In like manner, after a long time had passed, the king sent for his youngest daughter and repeated to her also the question which he had put to her elder sisters. She thought for a while, and replied:

"Indeed, father, the king's gift is precious, but God's gift is precious above all."

This answer greatly angered the king.

"Shameless girl!" he cried. "Begone! You are no child of mine. We shall see what gift God will give you!"

And the poor girl fled, sobbing and weeping, from the palace.

After wandering about for a while in the mountains she met a shepherd.

"Little father," she said, "I have no home; will you take me for your daughter?"

The good-hearted shepherd consented, and at nightfall they

came together to his cottage. From that day forth there she dwelt, and did the work of a housewife. One day, after some time had gone by, the poor man said:

"God willing, I will give you in marriage to my son. Would that please you?"

The girl was well content, and they set about preparing the poor betrothal as best they could. Some months later the shepherd fell sick, and very soon died, and thereupon all the work of the house passed to his son. But the young shepherd found great difficulty in looking after the family, and one day he left the village to look for work elsewhere. He set out with his two brothers, and they came to a certain country place where the people were dying of thirst. They had only one well, and because it gave no water, they were offering a reward of ten gold pieces to any brave man who would go down it. The young shepherd agreed to try, and clambered into the well. And there what did he see before him but a demon woman holding on one chain a beautiful girl, and on another a beautiful youth.

"Come, let us hear, Son of Adam," said the demon woman to the shepherd: "which of us is the more beautiful—this girl, this youth, or I?"

The young man answered instantly:

"Whomsoever the heart loves is beautiful."

The demon repeated her question three times, and three times he gave the same answer.

"Thou knowest, Son of Adam," said the demon; "ask of me what you will."

"Your good health first of all," said the shepherd, "and then water for the village."

"It is given," said the demon woman. "Take these three pome-granates also, and go."

No sooner was the shepherd out of the well than the water began to flow. The young man took the promised money and sent it home, together with the three pomegranates, in the care of one of his brothers, who, having earned nothing, had decided to return to the village. The shepherd himself, in search of yet more money, took the road again.

While he was on his way, his brother took the money and the pomegranates home, and left them with the shepherd's wife. Now it so happened that she had, that day, felt particularly thirsty, so she at once resolved to eat one of the pomegranates. She cut it open. Ah, what did she see? In place of every seed was there not a priceless diamond? Quite overjoyed, she ran straightaway to her mother-in-law, put one of the jewels in her hand, and sent her without delay to the goldsmiths'. The poor woman showed the diamond to them.

"I will sell it," she said, "for ten camel-loads of gold."

At last one goldsmith bought it for the price she asked, and she took the loads of gold back to the cottage. Thereupon the shepherd's wife sent for famous architects, and told them to build a palace, close to her father's, so splendid that it would make his look like a poultry yard. The architects built it in a very short time; the shepherd's wife had the cottage pulled down, and they all moved into the palace. She gave orders that every passing traveler should be stopped and given food and money. And so the fame of the palace was soon on everyone's lips.

The years went by, and one day the mistress of the palace was looking out of the window when she saw someone weeping in the place where the cottage had stood. Watching him closely, she saw that it was her husband the shepherd. At once she gave orders to the men-servants that without alarming him they should bring him in, and bathe and feed him, and that they should not let him go. When this had been done the guest was led in fear and trembling

228 • *King Lear*

into her presence. Suddenly he saw enthroned before him, richly dressed in furs and brocades, his own mother. He ran to her and kissed her hand; and then at her side he saw his wife. When they had embraced each other the young man asked how this wonderful palace had come to be. They told him the story of the pomegranate. He was enchanted to hear of it, and thereafter they lived together very joyfully.

The fame of this palace had now reached the ears of the king, and one day, disguising himself as a holy man, he took an attendant with him and set off to see for himself. His daughter, recognizing the attendant as they approached, and guessing that it was her father who had come, instantly ordered a table to be spread with every kind of dish. When the king, in his guise as a holy man, was received in the palace, and saw the feast prepared for him, he marveled. When they had eaten their fill, coffee was brought, but still the king could not bring himself to ask whose the palace might be. In the end he rose to depart. But his host, the former shepherd, cried:

"Holy father, my wife, alas, is very ill; will you not give her your blessing?"

"Assuredly," said the king, and went to see her. She was lying on a splendid couch, and rose to her feet as he entered.

"Dear father, may I kiss your hand?" she said.

When he realized that this was his own daughter, the king was filled with shame.

"Tell me, father dear," she said, "which is the more precious— God's gift or the king's?"

"You were right, my daughter," said the king. "God's gift is the most precious of all. Your husband shall inherit my kingdom, and may such good fortune always be yours."

And so they were all rejoiced, and lived happily ever after.

Jacob and Wilhelm Grimm
The Goose Girl at the Spring*

Once upon a time there was a very old woman who lived with a flock of geese in a lonely place on a mountain. She had a little house in this lonely spot, which was surrounded by a large forest. Every morning the old woman took her crutch and hobbled into the woods, where she was quite busy, much busier than one would have expected of someone her age. She gathered grass for her geese, picked wild fruit from the branches that her hands could still reach, and then carried everything home on her back. One would have thought that she would have collapsed to the ground under the heavy load, but she always brought it home safely. If she met people along the way, she would greet them in a friendly manner, "Good day, dear neighbor. Nice weather we're having today. Ah, you're wondering why I'm carrying the grass. Well, we all have burdens to bear on our backs." However, people did not like to encounter her, and when they had a choice, they took a different path. And, whenever a father chanced to meet her in the company of his son, he would say softly to him, "Beware of the old woman. She has cunning ways. She's a witch."

One morning a handsome young man was going through the forest. The sun shone brightly. The birds sang. A cool breeze caressed the leaves, and he was full of joy and good cheer. He had yet to come across anyone, when suddenly he spotted the old witch, who was kneeling on the ground and cutting grass with a sickle. She had already gathered a full load in her pack, and two baskets filled with wild pears and apples stood next to it.

*Jacob and Wilhelm Grimm, *The Complete Fairy Tales of the Brothers Grimm*, trans. Jack Zipes (New York: Bantam, 1992), 562–70. No. 179.

"My God, old woman," he said, "how can you possibly carry all that away?"

"I must carry it, dear sir," she answered. "Children of the rich don't have to do such things. But the peasants have a saying that goes:

'Watch out but don't look back
Your spine's curved like a sack.'

"Do you want to help me?" she asked as the young man continued to stand near to her. "You still have a straight back and young legs. It would be easy for you. Besides, my house is not very far from here. It's on a heath beyond that mountain over there. You could make it up there quickly, in a hop, skip, and a jump."

The young man felt sorry for the old woman. "I'll confess. My father is not a farmer," he answered, "but a rich count. However, so that you will see that farmers are not the only ones who can carry things, I shall take your bundle on my back."

"If that's your will," she responded, "then I am pleased. It will take a good hour of your time, but that should not matter to you. You must also carry the apples and pears over there."

The young count began to have some doubts when the woman mentioned an hour's walk, but she did not let him renege. She lifted the sack on his back and hung two baskets on his arm.

"You see," she said, "there's nothing to it."

"No, it's not all that light," responded the count, who had a pained expression on his face. "The bundle is very heavy. It feels as if it were packed with nothing but bricks, and the apples and pears feel as though they were made of lead. I can hardly breathe." He would have liked to set everything down, but the old woman did not let him.

"Just look," she said mockingly, "the young gentleman won't carry what an old woman like me has so often hauled. You're good with pretty words, but when it comes to serious action, you want to scoot away like the wind. Why are you standing around and dallying?" she continued. "Get a move on. Nobody's going to take the bundle off your back again."

As long as he walked on level ground, he could stand it, but as soon as they came to the mountain and had to climb, and the stones rolled out from under his feet as though they were alive, it was beyond his strength. Beads of sweat appeared on his forehead and trickled down his back, hot and cold.

"Old woman," he said, "I can't go any farther. I want to rest a while."

"Nothing doing," answered the old woman. "Once we've arrived, you can relax, but now you must keep marching. Who knows what good all this may do you?"

"Old woman, you're becoming shameless," said the count, and he wanted to throw off the pack. However, he struggled to no avail. The pack was stuck to his back as tightly as if it grew there. He twisted and turned, but he could not get rid of it. The old woman laughed at him and jumped delightedly with her crutch.

"Don't get mad, dear sir," she said. "Your face is turning as red as a tin rooster. Bear your burden with patience. When we get home, I'll certainly give you a good tip for your service."

What was he to do? He could only resign himself to his fate and plod along patiently after the old woman. She seemed to have become more and more nimble, while his load seemed to become heavier and heavier. Then, all at once, she took a leap and landed on top of the pack and sat there. Even though she was as thin as a rail, she weighed more than the plumpest peasant woman. The young man's knees wobbled, and when he did not continue, the old woman hit his legs with a branch and with stinging nettles. He groaned continually as he climbed the mountain, and just as he was about to collapse, he finally reached the old woman's house. When the geese spied the old woman, they spread their wings and necks in the air, ran toward her, and cackled greetings. The flock was followed by an old, old wench with a stick in her hand. She was big and strong, but ugly as sin.

"Mother," she said to the old woman, "did something happen to you along the way? You were gone so long."

"Heaven forbid, my little daughter," she responded. "Nothing bad happened to me. On the contrary, this kind gentleman here carried my load for me. Just think, he even carried me on his back when I became tired. The journey passed by quickly because we enjoyed ourselves and had fun with one another along the way."

The old woman finally slid off the young man and took the bundle from his back and the basket from his arm. She looked at him in a friendly way and said, "Now, sit down on the bench in front of the door and rest. You've earned your reward fairly, and you shall have it in due time."

Then she said to the goose girl, "Go into the house, my little daughter. It's not proper for you to be alone with a young man. No need to add oil to the fire. He could fall in love with you."

The count did not know whether he should weep or cry. Even if she were thirty years younger, he thought, my heart would never be moved by a treasure like that.

In the meantime, the old woman fondled her geese like children and then went into the house with her daughter. The young man stretched himself out on a bench underneath a wild apple tree. The air was warm and mild. All around him was a green meadow covered with cowslips, wild thyme, and a thousand other flowers. There was a clear brook that glistened with the sun's rays and rippled through the middle of the meadow. The white geese waddled back and forth or paddled in the water. "It's quite lovely here," he said. "But I'm so tired that I can't keep my eyes open. I'm going to sleep for a while. I can only hope that a gust of wind doesn't come and blow my feet out from under me. They feel as brittle as tinder wood."

After he had slept a while, the old woman came and shook him until he awoke. "Get up," she said. "You can't stay here. I confess I gave you a hard time, but it didn't cost you your life. Now you shall have your reward. Since you don't need money or land, I shall give you something else." Upon saying this, she placed a little box carved from a single emerald into his hand. "Take good care of it," she added. "It will bring you luck."

The count jumped up feeling that he had regained his strength and energy. He thanked the old woman for the present and set upon his way without turning around even once to look at the beautiful daughter. When he had gone some distance, he could still hear the merry cries of the geese.

The count must have wandered three days in the wilderness before he could find his way out. Eventually he reached a large city, and since he was a stranger, he was taken to the royal castle to meet the king and queen, who were sitting on their throne. The count knelt down before them, took the emerald box out of his pocket, and laid it at the queen's feet. She beckoned to him to stand up and hand her the little box. No sooner had she opened it and looked inside than she fell to the ground as if she were dead. The count was seized by the king's servants and was about to be taken to prison when the queen opened her eyes and cried out that they should release him. She ordered everyone to go outside and declared that she wanted to speak with the count in private.

When the queen was alone with him, she began to cry bitterly and said, "What's the use of all these splendors and honors that surround me when I awake every morning troubled and sorrowful! I had three daughters, and the youngest was so beautiful that the entire world considered her a miracle. She was as white as snow, as pink as apple blossoms, and her hair glittered like the rays of the sun. Whenever she cried, it was not tears that dropped from her eyes but pearls and jewels. On her fifteenth birthday the king summoned all three daughters to his throne. You should have seen how everyone gaped when the youngest entered: it was as if the sun had risen. The king said, 'My daughters, I don't know how much longer I have to live. So I shall decide today what each one of you is to receive after my death. You all love me, but whoever loves me most shall be given the best part of my realm.' Each of them said she loved him most of all. 'I want you to describe just how much you love me,' said the king. 'Then I'll be able to tell more clearly what you mean.' The oldest one said, 'I love my father as much as I love the sweetest sugar.' The second said, 'I love my father as much as I love my prettiest dress.' The youngest, however, kept quiet. Then her father asked, 'And you, my dearest child, how much do you love me?' 'I don't know,' she answered. 'I can't compare my love with anything.' Yet, her father insisted. She had to name something. Finally, she said, 'The best food has no taste without salt. Therefore, I love my father as much as I love salt.' When the king heard this, he became enraged and said, 'If you love me a much as you love salt, then your love shall also be rewarded with salt.'

"So he divided his kingdom between the two older daughters. However, he ordered a sack of salt bound to the back of his youngest daughter, and two servants were told to lead her out into the wild forest. We all pleaded and begged for her," the queen said, "but the king's rage could not be calmed. How she cried when she was forced to leave us! The entire way was strewn with pearls that fell from her eyes. Soon after, the king regretted his severity and had the entire forest searched for the poor child, but nobody could find her. When I think that wild animals may have eaten her, I don't know how to contain my grief. Sometimes I console myself with the hope that she is still alive and may have hidden herself in a large cave or has found shelter with merciful people. Now, you can imagine how I felt when I opened the emerald box, and there was a pearl just like the ones my daughter used to shed from her eyes, and you can also imagine how the sight of this stirred my heart. So you must tell me how you came upon this pearl."

The count told her he had received it from the old woman in the forest who had seemed uncanny to him and who he believed must be a witch. However, he had not seen a sign nor had he heard a thing about the queen's child. Nevertheless, the king and queen decided to seek out the old woman because they thought that they might obtain news of their daughter where the count had been given the pearl.

The old woman sat outside in her lonely place, spinning on her spinning wheel. It had already become dark, and a log burning on the hearth gave off a little light. All of a sudden there was a noise from the outside. The geese were coming home from the meadow, and their merry cries could be heard. Soon the daughter entered, but the old woman thanked her only by nodding her head a bit. The daughter sat down beside her, took her spinning wheel, and twisted the thread as nimbly as a young girl would. Thus they both sat for two hours without exchanging a word. Finally, something rustled at the window, and two fiery eyes glared inside. It was an old night-owl that uttered "*Tu whit-whoo*" three times. The old woman looked up just a little and said, "Now, my little daughter, it's time for you to go outside and do your work."

She stood up and went outside. Where did she go? Over the meadow toward the valley, farther and farther. Finally, she reached a spring surrounded by three old oak trees. In the meantime, the moon was round and large and had risen above the hill. It was so bright that one could easily have found a pin on the ground. The maiden removed the skin that covered her face, leaned over the spring, and began to wash herself. When she was finished, she dipped the skin in the water and laid it out on the ground so it could bleach and dry in the moonlight. But how the maiden was transformed! You've never seen anything like it in your life! After the gray wig had been taken off, her golden hair flared like sunbeams and spread like a cloak over her entire body. Her eyes sparkled like glistening stars in the sky, and her cheeks gleamed with the soft red glow of apple blossoms.

But the beautiful maiden was sad. She sat down and cried bitterly. One tear after another sprang from her eyes and rolled through her long hair down onto the ground. There she sat and would have remained for a long time if she had not heard a cracking and rustling in the branches of a nearby tree. Like a deer jolted by the shot of a hunter, she jumped up, and at the same time a black cloud passed over the moon. So the maiden immediately slipped back into the old skin and vanished like a light blown out by the wind. Trembling like an aspen leaf, she ran all the way home. The old woman was standing in front of the door, and the maiden wanted to tell her what had happened, but the old woman laughed in a friendly way and said, "I know everything already." She led the maiden into the room and started a new fire. However, she did not sit down at the spinning wheel again. Rather she fetched a broom and began to sweep and scrub. "Everything must be clean and neat," she said to the maiden.

"But, Mother," the maiden asked. "Why are you starting to work at such a late hour? What do you have in mind?"

"Do you know what time it is?" responded the old woman.

"Not past midnight yet," answered the maiden, "but it certainly must be past eleven."

"Don't you remember," continued the old woman, "that you came to me three years ago on this day? Your time is up. We can no longer stay together."

The maiden was scared and said, "Oh, Mother dear, do you want to throw me out? Where shall I go? I have neither home nor friends to turn to. I've done everything you've asked of me, and you've always been satisfied with me. Don't send me away."

The old woman did not want to tell the maiden what was in store for her. "My own stay here is over," the old woman said to her. "But before I leave, the house and room must be clean. Therefore, I don't want you to hinder my work, and don't worry on your own account. You shall find a roof to shelter you, and I'm sure you'll be satisfied with the wages that I'm about to give you."

"But tell me, what is going on?" insisted the maiden.

"And I'm telling you again, do not disturb my work. Don't say one more word. Just go into your room, remove the skin from your face, and put on the silk dress that you were wearing when you came to me. Then wait in your room until I call you."

But now I must say something about the king and queen who had departed with the count to seek out the old woman in her lonely place. The count had strayed from them in the forest during the night and had been forced to continue on his way alone. The next day it seemed to him that he was on the right path. He kept going until it became dark, and then he climbed up a tree and intended to spend the night there, for he was worried that he might get lost. When the moon cast its light on his surroundings, he spotted a shape meandering down the mountain. He could see that it was the goose girl whom he had previously encountered at the old woman's house, even though she was not carrying a stick in her hand. "Oho!" he exclaimed. "Here she comes. Once I catch one of the witches, I'll soon have the other in my hands as well." However, as he watched her go to the spring, take off the skin, and wash herself, his astonishment grew. Then when her golden hair swooped down her sides, he felt that she was more beautiful than anything else he had ever seen in the world. He hardly dared to breathe, but he did stick his head between the leaves as far as he could and looked straight at her. Whether he bent over too far, or whatever the cause, the branch suddenly cracked, and at the very same moment she slipped into the skin, jumped up like a deer, and disappeared from his sight just as the moon was covered by a cloud.

No sooner had she disappeared than the count climbed down from the tree and quickly rushed after her. He had not gone very far, when he noticed two figures wandering across the meadow in the twilight. It was the king and queen, who had glimpsed the light in the old woman's house from the distance and were heading straight for it. When the count told them about the miraculous things he had seen at the spring, they were sure that the goose girl was their lost daughter. Full of joy, they went on and soon arrived at the little house. The geese were sitting all around it with their heads tucked under their wings. Not one of them moved, as they were all fast asleep. The three travelers looked through the window and saw the old woman silently sitting and spinning. She nodded her head but did not look around. Everything was very clean in the room, as if the little fog men whose feet carry no dust lived there. However, the king and queen did not see their daughter. For a while they looked at everything, and finally they summoned up the courage to knock softly on the window. The old woman seemed to have expected them. She stood up and called out in a friendly way, "Come in, I already know who you are."

After they had entered the room, the old woman said, "You could have spared yourself the long journey if you had not unjustly banished your good and lovely child three years ago. Yet, the banishment has not harmed her. She has had to tend the geese for three years. She learned nothing evil in the process and kept herself pure of heart. You, however, have been punished sufficiently by the anguish you've suffered." Then she went to the door and called, "Come out, my little daughter."

The door opened, and the princess emerged with her golden hair and sparkling eyes. She was dressed in her silk gown, and it was as if an angel had descended from heaven into the room. She went directly to her father and mother and embraced and kissed them. They could not help weeping for joy. The young count was standing next to them, and when she noticed him, her cheeks turned as red as a moss rose. She herself did not know why. Then the king said, "My dear child, I have given away my kingdom. What am I to give you now?'

"She doesn't need anything," the old woman said. "I'm giving her the tears that she shed because of you. They are pure pearls, more beautiful than the ones that can be found in the ocean, and they are worth more than your entire kingdom. And as a reward for her work, I am going to give her my little house."

Just as the old woman said that, she vanished in front of their eyes. The walls rattled a little, and when they looked around, they saw that the little house had been transformed into a splendid palace. A royal table had been set for them, and servants were running all about the place.

The story does not end here, but my grandmother, who told me the tale, was losing her memory, and she forgot the rest. Yet, I believe that the beautiful princess married the count and that they remained together in the palace and lived in bliss as long as it pleased God. Whether the snow white geese that were kept at the little house were really girls that the old woman had taken under her care (nobody need take this amiss) and whether they regained their human shape and stayed on as servants for the young queen, I am not sure, but I suspect this was the case. One thing is sure: The old woman was not a witch, as people believed, but a wise woman who meant well. It was probably she who was at the birth of the princess and gave her the gift of weeping pearls instead of tears. Nowadays this does not happen anymore. Otherwise, the poor would soon become rich.

VII. CYMBELINE

§∽

C*ymbeline* is Shakespeare's most magisterial combination of folktale materials. In this late play, he combines one folktale plot, "The Wager on the Wife's Chastity" (ATU 882), with another, "Snow White" (ATU 709). Their point of connection in the play is a motif both tales share, the moment when the villain or villainess sends an agent to kill the heroine, but the agent instead allows her to go free and fakes the required evidence of her death. In the Grimms' "Snow White," this compassionate executioner is the huntsman who abandons Snow White in the forest and gives her stepmother a boar's liver and lungs to eat rather than the child's. The "Snow White" tale is closely related to another set of folktales that have also left their mark on *Cymbeline*, tales in which a sister leaves home, finds her long-lost brothers in the wilderness, and keeps house for them (as Snow White does for the dwarves) until disaster strikes.

"The Wager on the Wife's Chastity" folktale commonly begins with a marriage, often between a rich man and a poor woman. A man challenges the husband to a large-stakes bet that he can seduce the husband's wife. The man finds a way to fake carnal knowledge of the heroine. He either sneaks into her bedroom and spies on her or has a female accomplice do so. He then is able to report to the husband details of the woman's appearance, most damningly a mark on some private part of her body, and he often also presents some stolen personal possession of hers, such as a ring. The husband, emotionally and financially stricken from losing the bet, either sends an agent to kill his wife, or attacks her and leaves her for dead himself. The wife survives her husband's attempt on her life or is released by his agent. She then finds work, often disguised as a man and in a masculine profession. Eventually she is reunited with her husband, and is able to summon the villain and reveal the truth to everyone. The husband and wife resume their marriage.

Cymbeline follows the "Wager" plot closely. The play begins not with the marriage of the heroine, Imogen, but with the fallout from her marriage. Her father, King Cymbeline, is enraged by her marriage to Posthumus, "a poor but worthy gentleman" (1.1.7),* and has found occasion to banish him. Class disparity features in this marriage, as in many of the folktales, but here it is the bride who outranks the husband. Posthumus, having taken refuge in Rome, makes a wager with the villain Iachimo, who claims he can seduce Imogen with no more than a letter of introduction. Imogen roundly rejects Iachimo, but allows him to store a chest in her bedchamber. Iachimo conceals himself in the chest and emerges after Imogen is asleep. (The villain uses the same ploy in a Scottish version of the folktale not included here.†) He observes a distinctive mole beneath her left breast and steals a bracelet Posthumus gave Imogen as a love token before his departure. Posthumus, convinced and devastated by these false proofs, orders his faithful servant Pisanio to lure Imogen into the countryside and kill her. Pisanio instead supplies Imogen with boy's clothes and a plan—in the folktales the heroine takes care of these matters herself. Pisanio gives Posthumus a bloodied cloth as evidence of Imogen's death. The plot then becomes parallel to "Snow White," as I will discuss later, but the cross-dressed Imogen eventually enters into the service of the

---

*Shakespeare, *Cymbeline*, ed. Valerie Wayne. Wayne renders the heroine's name as "Innogen," which is how it appears in other historical and literary texts in Shakespeare's day. Other editors of the play have also made this decision (70–72). As the name appears as "Imogen" in Shakespeare's First Folio, our one textual authority for the play, I have used that spelling.

†"The Chest," in Campbell, *Popular Tales*, 2.9–23.

Roman ambassador to Britain, according to Pisanio's plan. When the Romans are captured by the British, with whom they are at war, Imogen finds herself back at her royal father's court, along with Posthumus and Iachimo. The truth comes out, Imogen and Posthumus are reconciled, and Iachimo is forgiven his misdeeds. Shakespeare most likely knew Boccaccio's version of "The Wager on the Wife's Chastity" in *The Decameron* (second day, ninth story). The "Wager" story also circulated in chapbooks (cheap printed editions) both before and after *Cymbeline*, and was a popular subject for medieval French romances.

The Chilean story here, "The Wager on the Wife's Chastity," has several notable parallels to *Cymbeline*. The heroine's gruff father is outraged by his daughter's marriage, much as King Cymbeline is. This paternal opposition doesn't last, however, and is due to the fact that his daughter is much poorer than his prospective son-in-law, the reverse of Princess Imogen's marriage to orphaned, impoverished Posthumus. The folktale husband enters into a wager with the would-be seducer of his wife, who uses an accomplice's wiles to steal the lady's ring and nightgown, and note a mole on her leg. The husband is convinced, as is Posthumus, by Iachimo's theft of Imogen's bracelet and knowledge of her mole. The folktale husband orders his employee to kill his wife, but this compassionate executioner instead lets her go and gives the husband false evidence of his wife's death, as does Pisanio. The heroine disguises herself as a man and finds manly work with a king whose son is fascinated by and attracted to her androgyny. Similarly, when Imogen is taken in by three outlaws, one declares, "Were you a woman, youth, / I should woo hard, but be your groom in honesty" (3.6.66–67). The folktale heroine eventually becomes king, and uses this power to locate her husband and uncover the truth. She retains her elevated status even when she becomes a wife again. After her identity is revealed, she is still called a king, in contrast to Imogen, who loses her status as royal heir at the end of the play because of the return of her long-lost brothers. "Oh, Imogen, / Thou hast lost by this a kingdom," says Cymbeline (5.5.371–72).

"The Innkeeper of Moscow," a German folktale, also begins with a poor woman marrying a wealthier man. In this case, the son of a rich merchant marries the family's maidservant of seven years. Posthumus, somewhat similarly, is a familiar figure to Imogen and her household, having grown up with her as a royal ward. The folktale's villain, to win his bet with the husband, hides under the heroine's bed at night, just as Iachimo hides in a trunk in Imogen's room. He steals her wedding ring and notes a mole beneath her breast, the same distinguishing mark that Imogen possesses and Iachimo exploits. When the heroine of the folktale misses her wedding ring, she has a duplicate made, which later makes her look guilty. The object that symbolizes her married chastity is not unique, pointing to its unsuitability as proof of fidelity, just as Desdemona's handkerchief, the loss of which convinces Othello that she has slept with another man, is twice intended to be copied (3.3.300, 3.4.178). *Cymbeline* deliberately recalls *Othello*, Shakespeare's earlier play about a woman framed for adultery, by giving *Cymbeline*'s villain the name Iachimo, a diminutive of the name Iago, the villain in *Othello*. "The Innkeeper of Moscow" takes place during wartime, just as much of *Cymbeline* unfolds during a war between the British and the Romans. The folktale wife disguises herself as a man, joins the army, and rises through the ranks to become a colonel and her husband's commanding officer. From this vantage point, she is able to uncover the villain's wrongdoing.

I have included Italo Calvino's "Wormwood" because it overlaps to some extent with the "Maiden Who Seeks Her Brothers" tales, which may also have left their mark on *Cymbeline* and are here represented by the Norwegian story "The Twelve Wild Ducks." "Wormwood" begins with a king who threatens to kill his unborn child if it proves to be a girl, as he has only daughters and wants a son. "The Twelve Wild Ducks" begins with a queen who says rash words because she wants her next child to be a girl, since she has only sons. The heroines of both "Wormwood" and "The Twelve Wild Ducks" grow up to be framed for infanticide. "Wormwood" is at root a chastity wager story, however, and another one in which a wealthy man marries what seems to be a poor girl, although she is, unbeknownst even to herself, a princess. The heroine, Wormwood, in this regard is much like Imogen's brothers, who are raised by a hermit in the wilderness, unaware that they are princes. As happens with Imogen and the heroines of the Chilean and German folktales, the villain who enters into the wager with Wormwood's husband is able to find out about her hidden mole. The famously convoluted ending of *Cymbeline*, an extravaganza of revelations so offensive to the playwright George Bernard Shaw that he rewrote it,* has nothing on the final scene of "Wormwood" for sheer strangeness. A talking lantern and oil cruet bring all secrets to light, and three men claim the heroine as their own: her father, her husband, and the man who rescued her when her husband left her for dead. This seems quite similar to the ending of Shakespeare's narrative poem *The Rape of Lucrece*, in which Lucrece's husband and father argue over to whom Lucrece, now dead, belongs. Ultimately, a third man, Brutus, claims Lucrece as a means to incite revolt against her rapist, Tarquin's, family.† I mention the parallel because *Lucrece* begins with something of a chastity wager, described in the poem's introductory Argument—men away on military duty fall to boasting about whose wife is most virtuous, and so decide to visit the women unannounced. Lucrece turns out to be the most virtuous, but the contest results in Tarquin conceiving a passion

---

* See the chapter on *Cymbeline* in Wilson, *Shaw on Shakespeare*, 43–67.
† Shakespeare, *Narrative Poems*, 117–20.

for her and ultimately raping her. Iachimo, spying on the sleeping Imogen, explicitly compares himself to Tarquin (2.2.12). "Wormwood" is one of several chastity wager stories in Calvino's excellent collection *Italian Folktales*. One of them, "The King of Spain and the English Milord," involves a heroine who is "white as ricotta and rosy as a rose," an overlap with Snow White's red and white beauty.[*]

The final chastity wager tale comes from a travelogue by J. M. Synge, the Irish author most famous for his play *The Playboy of the Western World*. Synge describes hearing a story told by an old man in the Aran Islands. This variant combines "The Wager on the Wife's Chastity" with a folktale Shakespeare used as a source for *The Merchant of Venice*, "A Pound of Flesh" (see chapter 4). An English ballad, "The Northern Lord," is another example of such a combination.[†] If Shakespeare was aware of the combination of the chastity wager and pound of flesh stories, perhaps it might have helped to inspire his combination of "Wager" with another folktale, "Snow White." "Wager" and "Snow White," however, do not seem to have been combined in folk tradition. Synge's version bears two particular resemblances to *Cymbeline*: a poorer man marries a wealthier woman, causing some trouble, and the villain conceals himself in a box that is then placed in the heroine's bedroom.

Cymbeline's other folktale plot derives from "Snow White," presumably the most familiar of all the folktales in this book for most of its readers. The version of the story we know best is the Brothers Grimm's, on which Walt Disney's 1937 animated film is based. The dominance of the Grimms' version can actually conceal *Cymbeline*'s resemblance to the folktale, as the play lacks a talking mirror,

[*] Calvino, *Italian Folktales*, 568.

[†] National Library of Scotland, Crawford.EB.872, EBBA 33579 in *English Broadside Ballad Archive*, ed. Patricia Fumerton, http://ebba.english.ucsb.edu/ballad/21895/xml (accessed August 14, 2017).

seven dwarves, and a poisoned apple. "Snow White," however, is a folktale found in many different countries and cultures, and while certain core elements define it, the details of the stories vary considerably. Again and again in "Snow White" stories, we see the heroine persecuted by a jealous female relative and forced to leave home. The villainess sends an agent to kill the heroine, but this compassionate executioner takes pity on her, allowing her to flee into the wilderness. There she encounters a group of men who live on the margins of society, because they are criminals, giants, dwarfs, djinn, and so on. These men take her in, and she acts as their housekeeper. The villainess learns that the heroine is alive and poisons her, perhaps several times, until she falls into a deathly unconsciousness. The heroine's adopted family does not bury her because she remains beautiful, and eventually she is found by a man who falls in love with her. She awakes from her death-sleep and marries him, and her persecutor is punished.

Cymbeline contains all of these episodes. As with some other Snow Whites, Imogen is reunited with her husband rather than married during the resolution of the plot.[*] Like Snow White, Imogen is persecuted by a jealous stepmother, the Queen, a practiced poisoner. Imogen flees her royal home, escaping into the wilderness. Pisanio has been given orders to kill her, but instead mercifully releases her. Imogen wanders, lost, until she comes to the home of three men who live as outlaws in a cave. They take her in, and she acts as their housekeeper. Eventually, she takes a poison concocted by the Queen, which Pisanio gave her in the mistaken belief that it was medicinal. Imogen appears dead, but her adopted family does not bury her. She wakes from her death sleep and is reunited with her husband, Posthumus. The Queen, her plans thwarted, goes mad and dies.

[*] Jones, *New Comparative Method*, 76.

Cymbeline in fact may be the earliest literary version of "Snow White." Elements of the folktale exist in earlier texts such as Xenophon of Ephesus's ancient Greek novel *An Ephesian Story* and Marie de France's medieval lai *Eliduc*, but these texts do not include all of the episodes listed in the preceding summary. *Cymbeline* is both earlier and more complete than Giambattista Basile's seventeenth-century novella "The Little Slave Girl" (second day, ninth story), which includes a number of "Snow White" motifs. Martin Butler, one of *Cymbeline*'s editors, writes that " 'Snow White' was not written down until the eighteenth century, but its resemblances to *Cymbeline* tempt one to speculate that it must have been in oral circulation much earlier."* The play's resemblance's to "Snow White" could also mean that *Cymbeline*, and not the eighteenth-century version, is the earliest literary example of the tale.

I have here included three versions of "Snow White," a Chilean version, a Tuscan version, and a Scottish version. In the Chilean "Blanca Rosa," taken from the same collection as "The Wager on the Wife's Chastity," the heroine takes refuge with outlaws, as does Imogen. Blanca Rosa sneaks in and eats the thieves' food, and when the men finally catch her, they take her for the Virgin Mary, come to chastise them for their wicked ways. Likewise, when old Belarius spots Imogen in his home he exclaims, "But that it eats our victuals, I should think / Here were a fairy. . . . By Jupiter, an angel!" (3.6.40–42). When the folktale heroine falls into her deathlike state, the robbers put her in a gold and silver coffin that they throw into the sea. Shakespeare includes a similar episode in *Pericles*, another late play with deep folktale affinities. Pericles's beloved wife, Thaisa, only apparently dead, is buried at sea with treasure in her coffin. As with Blanca Rosa, her coffin is recovered and she comes back to life. One of the most striking elements of "Blanca Rosa" is how it

---

*Butler, ed., *Cymbeline*, 7.

draws out the theme of necrophilia latent in "Snow White." In nearly all "Snow White" stories, a man falls in love with the heroine while she is apparently dead. In "Blanca Rosa," even more disturbingly, he strips the heroine of her clothes while she is unconscious. When he removes the hairpin that caused her sleep and she awakes, she is understandably alarmed and insists on leaving, until he sticks the pin back in her scalp and renders her unconscious again. Later, his malicious sisters strip the heroine and throw her into the street, further casting the disrobing of the helpless woman as a wicked act. Imogen wakes up without any assistance, but there is a scene in which a man becomes enamored of her as he gazes at her naked, unconscious form. This is what the villain Iachimo does when he spies on her as she sleeps, in the chastity wager plot.

The Tuscan tale "The Glass Coffin" was recorded by the Victorian writer Violet Paget, who later went on to write under the pseudonym Vernon Lee. In this story, after the jealous stepmother has sent the heroine away to be killed, she tells the heroine's father, the king, that the girl has run off to meet a lover. Imogen has fled the palace to meet her banished husband (she believes), as Cymbeline's court assumes. After being set free by a compassionate executioner, the folktale heroine finds a home in the wilderness. Seven brothers, robbers, live there, and she keeps house for them, just as Imogen keeps house for two brothers and their foster-father. The seven robber brothers ask the heroine which one of them she will marry, just as Guiderius mentions wooing and marrying the disguised Imogen in lines quoted earlier, but the heroine keeps her distance. Like Imogen, the heroine is poisoned by an act of kindness that unwittingly serves up the stepmother's poison. Pisanio gives Imogen the Queen's poison thinking it is a precious medicine. In "The Glass Coffin," an old woman innocently applies a poisonous hair cream, given to her by the stepmother, to the heroine.

I include a Scottish "Snow White" tale, "Lasair Gheug, the King of Ireland's Daughter," because in it the stepmother's hatred for the heroine begins as a competition over inheritance. Likewise, Cymbeline's Queen tries to do away with Imogen because she wants her own son to inherit the British throne. In most "Snow White" stories, the competition is over physical beauty, "who's the fairest of them all." There is no hint of this in *Cymbeline*, although both Imogen and the Queen are beautiful. Later in "Lasair Gheug," the stepmother does indeed consult with a talking trout about whether or not she is the most beautiful in the land. As Alan Bruford notes, "Lasair Gheug" combines elements of "Snow White" with elements of "The Maiden without Hands," a folktale discussed in chapter 3 of this book.* Just as "The Wager on the Wife's Chastity" can be found combined with "A Pound of Flesh," so "Snow White" is combined in "Lasair Gheug" with a folktale Shakespeare used for an earlier play.

Closely related to "Snow White" is a tale called "The Sister of Nine Brothers" (ATU 709A). This story begins with a girl leaving home and wandering in the wilderness, not because she has been banished by a murderously jealous stepmother, but because she is seeking her long-lost brothers. She finds them living together and joins them, acting as their housekeeper. Then she runs afoul of an ogre who sends her into a death-sleep until she is revived and married. The men with whom Imogen briefly lives in the woods, and for whom she keeps house, turn out to be her two long-lost brothers and the man who abducted and raised them. Perhaps Shakespeare was inspired by a tale like "The Sister of Nine Brothers," which does not begin like "Snow White," but ends like it. Another, more familiar folktale, "The Maiden Who Seeks Her Brothers" (ATU 451) begins much like "Sister of Nine Brothers": the birth of a baby girl causes, one way or another, her brothers' banishment from home. "Maiden Who Seeks Her Brothers" stories end quite differently from "Nine Brothers" and "Snow White," with the hero-

---

* Bruford, "Scottish Gaelic Version," 154.

ine taking a vow of silence to disenchant her bewitched brothers, nearly causing her own death. I include a Norwegian example of "The Maiden Who Seeks Her Brothers," Asbjørnsen and Moe's "The Twelve Wild Ducks." In it, the heroine's mother wishes for a daughter who is red, white, and black, just like Snow White's mother in the famous Grimm version.

Cymbeline's intricate intersection of "The Wager on the Wife's Chastity" and "Snow White" is Shakespeare's most thorough and accomplished combination of folk materials. The play's reflection of the "Brothers" folktales would perhaps not be lost on an audience primed to see *Cymbeline* as a folktale play. The play's first scene accomplishes such a priming. In it, the Queen insists she is not an evil stepmother, and a gentleman exclaims that it seems incredible that two princes would remain missing since infancy. These motifs are of course fairy tale staples, and despite the Queen's and gentleman's protestations, the play does feature a wicked stepmother and long-lost princes who are eventually found. Shakespeare's late romance is set not just in ancient Britain, but in the realm of old tales.

THE WAGER ON THE WIFE'S CHASTITY

Yolando Pino-Saavedra

The Wager on the Wife's Chastity*

There was once a gentleman named Manuel who lived alone in his home, where he kept a little store. One day he announced that the first girl to arrive in the morning had to be his wife, be she

*Yolando Pino-Saavedra, *Folktales of Chile* (Chicago: University of Chicago Press, 1967), 189–94. "Collected in January 1951 at the Gjüeimén farm, Ignao, Valdivia, from Escolástica Garrido, a day laborer's wife born in 1885" (273).

one-eyed, lame, poor, or whatever else. It chanced that a very poor girl came along. This girl was in fact so poor that when she entered a house, she had to go out backward, for she was dressed in front and had nothing to put on behind. But she was a pretty lass, and the young gentleman announced that her poverty didn't matter, she was to be his wife. He gave her a fine gift and told her to make herself a dress. The girl went home, hiding from her gruff old father, and told her mother to notify the old man that her suitor was coming to speak to him at twelve o'clock. Right on the dot, the young man arrived at the house and called out to see if anybody was at home. The old woman started out quite ashamed, for she, too, was dressed only in front and hadn't a stitch on behind. She came out forward and then backed up quickly into the house, letting out three good shouts for her husband. Finally the old fellow arrived, very surprised, with his hatchet on his shoulder.

"Don't be afraid, my little old man," said the youth. "I've come to greet you and ask for your daughter's hand in marriage."

The old man turned purple with rage and screamed, "Go away, sir! Get out of here, and don't come around to make fun of me!" He was so angry that he paid no attention to the stammered protests and even took a swing at the suitor with his hatchet. Then he summoned his daughter to find out just what this fellow had said to her.

"He told me he had made a promise," she said, "that the first girl who arrived at his store had to be his wife. I was the first, and I guess that's why he's here."

"But, daughter," said her father, "how are you going to marry if we're so poor?" By now the young man had pleaded so convincingly that the old man believed him. So, as the days went by, preparations were made for the wedding. The youth took the old people and their daughter to his house and dressed the father as a grand gentleman and the mother as a noble lady. Then they went to the registry and the priest and were duly married.

It came to pass that nobody saw this girl any more, for she was hidden in the house with her husband, who had put his father-in-law in charge of the store and his mother-in-law in charge of the household. The new wife had nothing to do, with maids and everything you could wish. One fine day an envious rich man came to the house just as the husband was about to make a little trip.

"I'll make you a bet, my friend," said the rich man, "that your wife will betray you while you're out sailing in your boat."

The husband set off without saying a word to his wife about the trip or the day he would return. She was very surprised by his sudden absence. As soon as he was gone, the other man spoke with an old sorceress and asked her what she could do to help him win the bet.

"That's the easiest thing there is," she cackled. "I'll go to lodge at that house tonight and get you into the bedroom by saying that I'm the aunt of the young wife." The horrid old woman managed to do just that. She embraced the girl with affection and began settling down for the night in the same room. But while the young woman wasn't watching, the old sorceress took a handful of bedbugs and scattered them in her sheets. In a jiffy, the girl was itching so she couldn't keep still. As she jumped up to shake out the bed, the old woman was watching her with great care and noticed a mole covered with sealing wax on her left leg. After the young bride had swept out all the mess in the bed, she fell into a deep sleep. There on her bedside table was her ring along with her nightgown and the seal that covered her mole. The old trickster tiptoed over, pocketed the articles, and skipped out of the house in the middle of the night.

The next day, the rich man had a rendezvous with the old woman and received the three articles. So it was that when the boat came in, he was waiting triumphantly at the dock for his friend. Each one had bet his whole ranch and fortune.

"Good morning, friend," called the man when the husband had docked. "How is everything? Ahem, I won the little bet, and here are the proofs." He produced the ring, the nightgown, and the seal from the girl's mole. "If you wish to know more, I can tell you that your wife has a brown mole on her leg."

The husband spoke not a word, but merely set off for his house, stooping with grief as he walked. He said a formal "good day" to his wife and not a peep more came out of him. Very surprised and hurt, she thought, "What on earth can be wrong with my husband? He has never been like this before."

The next morning he asked his wife to take a little stroll with him. He didn't mention where they were going, but told it only to a shoemaker he employed. When they came to the river bank, the husband got into a boat and told his wife to follow him. Then he said to the shoemaker, who was waiting nearby, "Kill this treacherous woman and bring me her eyes as proof." The shoemaker rowed away with the poor woman across the river.

"Ma'am," he said when they had reached the other bank, "the boss told me to pluck your eyes out, but I'm not going to do it. Instead I'll kill my dog and take her eyes to your husband."

"Oh, how can I thank you!" she cried. "Now, I want you to loan me your clothes, and you are to take mine."

The shoemaker returned to his employer and gave him the two eyes from his dog. Meanwhile the young wife had gone in search of work, dressed as a man and with her hair clipped short. She worked for a couple of days with a man who sold coal, but soon went on, always wandering and walking in her loneliness. Finally she drew near the palace of a certain king. The prince saw her and ran in to his father.

"Papa, a young man near the palace is looking for work, and he's very lovely and fine to look at."

"Give him a job," ordered the king. "Tomorrow, my son, you can take him to the mountains to round up some wild bulls and see if he's suited for work on horseback."

When dawn broke the next day, the prince went to the stables with the disguised girl. She saddled the best horse there was and tossed one rein over the edge of a fence, setting the horse right down on his backside.

"Good heavens!" exclaimed the prince, "it looks like this chap is more of a horseman than I am."

They rode away in search of the bull. With the first toss, the new cowhand lassoed a bull and pulled it down on its snout to the ground. The young prince was astonished by the ability of this young stranger. That night, back at the palace, he said to the king, "Papa, the young man is better than I with a lasso. But I swear he acts just like a woman."

"Go on, you silly boy," said the king. "How can a woman be so handy with a rope? Now, tomorrow you will invite him to go looking for some of the wildest colts we've got."

What do you suppose! The new cowhand had no sooner arrived at the pasture than she lassoed the wildest colt and brought it down on the spot. The prince reported this to his father, but still insisted that the youth made him think of a woman.

"You're on the wrong track, my lad," scoffed the king. "Take him to the dance tomorrow at that house where there are plenty of girls."

The next night, the mysterious youth went with the prince, drank until he had covered the table with empty bottles, and took one of the girls to dance. When it was late, he carried her off to bed. Immediately after they were out of sight of the prince, the girl revealed herself to the prostitute and gave her all the money in her pockets so she would keep the secret.

"How did it all go last night?" the king asked his son the next morning.

"How did it go! Lord, he was the first dancer on the floor. He drank everybody else under the table and took a girl to bed with him!"

The king could find no more proofs with which to test the cowhand, so he called him in and said, "Look here, young fellow, since you've been very useful in my house, I'm going to give you a palace as a reward." Saying that, he crowned the young girl and made her a king like himself.

Very soon after she became king, she sent her police out to search for a certain man named Manuel. When he arrived, the king said, "Good day, sir. I've sent for you because they told me you were married, and I want to know what you've done with your wife."

"Yes, sire," he answered. "I was married, but my woman did me wrong. That's why I sent her to be killed."

"Are you quite sure of that?" asked the king.

"Yes, I am, your majesty."

"And how was it? I mean, how did she betray you?"

He told the king the whole story, after which she sent her police with instructions to bring in the envious rich man at all costs. When he appeared, the king said, "Tell me a little something about this bet you made with the other gentleman."

"Yes, sire. I simply bet him that while he was away from home, his wife would be unfaithful. Nothing more." But eventually the king got the whole story out of him, and then the old sorceress was promptly summoned to the palace. When the old lady had confessed her part in the plot, the king declared that the rich man had to return everything he had won to the other man immediately. As for the wicked old woman, she was tied between the wildest colts in the kingdom and torn to pieces in the dust. Finally the young husband appeared at the palace again.

"Would you know your wife if you were to see her?" asked the king.

"Yes, your majesty. Seeing her, I'm sure I'd know her right away."

The king repeated the question three times, and each time the man assured him that he would certainly recognize his wife.

"I am she," declared the king, much to the poor man's bewilderment. With that, she sent him off to be washed, bathed, and dressed in the finest suit there was. The king and her husband lived on happily together, and I believe they haven't died yet.

Now the tale goes up a bean stalk so the next storyteller can spin us another.

Kurt Ranke

The Innkeeper of Moscow*

In the town of Moscow there once lived a rich merchant. He was old and had a grown son. One day he said to him, "Son, you should look for a wife."

The son said, "Father, I have made my choice, but I am afraid you will not agree."

"All right, tell me about it."

"I should like to marry the maidservant, whom we have had for seven years."

"Son, this is my very idea. Take her to church and marry her." The son did so.

They had been married for a year when he once went to a wine shop where he played cards and so on. It was nine o'clock, a quarter past nine, then he said, "I must go home, my wife will be waiting for me."

But the innkeeper broached another cask and said, "Don't be so kind to your wife; you will get home early enough. She is not as faithful as you believe."

*Kurt Ranke, *Folktales of Germany*, trans. Lotte Baumann (London: Routledge and Kegan Paul, 1966), 90–94. "Recorded in 1937 by the teacher Josef Stich in Neuhäusl, district of Rosshaupt, Czechoslovakia, from the German storyteller Franz Graf" (213).

"What are you talking about? I'll stake my whole fortune on my wife!"

"All right! You leave, and I shall sleep with your wife. But don't tell her about our bet." They wrote it all down, and the merchant went home.

In the morning he said to his wife, "Listen, I have to go away for six weeks, and you must keep everything in good order meanwhile." Then he left.

Whenever the wife needed wine for the shop, she sent the maidservant to the wine shop to get some. One time the innkeeper said to the maidservant, "Look here, you could easily make 5,000 florins. You are poor; what do you think about it?"

"I should like to, if it is easy enough for me to do."

"Can you lead me to your mistress's bedroom?"

"It is possible while she is at the table." She left the door open, and while her mistress was eating, the innkeeper got in and hid under the bed. The wife went to her bedroom at ten o'clock, locked the door, took her ring and everything off, and went to bed. He saw that she had a birthmark under her breast. She said her prayers and after a short while she fell asleep. Now he sneaked out, took her wedding ring, and went off with it. Good! If the merchant comes, he has won the bet!

Forty-eight hours later the merchant came back. He went to the wine shop, laughing in advance. "Well, how far have we got? I am sure to have won the bet!"

The innkeeper showed him the ring and told him about the birthmark. But let us see how things went on for the merchant's wife.

She was awake early in the morning. She washed, dressed, and wanted to wear her ring. It was gone! She thought, everything was locked, so the ring must have been stolen. She went to the goldsmith, had the same ring made again, and put it on her finger. When the merchant entered his shop, his first look went to his wife's hand. He saw that she had the ring. The real one was in his waistpocket.

Soon after this event he gave a dinner for the poor and said to his wife, "You put on your wedding dress, and I will put on my wedding suit. Then let us watch the poor." After the meal he took two pistols, and they went for a walk in the woods. He took her arm and they left. In the woods he called, "Stop!" He put his hand into the waistpocket. "Do you know this ring?" She grew white as a sheet. He said, "Well, I have made you rich, and you have deceived me terribly. Die!" He took his pistol, cocked it, took aim at her, but when he wanted it to fire, it did not go off. He threw it away and took the second one, but the same thing happened again. Then he said, "Now we are both beggars. You may go where you choose, and I shall go where I choose!"

Meanwhile his old father was anxiously waiting at home, but nobody came. Early in the morning he went to the police, and they searched all over, but there was no trace of the couple to be found.

The wife had gone to the right and the husband had gone to the left. At that time it was possible to enlist in the army without being examined. So she bought men's clothes—she still had some money left—put them on, and enlisted. She joined the cavalry. She had a clever head and soon became colonel.

Later on, her husband enlisted in the same squadron. Riding past him, she recognized her husband at first glance and took him as her officer's man. He was very meticulous and kept everything in good order; whenever there were women around, he left. Finally the colonel thought, you must find out why he behaves like this. He invited some handsome women, then he sent for his man and asked him to keep them company.

When he entered the room and saw the women, he went to the colonel and said, "Colonel, I feel sick and am unable to keep them company. I must go to bed." He lay down and ruminated.

In the morning the colonel sent for him, "You were not ill. Why did you not stay with them?"

He answered, "Colonel, please don't reopen old sores. They have long ago healed up but started bleeding again now."

"What bothers you about women? Express yourself freely, or you will be shot."

He sat down and pondered, "Colonel, I'd rather be shot than tear open this wound again."

"Come on, I want to know all about it!" When the man saw that it was no use, he began his story. He had married a maidservant, who had been in his house for seven years; she was poor but a real beauty. He had money and property. Once he left for six weeks, and meanwhile she had behaved in a scandalous way with an innkeeper. "Here, I still keep the wedding ring. When I came back, my wife had a false ring, and I was a beggar, because I had lost my money in a bet."

The colonel had grown as pale as death and shouted, "Four officers! Right on the spot! Tomorrow we must ride to town!" He chose four officers, and at six o'clock in the morning, they all came. The horses were brought from the stables; they mounted and rode to town at a trot.

They reached town at noon and went to the wine shop. They ate and drank. Then the colonel arose and said, "This is a fine shop over there."

"Yes," said the innkeeper, "I have gained it in one night. There was a merchant who trusted his wife. He left for six weeks, and I made a bet with him that I would sleep with his wife. And I won the bet."

The colonel said to the fellow, "What sort of maidservant did the wife have at that time?"

"A clever one. She owns the house over there."

"Go and fetch her. I must talk to her."

When she arrived, the colonel asked the innkeeper if he had a room, for the four officers wanted to talk to the girl. The innkeeper showed them a room without misgiving. When they had the maidservant in the room, the officers drew their sabers and asked her if she had served at the merchant's house.

"Why did you cheat the merchant? What have you done? Don't lie! I'll split your head with my saber!"

So she went down to her knees, "The innkeeper bribed me with 5,000 florins, so I let him into the bedroom. He hid under the bed. The mistress used to undress at night and to take her ring off. At night he got up, took the ring, and saw the birthmark on her chest." (The day after this confession, one of the officers went to her and said, "Here are another 1,000 florins for you, and I shall buy you another house.") When she had revealed everything, they went back to the main hall and called the innkeeper to account. At the beginning he tried to make denials, but the maidservant told him the whole story to his face. Now the innkeeper offered to return everything. "To return what? I am the wife!"

A woman had to come to examine her to see if she really was a woman. The innkeeper confessed everything and had to leave. They took his belongings and gave the rest to the poor.

She laid her saber down and received an enormous retirement pay—fancy her being a colonel of cavalry! She went back to the shop with her husband, and they lived happily. They had two children, a boy and a girl—real beauties they were. His father had long ago died from sorrow, and they erected a fine monument for him. And thus they lived in peace and harmony, and they are alive to this very day if they have not died since.

Italo Calvino

Wormwood*

Over and over it has been told that once upon a time there was a king and queen. Every time this queen had a baby, it was a girl. The king, who wanted a son, finally lost patience and said, "If you have one more girl, I shall kill it."

Just as she had feared, the poor wife ended up bearing another girl, but the prettiest child you ever saw. Lest her husband kill it, she said to its godmother, "Take this infant and do what you think best."

The godmother took it, saying to herself, "What am I to do with a baby girl?" She went into the country and laid it upon a wormwood bush.

There in the country lived a hermit. In his cave he had a doe suckling some newborn fawns. Every day the doe would go outside for something to eat. One evening when she returned to the cave, the fawns attempted to suckle, but the doe's udder was empty and the fawns went hungry. The same thing happened the next day, and the next, and the fawns were starving to death. Feeling sorry for them, the hermit followed the doe and discovered that she was going out every day to nurse a baby girl nestled in a wormwood bush. The hermit picked up the baby and carried her into the cave. He told the doe, "Nurse her here and divide your milk between her and your fawns."

The baby was gradually weaned and grew by leaps and bounds. The older she got, the lovelier she became. She did the hermit's housework, and the hermit came to cherish her as if she had been his very own daughter.

---

*Italo Calvino, *Italian Folktales*, trans. George Martin (New York: Harcourt Brace, 1980), 563–68. No. 157. Calvino's source is Giuseppe Pitrè's 1875 collection of folktales.

One day another king was out hunting, when right in the middle of everything a fierce storm came up; the wind blew, there was thunder and lightning, and it poured rain. The only available shelter was the hermit's cave. Seeing the king come in soaking wet, the hermit called, "Wormwood! Wormwood! Bring a chair, light the fire, and make His Majesty comfortable!"

"Wormwood?" said the king. "What kind of name is that, good hermit?"

So the hermit told of finding the child in a wormwood bush and naming her after it.

The minute he laid eyes on the girl, the king said, "Hermit, would you like to give her to me to take back to the palace? You are old; how can this child stay by herself like that in the country? I will provide her with teachers who will instruct her . . ."

"Majesty," replied the hermit, "I am devoted to the child, so for her own good I'm happy for her to go to the palace. The education Your Majesty is able to offer her is a far cry from what a poor hermit could give her."

The king bid the hermit goodbye, took Wormwood onto his horse, and rode away with her. At the palace he entrusted her to two noble ladies. Once he was thoroughly acquainted with the girl's merits, he said, "The best I can do by her is marry her and make her queen." He married her, and Wormwood became the realm's queen.

The king was madly in love with her. One day he said, "Wormwood, I am obliged to go away for a while. No matter how short a time I'll be away, it pains me more than I could ever say to leave you."

The king departed. One evening outside the kingdom, he found himself in the company of princes and knights, and each man began singing the praises of his own wife. "Go on, boast all you want," said the king, "but none of you could have a wife as wonderful as mine."

At that, one of the knights turned to him. "Majesty, I bet that if I went to Palermo in your absence, I could make time with your wife."

"Impossible!" replied the king. "Totally impossible!"

"Shall we bet on it?" urged the knight.

"Let's," answered the king.

They agreed on the stakes: a fief. They agreed on the length of time: one month. Then the knight departed. In Palermo he strolled day and night under the windows of the royal palace. The days went by without his getting so much as a glimpse of the queen: the windows were always shut.

Then one day as he was walking there, quite downcast, an old woman approached, begging for alms. "Get away from here," he said, "don't bother me!"

"What's troubling you, sir, and making you so gloomy?"

"Get away, let me alone!"

"Tell me what's bothering you, sir; maybe I can help you."

So the knight told her about the bet and his desire to enter the palace, or at least to find out what the queen looked like.

"Put your mind at rest, sir; I'll see to everything."

The old woman packed a basket with eggs and fruit, went to the palace, and asked to speak to the queen. When she was alone with the queen, she embraced her and whispered in her ear, "My daughter, you don't know me, but I'm a relative of yours, and it gives me joy to bring you these few things."

The queen was unacquainted with her relatives; for all she knew, the old woman could have been one. She therefore trusted her, invited her to live at the palace, and ordered everyone to respect her. At any hour of the day or night, the old woman was allowed to go in and out of the queen's room and do whatever she pleased.

One day while the queen was sleeping, the old woman entered her room. She approached the bed, peeped under the cover, and saw that the queen's bare back was graced by a very beautiful mole. Then with a pair of scissors the old woman cut the tiny hairs sprouting from the mole and put them away, after which she left the palace, quite pleased with herself. When the knight had these hairs in his possession and heard the old woman's description of the queen, he could no longer contain himself for joy. He rewarded the old woman with a goodly sum of money and departed. On the appointed day he went before the king and the other knights, who were quite anxious to know who would win the bet. The knight spoke: "Majesty, I apologize for what I'm about to tell you. Is it true, or isn't it, that your wife is such and such—" and he gave a minute description of her face.

"That is correct," replied the king, "but that proves nothing. You could have heard those things without ever actually seeing her in the flesh."

"In that case, Majesty, listen carefully: is it true, or isn't it, that your wife has a mole on her left shoulder?"

The king turned pale. "Well, yes."

The knight handed the king a locket. "Majesty, I hate to tell you, but here is proof that I have won the bet"—and with trembling hands the king opened the locket and saw the hairs from the queen's mole. He hung his head in silence.

Without delay the king returned to his palace. Happy to see him back after such a long absence, the queen came out to meet him, laughing. The king neither greeted nor embraced her. He ordered horses harnessed to a carriage and said to his wife, "Climb up," while he too climbed up and sat beside her, taking the reins himself.

Bewildered, the queen looked at him with apprehension, but the king didn't open his mouth. When they reached the foot of Mount Pellegrino, the king reined in the horses and said, "Get down." The queen alighted and the king, without dismounting, dealt her a resounding blow with his whip that knocked her down.

Then he whipped the horses to a gallop and disappeared from sight.

That day a doctor and his wife were on their way up to the Sanctuary of St. Rosalie, in fulfillment of a vow made before the birth of their son. Bringing up the rear was their Moorish slave, Alí. When they got to the foot of Mount Pellegrino they heard the sound of moaning. "Who can it be?" said the doctor. Going in the direction of the moans, they found a young woman lying on the ground, wounded and half dead. The doctor bandaged her up the best he could and said to his wife, "Let's put off our trip until another day and try to help this young woman. We'll carry her home and see if we can cure her."

That they did. Lodged and nursed by the doctor and his wife, the young woman got well. But no matter how many questions they put to her, she refused to talk about her past or say how her misfortune had come about. In spite of that, the doctor's wife, pleased over finding a young woman so good and virtuous, grew quite fond of her and engaged her as a maid.

One day the doctor said to his wife, "Dear, it is time we fulfilled our promise to St. Rosalie. We'll leave our little girl with the maid and depart with Alí."

The next morning they left early, while the maid and the little girl were still sleeping. After going a short distance, Alí slapped his forehead. "Master, Alí forget! No basket lunch!"

"Go back at once and get it!" said his master. "We'll wait for you here."

Now this slave, seeing how his owners had taken such a liking to the maid, had developed a mortal hatred for the poor young woman. Forgetting the lunch basket was a mere pretext. Running back home, he found the young woman and the child still sleeping. He approached with a butcher knife and slit the little girl's throat. Then he rejoined his owners.

When the young woman awakened she felt herself drenched with blood, then saw the child with its throat slit next to her. "Oh, my heavens!" she screamed. "Those poor, poor parents! Woe is me! What will I ever tell them?" In a panic, she opened a small window through which she fled into the countryside, running as fast as her legs would carry her. She came to a desolate plain, in the middle of which stood an old palace in partial ruin. The young woman entered it, but there was not a living soul in sight. She spied an old dilapidated sofa on which she sank down and promptly fell asleep, exhausted from fright and running.

Let us leave the young woman sleeping and turn back to that king who didn't want any daughters. In time his wife revealed that the daughter she had borne was not dead but had been entrusted to her godmother and heard from no more. The king couldn't rest after hearing that, and one day he said, "My wife, I'm leaving home and will only return when I have news of my daughter." After traveling far, he was overtaken by night on a desolate plain. He saw an old palace in partial ruin and went inside.

Let us leave this father in search of his daughter and go back to that king who had abandoned his wife at the foot of Mount Pellegrino. The more he thought about it, the more he was assailed with misgivings and remorse. "What if the knight was lying? What if my wife was actually innocent? Could she still be alive? Could she be dead by now? Here in this palace without her there's no peace for me. I shall go to the four corners of the globe and return only when I've had some news of her."

After traveling far, he was overtaken by night on a desolate plain. He saw an old palace in partial ruin and went inside. Another king was already there resting in an armchair. He took a seat nearby.

Let us leave that king and take up the doctor. Back from his pilgrimage, he entered his house expecting to see his little girl; instead, he found the house deserted and the child slain. His first impulse was to go and say to the slave, "Alí, we'll go after that wicked woman, to the ends of the earth if necessary, and we'll slay her the way she murdered our little girl."

So he set out. On a deserted plain night overtook him in the vicinity of an old palace in partial ruin. He entered and found two kings sitting in armchairs side by side. The doctor and Alí sat down in the two armchairs opposite them. So they sat, all four of them silent, each one lost in his own thoughts.

In the middle of the room was a lantern, which said, "I want oil."

Then into the room walked a little oil cruet, which said to the lantern, "Come on down lower."

The lantern let himself down, and the cruet poured oil into him. Then the cruet said to the lantern, "Have you anything of interest to tell me?"

"What would you like to hear? Yes, there is something that might interest you."

"Tell me."

"Listen," began the lantern, "there was a king who, wishing no more daughters, told his wife that if one more girl were born to her, he would kill the baby. To save the child, the wife had her whisked away. Listen to this: the child grew up and married a king. This king, misled by a knight, took her to Mount Pellegrino, struck her, and left her lying unconscious on the ground. A doctor came that way and heard a groan . . ."

Bit by bit as the lantern advanced in the story, the men seated in the armchairs looked up one by one, opened their eyes wide, and nearly jumped out of their seats at all they heard, while Alí shook like a leaf.

"Just listen to this," pursued the lantern. "What should the doctor and his wife see when they approached but a lovely young woman lying wounded on the ground. He took her home and later entrusted his little girl to her care. There was a slave who loathed the young woman, so what did he do but kill the little girl and make the blame fall on the young woman . . ."

"Poor young woman!" sighed the cruet. "And where is she now? Is she living or dead?"

"Sh . . ." said the lantern. "She's upstairs sleeping on a sofa. Here are her father the king and her husband the king who, regretful of the evil turns they have done her, are both out looking for her. And there's the doctor seeking to kill her, thinking she murdered his baby."

The father king and the husband king and the doctor had risen. The doctor immediately seized Alí, just barely in time to prevent his escape. All three of them fell on him and tore him apart.

Then they ran upstairs and knelt before the couch on which Wormwood was sleeping.

"She's mine!" said the father king. "She's my daughter!"

"She's mine!" said the husband king. "She's my wife!"

"She's mine!" said the doctor. "I saved her life!"

In the end she went to the king who was her husband. He invited her father and the doctor to the palace for a gala celebration of her return, and from then on they were all one happy family.

J. M. Synge
The Lady O'Conor*

There were two farmers in County Clare. One had a son, and the other, a fine rich man, had a daughter.

*J. M. Synge, *The Aran Islands* (Dublin: Maunsel, 1907), 18–24, https://babel .hathitrust.org/cgi/pt?id=ucl.31175001609034;view=1up;seq=36 (accessed April 21, 2017). Synge narrates an episode in which an old man tells him this story. I have supplied the story's title.

The young man was wishing to marry the girl, and his father told him to try and get her if he thought well, though a power of gold would be wanting to get the like of her.

"I will try," said the young man.

He put all his gold into a bag. Then he went over to the other farm, and threw in the gold in front of him.

"Is that all gold?" said the father of the girl.

"All gold," said O'Conor (the young man's name was O'Conor).

"It will not weigh down my daughter," said the father.

"We'll see that," said O'Conor.

Then they put them in the scales, the daughter in one side and the gold in the other. The girl went down against the ground, so O'Conor took his bag and went out on the road.

As he was going along he came to where there was a little man, and he standing with his back against the wall.

"Where are you going with the bag?" said the little man.

"Going home," said O'Conor.

"Is it gold you might be wanting?" said the man.

"It is, surely," said O'Conor.

"I'll give you what you are wanting," said the man, "and we can bargain in this way—you'll pay me back in a year the gold I give you, or you'll pay me with five pounds cut off your own flesh."

That bargain was made between them. The man gave a bag of gold to O'Conor, and he went back with it, and was married to the young woman.

They were rich people, and he built her a grand castle on the cliffs of Clare, with a window that looked out straightly over the wild ocean.

One day when he went up with his wife to look out over the wild ocean, he saw a ship coming in on the rocks, and no sails on her at all. She was wrecked on the rocks, and it was tea that was in her, and fine silk. O'Conor and his wife went down to look at the wreck, and when the lady O'Conor saw the silk she said she wished a dress of it.

They got the silk from the sailors, and when the Captain came up to get the money for it, O'Conor asked him to come again and take his dinner with them. They had a grand dinner, and they drank after it, and the Captain was tipsy. While they were still drinking, a letter came to O'Conor, and it was in the letter that a friend of his was dead, and that he would have to go away on a long journey. As he was getting ready the Captain came to him.

"Are you fond of your wife?" said the Captain.

"I am fond of her," said O'Conor.

"Will you make me a bet of twenty guineas no man comes near her while you'll be away on the journey?" said the Captain.

"I will bet it," said O'Conor; and he went away.

There was an old hag who sold small things on the road near the castle, and the lady O'Conor allowed her to sleep up in her room in a big box. The Captain went down on the road to the old hag.

"For how much will you let me sleep one night in your box?" said the Captain.

"For no money at all would I do such a thing," said the hag.

"For ten guineas?" said the Captain.

"Not for ten guineas," said the hag.

"For twelve guineas?" said the Captain.

"Not for twelve guineas," said the hag.

"For fifteen guineas," said the Captain.

"For fifteen I will do it," said the hag.

Then she took him up and hid him in the box. When night came the lady O'Conor walked up into her room, and the Captain watched her through a hole that was in the box. He saw her take off her two rings and put them on a kind of a board that was over her head like a chimney-piece, and take off her clothes, except her shift, and go up into her bed.

As soon as she was asleep the Captain came out of his box, and he had some means of making a light, for he lit the candle. He went over to the bed where she was sleeping without disturbing her at all, or doing any bad thing, and he took the two rings off the board, and blew out the light, and went down again into the box.[*]

When O'Conor came back the Captain met him, and told him that he had been a night in his wife's room, and gave him the two rings.

O'Conor gave him the twenty guineas of the bet. Then he went up into the castle, and he took his wife up to look out of the window over the wild ocean. While she was looking, he pushed her from behind, and she fell down over the cliff into the sea.

An old woman was on the shore, and she saw her falling. She went down then to the surf and pulled her out all wet and in great disorder, and she took the wet clothes off of her, and put on some old rags belonging to herself.

When O'Conor had pushed his wife from the window he went away into the land.

After a while the lady O'Conor went out searching for him, and when she had gone here and there a long time in the country, she heard that he was reaping in a field with sixty men.

She came to the field and she wanted to go in, but the gate-man would not open the gate for her. Then the owner came by, and she

---

[*]Here Synge breaks off from the story to describe the scene of storytelling:

> He [the storyteller] paused for a moment, and a deep sigh of relief rose from the men and women who had crowded in while the story was going on, till the kitchen was filled with people.
>
> As the Captain was coming out of his box the girls, who had appeared to know no English, stopped their spinning and held their breath with expectation.
>
> The old man went on—. (21)

told him her story. He brought her in, and her husband was there, reaping, but he never gave any sign of knowing her. She showed him to the owner, and he made the man come out and go with his wife.

Then the lady O'Conor took him out on the road where there were horses, and they rode away.

When they came to the place where O'Conor had met the little man, he was there on the road before them.

"Have you my gold on you?" said the man.

"I have not," said O'Conor.

"Then you'll pay me the flesh of your body," said the man.

They went into a house, and a knife was brought, and a clean white cloth was put on the table, and O'Conor was put upon the cloth.

Then the little man was going to strike the lancet into him, when says lady O'Conor—

"Have you bargained for five pounds of flesh?"

"For five pounds of flesh," said the man.

"Have you bargained for any drop of his blood?" said lady O'Conor.

"For no blood," said the man.

"Cut out the flesh," said lady O'Conor, "but if you spill one drop of his blood I'll put that through you." And she put a pistol to his head.

The little man went away and they saw no more of him.

When they got home to their castle they made a great supper, and they invited the Captain and the old hag, and the old woman that had pulled the lady O'Conor out of the sea.

After they had eaten well the lady O'Conor began, and she said they would all tell their stories. Then she told how she had been saved from the sea, and how she had found her husband.

Then the old woman told her story, the way she had found the lady O'Conor wet, and in great disorder, and had brought her in and put on her some old rags of her own.

The lady O'Conor asked the Captain for his story, but he said they would get no story from him. Then she took her pistol out of her pocket, and she put it on the edge of the table, and she said that anyone that would not tell his story would get a bullet into him.

Then the Captain told the way he had got into the box, and come over to her bed without touching her at all, and had taken away the rings.

Then the lady O'Conor took the pistol and shot the hag through the body, and they threw her over the cliff into the sea.

That is my story.[*]

SNOW WHITE

Yolando Pino-Saavedra
Blanca Rosa and the Forty Thieves[†]

A certain widower had a beautiful daughter called Blanca Rosa who was the living image of her mother. The mother, upon dying, had left the girl a little magic mirror and had told her daughter that if she ever wanted to see her, she need only take out her looking glass and it would give her her desire. After some time, the widower mar-

---

[*] Synge notes, "It gave me a strange feeling of wonder to hear this illiterate native of a wet rock in the Atlantic telling a story that is so full of European associations." He then goes on to note the histories of the chastity wager and pound of flesh plots (24).

[†] Yolando Pino-Saavedra, *Folktales of Chile* (Chicago: University of Chicago Press, 1967), 145–49. "Collected in 1949 by Marino Pizaro in Monte Patria, Coquimbo, from a schoolmistress, Amanda Flores" (267).

ried again, this time to a very envious woman. When the step-mother saw the daughter talking all day with her mirror, she took it away from her. This lady considered herself the most beautiful woman in the world. She asked the mirror, "Who is the most lovely of all women?" The mirror answered, "Your daughter." As the little glass didn't flatter her with the right answer, she became furiously envious and ordered her daughter killed. The men who were supposed to do the job abandoned the girl, and a little old man helped her.

Meanwhile the stepmother asked the mirror once again who was the most beautiful woman in the world. "Your daughter, who is still alive," was the answer. In a rage, she called for the little old man who had helped the girl and sentenced him to death if he didn't bring her the tongue and the eyes of her daughter. Now, the old fellow had a pet dog with blue eyes. Seeing that he couldn't defend the poor girl, he decided to kill the dog and convince the stepmother that he had followed orders. After this, he left Blanca Rosa to God's care in the forest. The stepmother was very pleased when he brought her the blue eyes and the tongue on a silver platter.

For a long while the life of Blanca Rosa was sad and full of pain, until one day she came upon the hideout of forty thieves. One morning when she had perched high in the crown of a tree, she observed a band of men leaving the forest. The girl climbed down to the den from which they had emerged and was dazzled and amazed to see all manner of jewels and delicious dishes. The good food was what she most wished for, so she crept in and ate to her heart's content, returning afterward to the treetop and falling into a deep sleep.

When the thieves returned to their lair, they found everything strewn about and suspected that somebody had found them out. The leader, however, didn't think so, but left a guard at the entrance just to make sure. When they had all gone off on their forays the next day, Blanca Rosa came down again. The guard saw her and was fascinated with such great beauty. He believed she was a being descended from heaven and dashed off pell-mell to give the rest the news. But when they returned to camp, nobody put much stock in what he said. After this, the chief ordered five men to stand guard and see about this strange apparition. All of them saw Blanca Rosa and reported the same news, believing that it was the Virgin of Heaven come to punish them. Meanwhile Blanca Rosa took pleasure in the hideout while the thieves were away. On their return, they found nobody. The chief himself decided to stand guard, for he couldn't be convinced of all these goings-on. Great was his surprise when he saw Blanca Rosa descend from the tree. Never before had he seen such a beautiful woman. He begged her pardon, thinking that she was surely the mother of God, and called his companions to repent and adore her. But Blanca Rosa, full of anguish, protested that she was not the Virgin, but rather only a poor orphan cast out of her stepmother's house. The only thing she wished was shelter so as not to die of hunger in her solitude. The thieves refused to believe this and continued to worship her as the Virgin. They built her a throne of gold, dressed her with the most lovely dresses, and adorned her with the most precious jewels. From that day on, Blanca Rosa lived happy and content among her robber "relatives."

It was rumored in the city that there was in the forest a den of thieves who adored a beautiful woman. When the stepmother got wind of this, she refused to believe it, and insisted that she was the only beautiful one in the world.

"Little mirror," she asked of the charm, "by the power God has given you, tell me who is the most beautiful of all."

"Blanca Rosa is the most beautiful woman," answered the little glass.

In desperation, the stepmother sought out a sorceress and offered her a great sum of money if she would only kill the lovely stepdaughter. The old witch searched through the forest until she found the hideout and, with lies, cajoleries, and flatteries, was able to see Blanca Rosa. When the old charmer was sure it was the right girl, she pretended to be a poor woman who wished to show her gratitude for some gold that the girl had once given her. She handed the girl a basket of fruit, but Blanca Rosa told the old woman to keep it, for she already had a great deal.

"If you won't accept this bit of fruit," croaked the old lady, "at least let me touch your dress and run my hand over your silky hair." She stroked Blanca Rosa's head and jabbed her with a magic needle. Instantly the girl dropped into a deep, deep sleep. The old hag slipped out in a wink and went to the stepmother to tell her that her daughter would trouble her no longer.

When the thieves arrived at the forest lair, they found their precious queen sleeping. As she didn't stir for many days, they believed her dead. After great weeping and many efforts to revive her, they resigned themselves to the task of the burial. Her outlaw friends placed her in a casket made of pure gold and silver, dressing her beautifully and adorning her with the most exquisite necklaces and pearls. They sealed her in against the least little drop of water and threw the casket into the sea.

Now there was in a certain city a prince who lived with his two old maid sisters and was very fond of fishing. One day he was out in his launch pulling in some nets when he saw in the waves something that sparkled and shone over the waters. Anxious to find out about this mystery, he called some fishermen to help him land the beautiful floating casket. They loaded it into his boat and he took it home, shutting himself in his own room. The casket was riveted so tight that he couldn't open it until he brought his whole tool kit to the task. After seven days and seven nights of labor, he removed the lid and found the girl dressed with such lovely garments and jewels. He tenderly removed the body and placed it on his bed, where he stripped it of its clothes and removed the jewels one by one, puzzling over the mystery of this person. When he found nothing, it occurred to him to comb her silken hair. The comb got snarled on a little bump, which the prince removed with a pair of tweezers. Immediately the fair girl sprang to life, and he realized that she had been bewitched all the time.

"Where are my thieves?" cried Blanca Rosa, seeing herself alone with this man she had never met, and totally nude. To console the distraught girl, the prince began to tell her the tale of how he had found her floating over the waves, assuring her that he was a good man and that there was nothing to fear. She would not be calmed and insisted on leaving, so the prince drove the needle back in her head and walked out to think what he could possibly do with the lovely maiden. Meanwhile the two old maid sisters were at their wit's end to see what their brother was doing locked in his room day and night. He hadn't even appeared to eat. They began to keep watch through the keyhole. Great was their shock when they spied a golden casket and heaps of jewels.

The prince returned to his room after long thought and removed the needle once again from Blanca Rosa's head. He told her he had not been able to find the forty thieves and asked her to remain in his house under his protection, as his wife. If she didn't wish to go into the street, she could remain in her room and nobody would know the secret.

One fine morning when the prince had gone off to fish and left the sad and melancholy Blanca Rosa in her room, the two sisters were seized with curiosity and opened the door. They were very indignant at seeing such a pretty girl seated on the bed. Immediately they stripped her of her fine clothing and necklaces and threw her nude into the street. Blanca Rosa frantically tried to hide and eventually arrived, breathless, at the house of an old cobbler. She was crying so bitterly that the old man took her in and hid her. The prince arrived home and found her room empty with the clothes strewn on the floor. Disconsolate, he wandered aimlessly in search of the lovely girl until someone told him of a beautiful young woman at the cobbler's house. Sure enough, he found Blanca Rosa there and took her joyfully back to his own place, where he began the preparations for the wedding. As a punishment for his sisters, the prince sent for two wild horses and had the old maids bound to them head and foot. The bucking broncos tore them into a thousand pieces. Immediately after this, the wedding was celebrated with great pomp. The forty thieves attended at Blanca Rosa's request and brought the bride many marvelous gifts. She and the prince lived very happily for all the rest of their lives.

Violet Paget

The Glass Coffin*

There was once a man who took a second wife, who was very spiteful and unkind toward her stepdaughter. She did everything in her power to make her husband hate the girl, but the girl was so good and so beautiful that it all proved useless. One day, therefore, the stepmother hired an assassin, who was to lead the girl into a wood and kill her, and bring her heart and her tongue to the stepmother, as a proof of his having done it. But when the murderer had led the girl into the wood, she begged him to spare her, and he was too much moved to kill her. So he killed a stag, cut out its tongue and

*[Violet Paget], *Tuscan Fairy Tales* (London: W. Satchell, [1880]), 93–101, https://babel.hathitrust.org/cgi/pt?id=coo.31924029931866;view=1up;seq =101 (accessed April 21, 2017). This book was published anonymously, but it is the work of Violet Paget, who wrote under the pseudonym Vernon Lee.

heart, and carried them to the stepmother, telling her that he had done his work. The stepmother believed it; and when her husband returned home and asked after the girl, she told him that his daughter had gone off with a lover, and no one knew whither.

The poor girl, meanwhile, wandered about the forest, till at last she came to a large and beautiful palace, all the doors of which were wide open. She entered, hoping to find somebody who might give her some food; but the palace was completely empty and excessively dirty. She found seven chairs, seven plates, seven knives and forks, and provisions for seven people. So she set about cleaning the rooms, made up seven beds, cooked a dinner for seven persons, and laid the table with seven places. Then she took a little gourdful of wine, a bit of cheese and a piece of bread, and made herself a little hut in the wood, where she spent the night.

The palace belonged to seven brothers, who went out every day to rob people, and returned home late every evening. Imagine their surprise and pleasure on finding the house clean, the beds made, the dinner cooked, and the table laid! They hunted all over the house, but could find no one; so they ate their dinner and went to bed. The next morning they went out as usual; and as soon as they were out of sight, the girl came out of her hut, entered the palace, made the beds, cooked the dinner, and laid the table, and returned to her hut, taking only a little gourd of wine, a piece of bread, and a bit of cheese. The seven robbers returned home, and again found their beds made and their dinner cooked. Thus it continued several days, until the curiosity of the robbers became too strong, and they determined that one of them should stay there during the daytime, and find out who this mysterious visitor might be. But he waited and waited—no one came; for the girl determined to clean the house only when they should all be asleep. So in the night she returned, cooked the dinner, and cleaned the rooms, and went away without having been seen. When the robbers found that the house had been cleaned and the dinner cooked during their sleep, they determined that one of them should stay up the following night; but he went to sleep, and the girl came and went unseen. This happened for six nights, until at last the youngest of the brothers placed himself across the doorway, and went to sleep there; as soon as the girl tried to pass, he woke up, caught hold of her, and called his brothers. Think how delighted they all were! They thanked her, entreated her to live with them, and bade her choose which of them she would marry. But she refused either to marry or to live with them; so it was settled that she should spend the night in her hut in the wood, and the day in the robbers' palace. They gave her lots of money, and got her everything she wished for; so she was very happy. But after some time she grew tired of being always alone, without a soul to speak to, so she asked an old beggar-woman, to whom she gave alms, to spend the mornings with her. They used to chat, and the old woman dressed the girl's hair, and got lots of money.

Now, it so happened that this old woman had formerly been accustomed to go once a week to the house of the stepmother, to get a present of old clothes and food. After the beggar-woman had made the girl's acquaintance, she ceased to go about asking for charity, because she got everything she wanted, so she ceased also to go to the house of the stepmother. One day the stepmother meets her, and asks her why she has not shown herself for so long; the old woman tells her that she has now as much of everything as she can possibly want, and tells her how she made the acquaintance of a beautiful girl living all by herself in a palace in the woods. The stepmother immediately suspected, from the description, that this must be her stepdaughter, and that the murderer she had hired must have deceived her. As the beggar-woman had told her that she combed and dressed the girl's hair, the stepmother gives her a magic ointment, and tells her that it is a very rare and precious pomatum, which will very much improve the girl's hair. The beggar-woman, suspecting nothing, takes the ointment, and the next day, as she is dressing the girl's hair, rubs some of it over her head. Immediately the girl falls down dead—stone dead.

When the old beggar-woman saw what had happened, she was so frightened that she ran away, leaving the girl dead on the floor. Conceive the surprise and grief of the seven robbers on their return home! They did all they could to bring her to life again; and when they saw it was all useless, they put her in a glass coffin, which they placed in the doorway, in order that they might always have the consolation of seeing her.

One day, as the robbers were out, who should pass by the house but the King's son. He sees a glass coffin, approaches, and beholds the most beautiful woman in the world. Immediately he falls madly in love with her; he calls for his coach, has the glass coffin put in, and drives to the palace. When the Queen-mother sees the coffin, she cries out that she will not let a dead woman be brought into her house.

"Carry her up to my room," insists the Prince; and so, despite the Queen, they carry her up and place her on a bed.

Then the Prince goes into the garden, and picks as many sweet-smelling flowers as he can possibly find. He boils them, and washes the body with the extract of all these sweet-smelling flowers. Scarcely has he touched the girl than she takes life again, and presently gets up, perfectly well and as beautiful as ever. The Prince married her, and she became Queen, and the wicked stepmother was burnt in the square.

("And what became of the seven robbers?"

"That I don't know; but I suppose the King made them viceroys, or *gransignori* of some sort.")

I may remark, by way of note, that although these seven brothers were called robbers by the narrator, she seemed to consider them as highly respectable persons, and was much puzzled when I asked her how robbers could be anything but rascals. I fancy the explanation of this anomaly must be sought for in the fact that these brothers were originally *outlaws*, and that as after some time outlaws ceased to exist, and the fact of their having existed was forgotten by the people, they were turned into *robbers*.

Alan Bruford

Lasair Gheug, the King of Ireland's Daughter*

There was a king once, and he married a queen, and she had a daughter. The mother died then, and he married another queen. The queen was good to her stepdaughter. But one day the *eachrais ùrlair*† came in, and she said to the queen that she was a fool to be so good to her stepdaughter "when you know that the day the king dies, your share of the inheritance will be a small one to your stepdaughter's share."

"What can be done about it?" said the queen. "If my stepdaughter does well, I will get a share."

"If you give me what I ask," said the *eachrais ùrlair*, "I will do something about it."

---

* Alan Bruford, "A Scottish Gaelic Version of 'Snow White,'" *Scottish Studies* 9 (1965): 153–74. From the Scottish Studies website, http://journals.ed.ac.uk /ScottishStudies/about/policies. The "story is part of a manuscript collection of folktales and other traditions from Atholl made in 1891 by Lady Evelyn Stewart-Murray.... This story was taken down on Wednesday, 3rd June 1891, from the telling of Mrs. MacMillan, Bridge Cottage, Strathtay, one of Lady Evelyn's best informants" (153). The notes that follow are Bruford's.

† The *eachrais ùrlair* (*eachlach ùrlair*) is a commonplace of Gaelic folktales: she is the character who first inspires the stepmother to wickedness. Sometimes she is called the "henwife" (*cailleach nan cearc*) as in Irish versions.

"What would you want, old woman?" said the queen.

"I have a little saucepan, I only put it on occasionally: I want meal enough to thicken it, and butter enough to thin it, and the full of my ear of wool."

"How much meal will thicken it?"

"The increase of seven granaries of oats in seven years."

"How much butter will thin it?" said the queen.

"The increase of seven byres of cattle in seven years."

"And how much wool will your ear hold?"

"The increase of seven folds of sheep in seven years."

"You have asked much, old woman," said the queen, "but though it is much, you shall have it."

"We will kill the king's greyhound bitch and leave it on the landing of the stairs, so that the king thinks that it is Lasair Gheug who has done it. We will make Lasair Gheug swear three baptismal oaths, that she will not be on foot, she will not be on horseback, and she will not be on the green earth the day she tells of it."*

The king came home, and saw the greyhound bitch on the landing. Roared, roared, roared the king: "Who did the deed?"

"Who do you think, but your own eldest daughter?" said the queen.

"That cannot be," said the king, and he went to bed, and he ate not a bite, and he drank not a drop: and if day came early, the king rose earlier than that, and went to the hill to hunt.

In came the *eachrais ùrlair*. "What did the king do to his daughter last night?" she asked.

"He did nothing at all, old woman," said the queen. "Go home, and never let us see you again after the rage you put the king in last night."

---

*The oath she swears is normally not to tell the truth to any Christian soul: hence the insistence on the unchristened children later in the story, though they are not really required in this version.

"I will be bound that he will kill his daughter tonight," said the *eachrais ùrlair*. "We will kill the king's graceful black palfrey, and leave it on the landing. We will make Lasair Gheug swear three baptismal oaths, that she will not be on foot, she will not be on horseback, and she will not be on the green earth the day she tells of it."

The king came home, and saw the graceful black palfrey on the landing. Roared, roared, roared the king: "Who did the deed?"

"Who do you think, but your own eldest daughter?" said the queen.

"That cannot be," said the king, and he went to bed, and he ate not a bite, and he drank not a drop: and if day came early, the king rose earlier than that, and went to the hill to hunt.

In came the *eachrais ùrlair*. "What did the king do to his daughter last night?"

"He did nothing at all, old woman," said the queen. "Go home, and don't come here again, after the rage you put the king in last night."

"I will be bound," said the *eachrais ùrlair*, "that he will kill his daughter tonight. We will kill your own eldest son," said she, "and leave him on the landing. We will make Lasair Gheug swear three baptismal oaths, that she will not be on foot, she will not be on horseback, and she will not be on the green earth the day she tells of it."

The king came home, then, and saw his eldest son on the landing. Roared, roared, roared the king: "Who did the deed?"

"Who do you think, but your own eldest daughter?" said the queen.

"That cannot be," said the king, and he went to bed, and he ate not a bite, and he drank not a drop: and if day came early, the king rose earlier than that, and went to the hill to hunt.

In came the *eachrais ùrlair*. "What did the king do to his daughter last night?"

"He did nothing at all, old woman," said the queen. "Go home, and don't come here again, after the rage you put the king in last night."

"I will be bound," said the *eachrais ùrlair*, "that he will kill his daughter tonight. You must pretend that you are sick, sore, and sorry."

Men leapt on horses and horses on men to look for the king. The king came. He asked the queen what in the seven continents of the world he could get to help her, that he would not get.

"There is something to help me," said she, "but what will help me you will not give me."

"If there is something to help you," said he, "you shall have it."

"Give me the heart of Lasair Gheug, the king of Ireland's daughter," said the queen.

"Well," said the king, "it hurts me to give you that, but you shall have that," said the king. He went to the squinting sandy cook and asked if he would hide his child for one night.

"I will," said the cook. They killed a sucking pig, and they took out the heart and liver. They put its blood on Lasair Gheug's clothes. The king went home with the heart and the liver, and gave it to the queen. Then the queen was as well as she had ever been.

The king went again to the squinting sandy cook, and he asked him if he would hide his child for one night again. The cook said he would. Next day the king took with him the best horse in the stable, a peck of gold, a peck of silver, and Lasair Gheug. He came to a great forest, with no edge and no end, and he was going to leave Lasair Gheug there. He cut off the end of one of her fingers.

"Does that hurt you, daughter?" he said.

"It doesn't hurt me, father," she said, "because it is you who did it."

"It hurts me more," said the king, "to have lost the greyhound bitch." With that he cut off another of her fingers.

"Does that hurt you, daughter?" he said.

"It doesn't hurt me, father, because it is you who did it."

"It hurts me more than that to have lost the graceful black palfrey." With that he cut off another of her fingers.

"Does that hurt you, daughter?" said the king.

"It doesn't hurt me, father," said she, "because it is you who did it."

"It hurts me more," said he, "to have lost my eldest son." He gave her the peck of gold and the peck of silver, and he left her there. He went home, and he lay down on his bed, blind and deaf to the world.

Lasair Gheug was frightened in the forest that wild beasts would come and eat her. The highest tree she could see in the forest, she climbed that tree. She was not there long when she saw twelve cats coming, and a one-eyed gray cat along with them. They had a cow and a cauldron, and they lit a fire at the foot of the tree she was in. They killed the cow and put it in the cauldron to cook. The steam was rising, and her fingers were getting warm. She began to bleed, and drop after drop fell in the cauldron. The one-eyed gray cat told one of the other cats to go up the tree and see what was there: for king's blood or knight's blood was falling into the cauldron. The cat went up. She gave it a handful of gold and a handful of silver not to tell that she was there. But the blood would not stop. The one-eyed gray cat sent everyone up, one after the other, until all twelve had been up, and they all got a handful of gold and a handful of silver. The one-eyed gray cat climbed up himself, and he found Lasair Gheug and brought her down.

When the supper was ready, the one-eyed gray cat asked her whether she would have her supper with him, or with the others. She said she would rather have supper with him, he was the one she liked the look of best. They had their supper, and then they were going to bed. The one-eyed gray cat asked which she would rather, to go to bed with him, or to sleep with the others. She said she would rather go with him, he was the one she liked the look of best. They went to bed, and when they got up in the morning, they were in Lochlann. The one-eyed gray cat was really the king of Lochlann's son, and his twelve squires along with him. They had been bewitched by his stepmother, and now the spell was loosed.

They were married then, and Lasair Gheug had three sons. She asked the king for a favor not to have them christened.

There was a well in the king of Ireland's garden, and there was a trout in the well, and the queen used to go every year to wash in the well. She went there this time, and when she had washed, she said to the trout, "Little trout, little trout," said she, "am not I," said she, "the most beautiful woman that ever was in Ireland?"

"Indeed and indeed then, you are not," said the trout, "while Lasair Gheug, the king of Ireland's daughter, is alive."

"Is she alive still?" said the queen.

"She is, and will be in spite of you," said the trout. "She is in Lochlann, and has three unchristened children."

"I will set a snare to catch her," said the queen, "and a net to destroy you."

"You have tried to do that once or twice before," said the trout, "but you haven't managed it yet," said he, "and though I am here now, many is the mighty water I can be on before night comes."

The queen went home, and she gave the king a piece of her mind for making her believe that he had given her Lasair Gheug's heart and liver when she was alive and well in Lochlann still. She wanted the king to go with her to see Lasair Gheug, but the king would not budge, and he would not believe that she was there. She sent her twelve maids-in-waiting to Lochlann, and she gave a box to her own maid to give Lasair Gheug, and she asked her to tell her not to open it until she was with her three unchristened children.

Lasair Gheug was sitting at the window sewing. She saw her father's banner coming. In her delight she did not know whether to run out of the door or fly out of the window. They gave her the box, and she was so delighted with it that she did not wait to be with her three unchristened children. She opened the box when the others had gone home. When she opened the box, there were three grains in it . . . one grain of ice stuck in her forehead and another in each of her palms, and she fell dead and cold.

The king came home and found her dead. That would have beaten a wiser man than he. He was so fond of her, he would not let her be buried. He put her in a leaden coffin and kept it locked up in a room. He used to visit her early and late. He used to look twice as well when he went in as when he came out. This had been going on for a while when his companions persuaded him to marry again. He gave every key in the house to the queen, except the key of that room. She wondered what was in the room, when he looked so poorly coming out, compared with the way he was when he went in. She told one of the boys one day, if he was playing near the king, to see if he could manage to steal the key out of his pocket. The lad stole the key and gave it to his stepmother. She went in, and what was there, but the king's first wife. She looked her over: she saw the grain of ice in her forehead and she took a pin and picked it out. The woman in the coffin gave a sigh. She saw another one in one of her palms, and took it out. The woman sat up. She found another one in the other palm, and took it out. Then she was as well as she had ever been. She brought her out with her and put her in another room. She sent the boy with the key to meet his father coming home and put it back in his pocket without his knowledge.

The king came home. The first thing he did was to go inside that room as usual. There was nothing there. He came out then to ask what had happened to the thing that had been in that room. The queen said she had never had the key of that room. She asked what had been in that room. He said it was his first wife, and with the love he had for her he would not bury her: he liked to see her, dead though she was.

"What will you give me," said the queen, "if I bring you her alive?"

"I don't expect to see her alive," said he, "but I would be glad to see her even though she were dead."

The queen went then and brought her in on her arm, alive and well. He did not know whether to laugh or cry with his delight. The other queen said then that she might as well go home, there was no more need for her there. Lasair Gheug said that she was not to go home: she should stay along with her, and should have food and drink as good as herself, every day as long as she lived.

At the end of this another year had gone by. The queen of Ireland went to the well to wash there again.

"Little trout, little trout," said she, "am not I the most beautiful woman that ever was in Ireland?"

"Indeed and indeed you are not," said the trout, "while Lasair Gheug, the king of Ireland's daughter, is alive."

"Is she alive still?" said she.

"Oh yes, and she will be in spite of you," said the trout.

"I will set a snare to catch her," said the queen, "and a net to destroy you."

"You have tried to do that once or twice before," said the trout, "but you haven't managed it yet," said he. "Though I am here now, many is the mighty water I can be on before night comes."

The queen went home then, and she got the king moving, and they went to visit Lasair Gheug. Lasair Gheug was sitting at the window this time, but she showed no pleasure at all at the sight of her father's banner.

When Sunday came, they went to church. She had sent people to catch a wild boar that was in the wood, and others to get faggots and sticks and stuff to make a big fire. She got the wild boar: she got on to the boar's back, went in at one door of the church and out at the other door. She called her three unchristened children to her side.

"I am not going to tell my story to anyone at all," said she, "but to you three unchristened children."

"When I was in my own father's kingdom in Ireland, my step-mother and the *eachrais ùrlair* killed my father's greyhound bitch and left it on the landing. They made me swear three baptismal oaths, that I would not be on foot, I would not be on horseback, and I would not be on the green earth the day I told of it. But I am on the wild boar's back. They expected that my father would kill me, but my father has not killed me yet."

She went in at one door, and she went out at the other door, and she called her three unchristened children along with her.

"I am not going to tell my story to anyone at all," said she, "but to you three unchristened children."

"When I was in my own father's kingdom in Ireland, my step-mother and the *eachrais ùrlair* killed my father's graceful black pal-frey and left it on the landing. They made me swear three baptismal oaths, that I would not be on foot, I would not be on horseback, and I would not be on the green earth the day I told of it. But I am on the wild boar's back. They expected that my father would kill me, but my father has not killed me yet."

She went in at one door, and she went out at the other door, and she called her three unchristened children along with her.

"I am not going to tell my story to anyone at all," said she, "but to you three unchristened children."

"When I was in my own father's kingdom in Ireland, my step-mother and the *eachrais ùrlair* killed my eldest brother and left him on the landing. They made me swear three baptismal oaths, that I would not be on foot, I would not be on horseback, and I would not be on the green earth the day I told of it. But I am on the wild boar's back. They expected that my father would kill me, but my father has not killed me yet. Now," said she, "I have nothing more to tell you."

The wild boar was set free. When they came out of the church, the queen of Ireland was caught and burnt in the fire.

When the king was going home, he said to his daughter, Lasair Gheug, that she had done ill by him: he had come from home with a wife, and he was going home now without one. And Lasair Ghueg said: "It wasn't that way: you came here with a monster, but I have a woman friend, and you shall have her, and you will go home with a wife." And they made a great, merry, mirthful, happy, hospitable, wonderful wedding: it was kept up for a year and a day. I got shoes of paper there on a glass pavement, a bit of butter on an ember, porridge in a creel, a greatcoat of chaff, and a short coat of buttermilk. I hadn't gone far when I fell, and the glass pavement broke, the short coat of buttermilk spilt, the butter melted on the ember, a gust of wind came and blew away the greatcoat of chaff. All I had had was gone, and I was as poor as I was to start with. And I left them there.

THE MAIDEN WHO SEEKS HER BROTHERS

Peter Christian Asbjørnsen and Jørgen Moe
The Twelve Wild Ducks*

Once on a time there was a Queen who was out driving, when there had been a new fall of snow in the winter; but when she had

---

*Peter Christian Asbjørnsen and Jørgen Moe, *Popular Tales from the Norse*, trans. George Webbe Dasent (New York: G. P. Putnam, 1912), 51–59, https:// babel.hathitrust.org/cgi/ pt?id=hvd.32044013690508;view=1up;seq=241 (accessed April 21, 2017).

gone a little way, she began to bleed at the nose, and had to get out of her sledge. And so, as she stood there, leaning against the fence, and saw the red blood on the white snow, she fell a-thinking how she had twelve sons and no daughter, and she said to herself—

"If I only had a daughter as white as snow and as red as blood, I shouldn't care what became of all my sons."

But the words were scarce out of her mouth before an old witch of the Trolls came up to her.

"A daughter you shall have," she said, "and she shall be as white as snow, and as red as blood; and your sons shall be mine, but you may keep them till the babe is christened."

So when the time came the Queen had a daughter, and she was as white as snow, and as red as blood, just as the Troll had promised, and so they called her "Snow-white and Rosy-red." Well, there was great joy at the King's court, and the Queen was as glad as glad could be; but when what she had promised to the old witch came into her mind, she sent for a silversmith, and bade him make twelve silver spoons, one for each prince, and after that she bade him make one more, and that she gave to Snow-white and Rosy-red. But as soon as ever the Princess was christened, the Princes were turned into twelve wild ducks, and flew away. They never saw them again,—away they went, and away they stayed.

So the Princess grew up, and she was both tall and fair, but she was often so strange and sorrowful, and no one could understand what it was that failed her. But one evening the Queen was also sorrowful, for she had many strange thoughts when she thought of her sons. She said to Snow-white and Rosy-red—

"Why are you so sorrowful, my daughter? Is there anything you want? if so, only say the word, and you shall have it."

"Oh, it seems so dull and lonely here," said Snow-white and Rosy-red; "everyone else has brothers and sisters, but I am all alone; I have none; and that's why I'm so sorrowful."

"But you *had* brothers, my daughter," said the Queen; "I had twelve sons who were your brothers, but I gave them all away to get you"; and so she told her the whole story.

So when the Princess heard that, she had no rest; for, in spite of all the Queen could say or do, and all she wept and prayed, the lassie would set off to seek her brothers, for she thought it was all her fault; and at last she got leave to go away from the palace. On and on she walked into the wide world, so far, you would never have thought a young lady could have strength to walk so far.

So, once, when she was walking through a great, great wood, one day she felt tired, and sat down on a mossy tuft and fell asleep. Then she dreamt that she went deeper and deeper into the wood, till she came to a little wooden hut, and there she found her brothers; just then she woke, and straight before her she saw a worn path in the green moss, and this path went deeper into the wood; so she followed it, and after a long time she came to just such a little wooden house as that she had seen in her dream.

Now, when she went into the room there was no one at home, but there stood twelve beds, and twelve chairs, and twelve spoons—a dozen of everything, in short. So when she saw that she was so glad, she hadn't been so glad for many a long year, for she could guess at once that her brothers lived here, and that they owned the beds, and chairs, and spoons. So she began to make up the fire, and sweep the room, and make the beds, and cook the dinner, and to make the house as tidy as she could; and when she had done all the cooking and work, she ate her own dinner, and crept under her youngest brother's bed, and lay down there, but she forgot her spoon upon the table.

So she had scarcely laid herself down before she heard something flapping and whirring in the air, and so all the twelve wild ducks came sweeping in; but as soon as ever they crossed the threshold they became Princes.

"Oh, how nice and warm it is in here," they said. "Heaven bless him who made up the fire, and cooked such a good dinner for us."

And so each took up his silver spoon and was going to eat. But when each had taken his own, there was one still left lying on the table, and it was so like the rest that they couldn't tell it from them.

"This is our sister's spoon," they said; "and if her spoon be here, she can't be very far off herself."

"If this be our sister's spoon, and she be here," said the eldest, "she shall be killed, for she is to blame for all the ill we suffer."

And this she lay under the bed and listened to.

"No," said the youngest, " 'twere a shame to kill her for that. She has nothing to do with our suffering ill; for if any one's to blame, it's our own mother."

So they set to work hunting for her both high and low, and at last they looked under all the beds, and so when they came to the youngest Prince's bed, they found her, and dragged her out. Then the eldest Prince wished again to have her killed, but she begged and prayed so prettily for herself.

"Oh! gracious goodness! Don't kill me, for I've gone about seeking you these three years, and if I could only set you free, I'd willingly lose my life."

"Well!" said they, "if you will set us free, you may keep your life; for you can if you choose."

"Yes; only tell me," said the Princess, "how it can be done, and I'll do it, whatever it be."

"You must pick thistle-down," said the Princes, "and you must card it, and spin it, and weave it; and after you have done that, you must cut out and make twelve coats, and twelve shirts, and twelve neckerchiefs, one for each of us, and while you do that, you must neither talk, nor laugh, nor weep. If you can do that, we are free."

"But where shall I ever get thistle-down enough for so many neckerchiefs, and shirts, and coats?" asked Snow-white and Rosy-red.

"We'll soon show you," said the Princes; and so they took her with them to a great wide moor, where there stood such a crop of thistles, all nodding and nodding in the breeze, and the down all floating and glistening like gossamers through the air in the sunbeams. The Princess had never seen such a quantity of thistle-down in her life, and she began to pluck and gather it as fast and as well as she could; and when she got home at night she set to work carding and spinning yarn from the down. So she went on a long, long time, picking, and carding, and spinning, and all the while keeping the Princes' house, cooking, and making their beds. At evening home they came, flapping and whirring like wild ducks, and all night they were Princes, but in the morning off they flew again, and were wild ducks the whole day.

But now it happened once, when she was out on the moor to pick thistle-down,—and if I don't mistake, it was the very last time she was to go thither,—it happened that the young King who ruled that land was out hunting, and came riding across the moor, and saw her. So he stopped there and wondered who the lovely lady could be that walked along the moor picking thistle-down, and he asked her her name, and when he could get no answer, he was still more astonished; and at last he liked her so much, that nothing would do but he must take her home to his castle and marry her. So he ordered his servants to take her and put her up on his horse. Snow-white and Rosy-red she wrung her hands, and made signs to them, and pointed to the bags in which her work was, and when the King saw she wished to have them with her, he told his men to take up the bags behind them. When they had done that the Princess came to herself, little by little, for the King was both a wise man and a handsome man too, and he was as soft and kind to her as a doctor. But when they got home to the palace, and the old Queen, who was his stepmother, set eyes on Snow-white and Rosy-red, she got so cross and jealous of her because she was so lovely, that she said to the king—

"Can't you see now, that this thing whom you have picked up, and whom you are going to marry, is a witch? Why, she can't either talk, or laugh, or weep!"

But the King didn't care a pin for what she said, but held on with the wedding, and married Snow-white and Rosy-red, and they lived in great joy and glory; but she didn't forget to go on sewing at her shirts.

So when the year was almost out, Snow-white and Rosy-red brought a Prince into the world; and then the old Queen was more spiteful and jealous than ever, and at dead of night she stole in to Snow-white and Rosy-red, while she slept, and took away her babe, and threw it into a pit full of snakes. After that she cut Snow-white and Rosy-red in her finger, and smeared the blood over her mouth, and went straight to the King.

"Now come and see," she said, "what sort of a thing you have taken for your Queen; here she has eaten up her own babe."

Then the king was so downcast, he almost burst into tears, and said—

"Yes, it must be true, since I see it with my own eyes; but she'll not do it again, I'm sure, and so this time I'll spare her life."

So before the next year was out she had another son, and the same thing happened. The King's stepmother got more and more jealous and spiteful. She stole into the young Queen at night while she slept, took away the babe, and threw it into a pit full of snakes, cut the young Queen's finger, and smeared the blood over her mouth, and then went and told the King she had eaten up her own child. Then the King was so sorrowful, you can't think how sorry he was, and he said—

"Yes, it must be true, since I see it with my own eyes, but she'll not do it again, I'm sure, and so this time too I'll spare her life."

Well, before the next year was out, Snow-white and Rosy-red brought a daughter into the world, and her, too, the old Queen took and threw into the pit full of snakes, while the young Queen slept. Then she cut her finger, smeared the blood over her mouth, and went again to the King and said—

"Now you may come and see if it isn't as I say; she's a wicked, wicked witch, for here she has gone and eaten up her third babe too."

Then the King was so sad, there was no end to it, for now he couldn't spare her any longer, but had to order her to be burnt alive on a pile of wood. But just when the pile was all ablaze, and they were going to put her on it, she made signs to them to take twelve boards and lay them round the pile, and on these she laid the neckerchiefs, and the shirts, and the coats for her brothers, but the youngest brother's shirt wanted its left arm, for she hadn't had time to finish it. And as soon as ever she had done that, they heard such a flapping and whirring in the air, and down came twelve wild ducks flying over the forest, and each of them snapped up his clothes in his bill and flew off with them.

"See now!" said the old Queen to the King, "wasn't I right when I told you she was a witch; but make haste and burn her before the pile burns low."

"Oh!" said the King, "we've wood enough and to spare, and so I'll wait a bit, for I have a mind to see what the end of all this will be."

As he spoke, up came the twelve princes riding along, as handsome well-grown lads as you'd wish to see; but the youngest prince had a wild duck's wing instead of his left arm.

"What's all this about?" asked the Princes.

"My Queen is to be burnt," said the King, "because she's a witch, and because she has eaten up her own babes."

"She hasn't eaten them at all," said the Princes. "Speak now, sister; you have set us free and saved us, now save yourself."

Then Snow-white and Rosy-red spoke, and told the whole story; how every time she was brought to bed, the old Queen, the King's stepmother, had stolen into her at night, had taken her babes away, and cut her little finger, and smeared the blood over her mouth; and then the Princes took the King, and showed him the snake-pit where three babes lay playing with adders and toads, and lovelier children you never saw.

So the King had them taken out at once, and went to his stepmother, and asked her what punishment she thought that woman deserved who could find it in her heart to betray a guiltless Queen and three such blessed little babes.

"She deserves to be fast bound between twelve unbroken steeds, so that each may take his share of her," said the old Queen.

"You have spoken your own doom," said the King, "and you shall suffer it at once."

So the wicked old Queen was fast bound between twelve unbroken steeds, and each got his share of her. But the King took Snow-white and Rosy-red, and their three children, and the twelve Princes; and so they all went home to their father and mother, and told all that had befallen them, and there was joy and gladness over the whole kingdom, because the Princess was saved and set free, and because she had set free her twelve brothers.

VIII. The Tempest

We might not expect to find "The Magic Flight" folktale (ATU 313) in *The Tempest*, because the play is famous for what might be the most pointedly unmagical flight in world literature. Prospero leaves the island only after he has renounced his sorcery, broken his magic staff, and drowned his book of enchantments. The magician in "The Magic Flight" folktale also ends the story overpowered and, in some versions, dead. The magician's daughter, having deceived and overmastered her father, uses powerful magic to flee with her beloved. She seems quite unlike Prospero's daughter Miranda, who has no magic and is manipulated by her father even when she believes she is rebelling against him. The Miranda-Ferdinand strand of the play begins like "The Magic Flight" folktale, but the folktale plot is stopped in its tracks by Prospero's overweening dominance.

"The Magic Flight" is popular and widespread, and versions differ wildly from each other, as many different motifs accumulate around a central core of incidents. In this central plot, a young man arrives at the home of a magician. The magician orders him to perform impossible tasks, under threat of death. The magician's daughter, however, falls in love with the young man, and uses her own supernatural powers to complete the tasks. The hero and heroine flee the magician's house, but he pursues them. The magician's daughter uses magic to evade capture, either throwing objects behind them that metamorphose into huge obstacles, or transforming herself and the young man so that they are unrecognizable. The couple marries, sometimes after additional trials.

In *The Tempest*, Ferdinand is shipwrecked on Prospero's island and separated from his father and the rest of their party, just as in the folktale the young man finds himself in the wizard's domain. Ferdinand meets Miranda, the magician's daughter, and the two fall in love at first sight. Prospero, however, accuses Ferdinand of being a spy, magically disarms him, and orders him to stack thousands of logs. (In the folktale, the hero is very frequently charged with reducing a forest to bundles of firewood or the like.) At this point in the play, however, the folktale plot hits an impasse. Miranda offers to help Ferdinand with his chore, but simply by manually stacking the logs herself, since she has no supernatural abilities. Ferdinand steadfastly refuses her help. Prospero, moreover, has only been pretending to plague Ferdinand. Actually, he has been masterminding the marriage of his daughter to Ferdinand, the heir apparent to the crown of Naples. Prospero only pretends to be the enemy of the young prince and young love. While Ferdinand and Miranda believe themselves to be, like the folktale couple, carrying on a clandestine courtship despite a sorcerer's persecution, they are not.

The Tempest is just one of several seventeenth-century European literary adaptations of "The Magic Flight." Jacob Ayrer's German play *The Fair Sidea*, sometimes cited as an analogue or possible source of *The Tempest*, follows the folktale closely. Giambattista Basile's *Tale of Tales* contains three separate versions of the story.[*] Marie-Catherine d'Aulnoy's fairy tale "The Bee and the Orange Tree," included here, is an elaborate riff on the folktale. Another literary version of "The Magic Flight" is in the eleventh-century Indian *Ocean of the Streams of Story*.[†] Folklorists and classicists have

---

[*] Basile, *Tale of Tales*: "The Dove," 2.7 (184–94); "Rosella," 3.9 (273–79); "Petrosinella," 2.1 (147–51).

[†] Somadeva, *Kathā Sarit Sāgara*, 355–69. "Story of Śṛingabhuja and the Daughter of the Rākshasa," vol. 1, book 7, chapter 39.

long noted the resemblance of the Jason and Medea myth to "The Magic Flight." Shakespeare seems to have noticed the connection too, as he refers several times in *The Tempest* to Medea. Likewise, d'Aulnoy namechecks Jason and his quest for the golden fleece in "The Bee and the Orange Tree," and the unusual name Ayrer gave to his play's heroine, Sidea, may echo the name Medea.

Two British versions of "The Magic Flight" are included here. In Joseph Jacobs's English "Nix Nought Nothing," the young man falls prey to a giant because of a mistake committed by the boy's father. Likewise, Prospero shipwrecks and tests Ferdinand because his father, Alonso, aided and abetted Prospero's overthrow as Duke of Milan. The giant in "Nix" dies during the course of the magic flight, and Prospero also confronts his own mortality as his daughter leaves to marry, saying that every third thought will be of his grave (5.1.312). The folktale hero, however, joyfully reunites with his parents, just as Ferdinand and his father rejoice at their reunion, each having thought the other drowned.

The Scottish tale "Green Sleeves" represents a subset of "Magic Flight" stories that bear some resemblance to the great fourteenth-century romance *Sir Gawain and the Green Knight*. In *Sir Gawain*, an uncanny green man challenges Gawain to a game, and then to find his home within a year and a day, where death most likely awaits the knight, as in "Green Sleeves" (as well as in "Jack Beats the Devil," also here). In "Green Sleeves," the title character's daughter in the form of a bird leads the young man to her father's home. In *The Tempest*, the airy spirit Ariel lures Ferdinand to Prospero with a song. The motif in which a bird, whether an avatar of the heroine or not, leads the hero to the sorcerer's abode dates back to *Ocean of the Streams of Story*, and we will see it again in "Jack Beats the Devil." The hero of "Green Sleeves" is given torturous lodging and inedible food, just as Prospero threatens Ferdinand that "I'll manacle thy neck and feet together; / Sea water shalt thou drink; thy food shall be / The fresh-brook mussels, withered roots, and husks / Wherein the acorn cradled" (1.2.462–65). Perhaps the most striking similarity of "Green Sleeves" to *The Tempest* is that the heroine magically completes the task her father has assigned the hero by summoning legions of fairies, just as Prospero's magic is accomplished by elves, spirits native to the island. In the Brothers Grimm's "The Two Kings' Children," autochthonous gnomes or *Eerdmännekens* (literally, "little earth-men") perform the tasks.[*] "Green Sleeves" contains a "forgotten bride" episode common to "Magic Flight" tales, in which the heroine disposes of various suitors or "false bridegrooms," just as Miranda is sought by the anti-heroes Caliban and Stephano.

In the next three versions of "The Magic Flight" included here, the Grimms' "The Two Kings' Children," Zora Neale Hurston's "Jack Beats the Devil," and d'Aulnoy's "The Bee and the Orange Tree," the hero must undertake a perilous water-crossing to reach the magician's home, just as Ferdinand is shipwrecked on Prospero's island. In the Grimms' and Hurston's tales, the young man must clear a forest and reduce it to stacks of firewood, suggestive of Ferdinand's log-bearing. In "The Two Kings' Children" and "The Bee and the Orange Tree," the sorcerer has a wife even shrewder and more powerful than her husband. Prospero has no wife, but *The Tempest* is haunted by the memory of the witch Sycorax, Caliban's mother.

D'Aulnoy's "The Bee and the Orange Tree" is the longest tale included in this anthology, but its resemblances to *The Tempest* warrant its inclusion here. Both d'Aulnoy's heroine and later her future husband are shipwrecked on an island inhabited by ogres, just as Miranda and Ferdinand are shipwrecked on the magic island. The heroine, Princess Aimée, is appareled in a manner that

[*] Jacob and Wilhelm Grimm, *Kinder- und Hausmärchen*, 2.253.

suggests Native Americans, with her animal skin garments and her bows and arrows. She is referred to as a savage repeatedly. *The Tempest* famously also suggests New World contexts, as when Trinculo and Stephano mistake Caliban for an Indian. Aimée is nearly forced to marry the ogre's son, a threat to her royal marriage prospects like that of Caliban to Miranda's, as Caliban first attempts to rape Miranda and then promises her as a prize to Stephano if he kills Prospero. The hero of d'Aulnoy's story spends some time transformed into a tree, his consciousness imprisoned in arboreal form, as Ariel is trapped in a pine tree for years before the play begins. A little rhyming sermon on premarital chastity ends the tale, just as Prospero's masque for the young couple is one of his many ways of insisting they wait until the wedding night.

THE MAGIC FLIGHT

Joseph Jacobs
Nix Nought Nothing*

There once lived a king and a queen as many a one has been. They were long married and had no children; but at last a baby boy came to the queen when the king was away in the far countries. The queen would not christen the boy till the king came back, and she said, "We will just call him Nix Nought Nothing until his father comes home." But it was long before he came home, and the boy had grown a nice little laddie. At length the king was on his way back; but he had a big river to cross, and there was a whirlpool, and he could not get over the water. But a giant came up to him, and

*Joseph Jacobs, *English Fairy Tales*, illus. John Dixon Batten (London: David Nutt, 1890), 33–39, https://babel.hathitrust.org/cgi/pt?id=hvd.32044024186231 ;view=1up;seq=55 (accessed April 21, 2017).

said: "I'll carry you over." But the king said: "What's your pay?" "O give me Nix, Nought, Nothing, and I will carry you over the water on my back." The king had never heard that his son was called Nix Nought Nothing, and so he said: "O, I'll give you that and my thanks into the bargain." When the king got home again, he was very happy to see his wife again, and his young son. She told him that she had not given the child any name, but just Nix Nought Nothing, until he should come home again himself. The poor king was in a terrible case. He said: "What have I done? I promised to give the giant who carried me over the river on his back Nix Nought Nothing." The king and the queen were sad and sorry, but they said: "When the giant comes we will give him the hen-wife's boy; he will never know the difference." The next day the giant came to claim the king's promise, and he sent for the hen-wife's boy; and the giant went away with the boy on his back. He traveled till he came to a big stone, and there he sat down to rest. He said:

"Hidge, Hodge, on my back, what time of day is that?"

The poor little boy said: "It is the time that my mother, the hen-wife, takes up the eggs for the queen's breakfast."

The Giant was very angry, and dashed the boy's head on the stone and killed him.

So he went back in a tower of a temper, and this time they gave him the gardener's boy. He went off with him on his back till they got to the stone again when the giant sat down to rest. And he said: "Hidge, Hodge, on my back, what time of day do you make that?"

The gardener's boy said: "Sure it's the time that my mother takes up the vegetables for the queen's dinner."

Then the giant was right wild and dashed his brains out on the stone.

Then the giant went back to the king's house in a terrible temper and said he would destroy them all if they did not give him Nix Nought Nothing this time. They had to do it; and when he came to the big stone, the giant said: "What time of day is that?" Nix Nought Nothing said: "It is the time that my father the king will be sitting down to supper." The giant said: "I've got the right one now"; and took Nix Nought Nothing to his own house and brought him up till he was a man.

The giant had a bonny daughter, and she and the lad grew very fond of each other. The giant said one day to Nix Nought Nothing: "I've work for you tomorrow. There is a stable seven miles long and seven miles broad, and it has not been cleaned for seven years, and you must clean it tomorrow, or I will have you for my supper."

The giant's daughter went out next morning with the lad's breakfast, and found him in a terrible state, for always as he cleaned out a bit, it just fell in again. The giant's daughter said she would help him, and she cried all the beasts in the field, and all the fowls of the air, and in a minute they all came, and carried away everything that was in the stable and made it all clean before the giant came home. He said: "Shame on the wit that helped you; but I have a worse job for you tomorrow." Then he said to Nix Nought Nothing: "There's a lake seven miles long, and seven miles deep, and seven miles broad, and you must drain it tomorrow by nightfall, or else I'll have you for my supper." Nix Nought Nothing began early next morning and tried to lave the water with his pail, but the lake was never getting any less, and he didn't know what to do; but the giant's daughter called on all the fish in the sea to come and drink the water, and very soon they drank it dry. When the giant saw the work done he was in a rage, and said: "I've a worse job for you tomorrow; there is a tree, seven miles high, and no branch on it, till you get to the top, and there is a nest with seven eggs in it, and you must bring down all the eggs without breaking one, or else I'll have you for my supper." At first the giant's daughter did not know how to help Nix Nought Nothing; but she cut off first her fingers and then her toes, and made steps of them, and he clomb the tree and got all the eggs safe till he came just to the bottom, and then one was broken. So they determined to run away together and after the giant's daughter had tidied up her hair a bit and got her magic flask they set out together as fast as they could run. And they hadn't got but three fields away when they looked back and saw the giant walking along at top speed after them. "Quick, quick," called out the giant's daughter, "take my comb from my hair and throw it down." Nix Nought Nothing took her comb from her hair and threw it down, and out of every one of its prongs there sprung up a fine thick briar in the way of the giant. You may be sure it took him a long time to work his way through the briar bush and by the time he was well through Nix Nought Nothing and his sweetheart had run on a tidy step away from him. But he soon came along after them and was just like to catch 'em up when the giant's daughter called out to Nix Nought Nothing, "Take my hair dagger and throw it down, quick, quick." So Nix Nought Nothing threw down the hair dagger and out of it grew as quick as lightning a thick hedge of sharp razors placed criss-cross. The giant had to tread very cautiously to get through all this and meanwhile the young lovers ran on, and on, and on, till they were nearly out of sight. But at last the giant was through, and it wasn't long before he was like to catch them up. But just as he was stretching out his hand to catch Nix Nought Nothing his daughter took out her magic flask and dashed it on the ground. And as it broke out of it welled a big, big wave that grew, and that grew, till it reached the giant's waist and then his neck, and when it got to his head, he was drowned dead, and dead, and dead indeed. So he goes out of the story.

But Nix Nought Nothing fled on till where do you think they came to? Why, to near the castle of Nix Nought Nothing's father and mother. But the giant's daughter was so weary that she couldn't move a step further. So Nix Nought Nothing told her to wait there while he went and found out a lodging for the night. And he went on toward the lights of the castle, and on the way he came to the cottage of the hen-wife whose boy had had his brains dashed out by the giant. Now she knew Nix Nought Nothing in a moment, and hated him because he was the cause of her son's death. So when he asked his way to the castle she put a spell upon him, and when he got to the castle, no sooner was he let in than he fell down dead asleep upon a bench in the hall. The king and queen tried all they could do to wake him up, but all in vain. So the king promised that if any lady could wake him up she should marry him. Meanwhile the giant's daughter was waiting and waiting for him to come back. And she went up into a tree to watch for him. The gardener's daughter, going to draw water in the well, saw the shadow of the lady in the water and thought it was herself, and said: "If I'm so bonny, if I'm so brave, why do you send me to draw water?" So she threw down her pail and went to see if she could wed the sleeping stranger. And she went to the hen-wife, who taught her an unspelling catch that would keep Nix Nought Nothing awake as long as the gardener's daughter liked. So she went up to the castle and sang her catch and Nix Nought Nothing was wakened for a bit and they promised to wed him to the gardener's daughter. Meanwhile the gardener went down to draw water from the well and saw the shadow of the lady in the water. So he looks up and finds her, and he brought the lady from the tree, and led her into his house. And he told her that a stranger was to marry his daughter, and took her up to the castle and showed her the man: and it was Nix Nought Nothing asleep in a chair. And she saw him, and cried to him: "Waken, waken, and speak to me!" But he would not waken, and soon she cried:

> "I cleaned the stable, I laved the lake, and I clomb the tree,
>> And all for the love of thee,
>> And thou wilt not waken and speak to me."

The king and the queen heard this, and came to the bonny young lady, and she said:

"I cannot get Nix Nought Nothing to speak to me for all that I can do."

Then were they greatly astonished when she spoke of Nix Nought Nothing, and asked where he was, and she said: "He that sits there in the chair." Then they ran to him and kissed him and called him their own dear son; so they called for the gardener's daughter and made her sing her charm, and he wakened, and told them all that the giant's daughter had done for him, and of all her kindness. Then they took her in their arms and kissed her, and said she should now be their daughter, for their son should marry her. But they sent for the hen-wife and put her to death. And they lived happy all their days.

Peter Buchan

Green Sleeves[*]

There was a king dwelt in Scotland who had a son that delighted much in gambling, and his chief amusement was that of skittles. Having practiced it much he became so dexterous a player that no one could be found to contend with him. One day, however, as he went out alone, regretting the want of a partner, an old man appeared, and offered to play with him on the following terms: that whoever won the game should have it in his power to ask of the

[*] Peter Buchan, *Ancient Scottish Tales: An Unpublished Collection Made by Peter Buchan, with an Introduction by John A. Fairley* (Peterhead, Scotland, 1908), 40–47, https://babel.hathitrust.org/cgi/pt?id=nyp.33433086946278;view=1up;seq=48 (accessed April 21, 2017). Buchan was a printer and ballad collector who collected and recorded these tales from 1827–29 (1–2). I have added paragraph breaks and put direct speech in quotation marks.

other what he pleased, and the loser to be strictly bound to the observance of the same, under pain of death. This being mutually agreed to, they began, when the old man was more successful than the prince, and won the game.

The prince was at this a good deal disconcerted, and said he was the first person in Scotland who had ever beat him. The terms of the game, as before explained, were to the loser to do whatever was asked by the gainer. The old man then commanded him to tell him his name and place of abode before that day twelve months, or to suffer death. The prince upon hearing these hard requests, went home and went to bed, but would tell no one the cause of his anguish, although often interrogated by his nearest relations. At length the king, his father, would needs know the nature of his complaint, and commanded him to inform him forthwith, which he did as already related, viz, that an old man with whom he had played a game at skittles had commanded him to be able to tell him his name and the place of his abode, before the end of the year, being the terms on which they had played. The king then said it would be much better to go in pursuit of these particulars than lie desponding on a bed of sickness.

According to his father's advice, he arose next morning, and traveled the longest summer day in June, till he came to a cottage, at the end of which, on a turf seat, sat an old man, who addressed the prince familiarly saying, "Well, my prince, you are come seeking that rogue Green Sleeves; but although I am upward of two hundred years old, I never saw him but twice, and a little ago he passed this house; I cannot, however, tell you where he dwells; but my brother who stays about two hundred miles farther off, and is four hundred years older than I am, perhaps can tell you, and if you will stay all night at my house, I will put you on a plan to go to him quickly." The prince took lodging accordingly, and was well entertained. Tomorrow he was led to an adjoining house, and given by the cottager a round ball with a pair of slippers. The ball he was to roll before him, and the slippers would follow. But on arriving at his brother's cottage, he was to give the slippers and ball a kick, when they would return again to their rightful owner.

The prince accordingly went as directed, and found the second old man sitting by his own door, who said, "Well, prince, I see you have found me, and I know whom you seek; it is that scoundrel Green Sleeves. You have been at my brother's, but I cannot tell you where he stays more than he does; but I shall give you another pair of slippers and a ball which will take you to another brother that lives about eight hundred miles off, and about a thousand years older; he will likely be able to tell you where he dwells."

He, as formerly, goes again on his adventure, and found the old man, who seemed rather sulky, saying, he knew what he wanted, and if he would stay with him till tomorrow, he would endeavor to put him upon a plan to find him out. Tomorrow comes, when the prince was taken to a different apartment of the house where he had slept, and addressed by the old man thus: "As there are three of Green Sleeves's daughters come to the river Ugie to bathe under the disguise of swans' feathers, you will get behind a hedge of the black sloe-berry tree, and there you will be able to observe all their motions without being seen. As soon as they have stript themselves of their swan-skins and laid them down, there is one with a blue wing, which you will immediately take up and retain."

The prince went as directed, and hid himself behind the sloe-thorn hedge, when he saw three of the most beautiful swans come and hover over the river for a little time, at length alighted and threw off their swan-skins, when he snatched up the one with the blue wing. After they had continued for some time in the water, they prepared to proceed directly home; but as the one who had the skin with the blue wing could not find hers, she was at a loss what to do, more particularly as the other two told her they would not wait, but go home without her. On looking wistfully around her, she spied the prince, whom she knew, and asked him if he had her swan-skin. He acknowledged the theft, and said, if she would tell him where Green Sleeves stayed, he would deliver unto her the skin. This she said she durst not venture to do, but upon his immediately giving it up, she would teach him how to discover the place of his retreat if he would follow her directions.

He then gave her the skin, and she directed him as follows: "First you will come to a river which you will easily cross, but the second will appear more difficult, as it will be raging and foaming up from the bottom; this you must not heed, but venture in, when I will stand by you, and cause a wind to blow upon your clothes which will immediately dry them." He found the waters as described, but got more easily over them than he imagined, as he was attended by the lady, who whistled him over, and dried his clothes agreeably to the contract.

On his arriving at the opposite shore, he spied a castle, which he took to be the residence of Green Sleeves. This castle he walked round and round, but could find no entrance; at one of the corners he discovered a little bell which he rang, and which brought to his view the porter, who surlily asked what he wanted. The prince replied that it was Green Sleeves. Green Sleeves next made his appearance, and said, "Well, my prince, you have at length found me out." On being invited into the castle, he espied an old woman sitting among the ashes, whom Green Sleeves commanded for an old hag to rise up immediately and let the prince sit down. She did as required, but the dust that flew from her clothes was likely to smother him. He next commanded her to go and give the prince some meat, when she brought him a few fish skins and old molded bread, which he said his delicate stomach could not use. Green Sleeves replied, there was no matter, he could go to bed supperless, as he had to rise in the morning and do a job for him.

On going to bed, it was composed of pieces of broken glass, such as bottles, and the like, which prevented him from lying down, as the more he attempted to clear away the rubbish, it accumulated the more; but on looking around him he spied Blue Wing through a small aperture in the door, who bade him cheer up and not be afraid, as she would be his friend and assist him in the time of need; and, as a proof of the reality of her promise, she immediately transformed his apartment into one of the finest rooms imaginable, with a soft and easy bed for his accommodation. In the morning when he arose, everything appeared as it was before, so that, when Green Sleeves appeared, and asked him how he had slept, he was told that it was impossible for anyone to have slept on such a bed, and he considered his treatment very harsh, adding at the same time that if he (the prince) had gained the game, he would not have used him so cruelly.

Green Sleeves, however, persisted in giving him another task to perform, which he thought would not be in the power of man to accomplish, and that was to build a house about a thousand miles long, as many broad, and as many high, to be covered over with feathers of every kind of bird that flew; and to have a stone in it out of every quarry in the world, and to be ready before twelve o'clock next day; or it was to cost him his life. On hearing of this, he was sadly distressed, and knew not what to do, when Blue Wing appeared and requested him not to do anything toward the rearing of it, as it was impossible for him to accomplish it alone. She then opened a box, out of which started some thousands of fairies, who immediately commenced working, and had the house all finished against the time appointed by Green Sleeves, who appeared and remarked, that he had finished his task as commanded; he would therefore go home to his supper and bed, as he had another task for him to perform on tomorrow. His supper and bed were composed of the same substance as they were before, when Blue Wing appeared and changed both into what were more suitable and agreeable for a princely stomach and constitution.

On the morning when he arose, Green Sleeves said he had a cask of lintseed to sow which he must sow, reap, and have the seed in the cask in the same condition as that which he gave him out, before tomorrow night. Blue Wing then came in as before, and again set her little fairy emissaries to work; part of them cultivating the ground, part sowing the seed, part reaping, and so on, till the whole were finished by the evening. Thus being done, he waited in the fields till Green Sleeves appeared; who, when he had observed that the work was finished, he ordered him home to his supper and bed, which was as usual, but Blue Wing still continued his friend, and gave him a comfortable supper and bed as before.

In the morning, Green Sleeves had another task for him to perform, which, if he accomplished aright, it was to be the last. He was then put to clean the stable where there had stood for two hundred years, two hundred horses, and to find among the dung a gold needle which had been lost by his grandmother, about a thousand years before. The task, like all the former ones which had been imposed upon him, was impossible for him to accomplish alone; but Blue Wing coming in at the time, again set all her little family to work, and cleaned the stable of its rubbish, found the long lost needle, and gave it to the Prince, with an injunction not to let her father know that she assisted him in any manner of way, should he put such a question to him, or even insinuate as much. The whole being now finished, Green Sleeves came in, and on receiving the golden needle said, he supposed his daughter Blue Wing had greatly assisted him in all his tasks, or he never would have got them accomplished. But the prince, as desired, denied it.

Blue Wing also informed the prince that her father would offer one of his daughters to him in marriage, but to be sure to accept of none of them, for if he did, they would immediately murder him; but as it would be somewhat difficult for him to know them, as he would only see them through a small hole in a door, she would tie a blue thread around her finger, and hold it out, so that he might take hold of it, and cause her father to open the door, as he wanted her in marriage; for, if he once let go the finger she was lost to him forever. All as Blue Wing foretold him came to pass, for Green Sleeves caused first the one daughter and then the second pass before him; but he would accept of none of them till Blue Wing came, who held out her finger, when he seized it, and commanded the door to be opened. Her father taunted him a good deal about his foolish choice, saying the other two were more handsome and wise women, and that he had made choice of the worst of the three; but being determined to stick to his agreement, he retained her.

Next morning the wedding was to be solemnized, but Blue Wing had previously taught the prince not to drink any of the wine at the marriage feast, as it would be poisoned, but to have a horn prepared by their sides, into which they were to pour the wine. This being done, Blue Wing baked three magical cakes with the wine, and hung one to each of the bed posts in which they were to sleep that night, which would make answer to any question put to them. The prince and Blue Wing, instead of going to bed as anticipated by Green Sleeves, mounted two of the best horses in the stable, and with all haste rode off. Green Sleeves, imagining that the prince and Blue Wing would be now asleep in bed, as he had determined to murder them, went to the bedside and asked if they were asleep; when one of the cakes replied they were not, and seemed very much displeased at the untimely visit. A little time after he went a second time, and received the same repulse, and so on a third time, when the cake in the back of the bed informed him his daughter and the prince were gone off long ago, and were now many hundred miles distant. This enraged him greatly, and so violent was his passion that he determined to devour the old woman, as he said she was art and part in the knowledge of their flight.

He then put on his boots of seven leagues, and followed them with all speed. On their observing him coming up so fast, they were afraid that they would now be murdered, but Blue Wing said to the prince, put your hand into one of the horses' ears and he would find a small piece of wood, which, on throwing over his left shoulder, would immediately turn into a great wood. This having the desired effect, Green Sleeves had to return and call all his hewers of wood to cut it down. The field was no sooner cleared of the wood than he pursued them again with all vigor.

On his coming up with them a second time, the prince became fearful; but to allay his fears, the now princess (Blue Wing) desired him to put his hand into the horse's other ear, where he would find a small stone, which, when taken out and thrown over his left shoulder, as he had done the piece of wood, there would arise a very great rock. This also being done, Green Sleeves had a second time to return back and call all his quarriers to cut away the rock.

He then pursued as formerly; but when he was nearly up with the prince and princess, there being a drop of water at the horse's nose, it was thrown as the others had been, over the prince's left shoulder, when instantly there appeared a great river, which made him return a third time for all his ship carpenters to build him a ship for to sail over it. He again mastered this difficulty, and got over the river, pursuing with all his might the fugitive prince and princess. The prince now became more fearful than ever, thinking all their means and sources of escape had been exhausted, and nothing but inevitable death awaited them. The princess still informed him there was a way left them for deliverance, and desired him to go to the top of a high hill as fast as possible, and there he would find an egg in a certain bird's nest, which he would take out, and if he struck her father on a particular part of his breast, he would fall immediately; but if he chanced to miss that spot, they were both gone. The prince, as good fortune still attended him, found the egg, which had the desired effect, for he had no sooner thrown it than Green Sleeves fell, which rid them of a very troublesome enemy.

They now pursued their journey in peace, till within a few miles of his father's kingdom, when she requested him to pursue his route alone, but to inform his parents on his first arrival at the court, the good services she had performed for him, then would they call her with great honor and respect; but if she were to go with him immediately they would conceive her to be some lightsome leman.* She also warned him to beware of allowing anyone to kiss him; for if he did, he would then think no more of her, but forget all that she had done for him. This he determined to keep in mind; but unluckily a little lap-dog in the height of his kindness kissed the prince, which had the effect as foretold by the princess, of making him forget his princess, Blue Wing.

The princess having continued for a long time in the place where she had been left, went up into a tree near a goldsmith's house, from whence came the house maid with a pitcher to draw water from a well beneath the tree, but seeing the shadow of the princess in the water, and thinking it to be her own, she got quite vain, broke the pitcher, and said it was a shame for such a beauty to act in the capacity of a servant to such a mean man. She therefore went away to seek a better fortune, and not returning, the housekeeper came to the well next, when being puffed up with the same vain and false delusions, went also away to another place. The goldsmith now wondering much at their long stay, went himself to the well, where seeing the likeness of a female in the water, suspected the cause of their disappearance, and remarked to himself that if he had not

---

*That is, some frivolous paramour.

known himself to be a man, he also would have been deceived so looking up to the tree, saw the princess, whom he charged with being the cause of his servants absenting themselves from his service. She replied that she could not help their indulging in such foolish notions; but if he would take her home to his dwelling, she would endeavor to make up for his loss by her steady perseverance in the way to please him. He accordingly agreed, and home they went together.

She continued in his service till it happened on a day that the young prince, her husband, was going to be married, he sent his groom to the goldsmith to get ready gold mounting for the horses; but he seeing the princess in the capacity of a menial, was so taken with her beauty, that he made love to her, and offered her a considerable sum of money if she would consent to lie with him all that night. This she agreed to, but upon conditions that she was to undress and go first to bed. This being done, she said she had forgot to set down some water by her master's bedside, and must needs to rise and do it; but to prevent her from rising up, he went to do it, which was no sooner done than she commanded him to stand still in the posture he went, and to continue that way all night. He endeavored with all his might to set himself at liberty, but could not succeed. He then offered her all the money they had agreed upon for the bedding, to set him free, and he would never make such another proposal to her. Upon these terms she liberated him, refusing his money, but requesting him to publish her beauty and powers wherever he went, and whenever he had an opportunity, particularly before all the noblemen in the court. As soon as at liberty, he did as he had promised, when the duke of Marlborough went to find her out, which was easily done.

He, like the groom, bargained with her for a very large sum of money to have the pleasure of sleeping with her that night. However, as on the former occasion, she went first to bed, and observed to the duke that she had forgot to cover up the fire for fear of danger; but he agreed to do it to prevent her from her rising from bed. He had no sooner taken the shovel in his hand to perform the work than she commanded him to work in that manner all the night, or till she released him. He soon saw he was duped, and begged her to free him from such an ignominious task, and she should have all the money agreed for, and not be subject to lie with him as proposed. She refused the money, and set him at liberty upon conditions of his taking her as his partner to a splendid ball that was to take place at court shortly afterward. This he promised faithfully to perform, and when the ball commenced, the duke had one of the most handsome and beautifully dressed partners in all the hall.

After they had danced till all parties were wearied, it was proposed that they should sing a song, or tell a tale about for their future amusement. Everyone having sung a song, or told a tale, it came to the princess's turn, when she was reminded of her duty, but instead of singing, or telling a tale herself, she put down on the floor a golden cock and hen, with a few particles of bere* and oats. The hen began to abuse the cock thus: "You are now like some other people in this world, you soon begin in the time of your prosperity to forget what I have done for you in the time of your adversity; how I built a house for you, sowed the lintseed, and cleaned the stable, and found the golden needle." These put the prince in remembrance of everything that had taken place regarding himself, and that the lady was no other than his favorite Blue Wing, to whom he had formerly been married. The other lady was set at liberty, and the princess, Blue Wing, reinstated, with all the honors and joys that love and gratitude could devise. They lived together many years happy, and saw a thriving and beautiful generation rise up in their place, who did honor to their education and talents.

---

*Barley.

Jacob and Wilhelm Grimm
The Two Kings' Children*

Once upon a time there was a king who had a little boy, and according to the constellation of the stars, it was predicted that he would be killed by a stag when he turned sixteen. One day, when he had reached that age, the huntsmen went out hunting with him in the forest, but the prince got separated from them. Suddenly he saw a big stag and kept trying to shoot it without much success. Finally, the stag ran away and led him on a chase until they were out of the forest. All at once, a big lanky man was standing there instead of the stag and said, "Well, it's a good thing I got you now. I wore out six pair of glass skates chasing after you and could never catch you."

He took the prince with him and dragged him across a large lake, toward a big royal castle. Once there the prince had to sit down at a table and eat something with the man. After they had eaten together, the king said, "I've got three daughters, and I want you to watch over the oldest one for me from nine in the evening until six in the morning. Each time the clock strikes the hour, I shall come and call you. If you don't answer me, you'll be put to death in the morning. However, if you answer me, you shall have my daughter for your wife."

When the young people went up to the bedchamber, there was a stone statue of Saint Christopher standing there, and the king's daughter said to him, "My father will come at nine o'clock and every hour until the clock strikes six. If he asks anything, I want you to answer him in place of the prince."

The stone Saint Christopher nodded his head very fast, then more and more slowly until he finally came to a stop.

*Jacob and Wilhelm Grimm, *The Complete Fairy Tales of the Brothers Grimm*, trans. Jack Zipes (New York: Bantam, 1992), 408–14. No. 113.

The next morning the king said to the young prince, "You've done well, but I can't give you my daughter. Now, I want you to watch over my second daughter. Then I'll consider giving you my oldest daughter for your wife. I shall come every hour on the hour, and when I call, you must answer me. If you don't answer me, your blood will flow."

The prince went with the second daughter up to the bedchamber, where there was a stone statue of Saint Christopher, much larger than the first, and the king's daughter said to him, "If my father asks a question, I want you to answer."

The big stone Saint Christopher nodded his head very fast, then more and more slowly until he came to a stop. The prince lay down on the threshold, put his hand under his head, and went to sleep.

The next morning the king said to him, "You've done well, but I can't give you my daughter. Now, I want you to watch over my youngest daughter. Then I'll consider giving you the second for your wife. I shall come every hour, and when I call, answer me. If you don't answer me when I call, your blood will flow."

Again the prince went with the youngest daughter up to the bedchamber, and there stood a Saint Christopher, much bigger and taller than the other two. The king's daughter said to him, "If my father calls, I want you to answer."

The big, tall Saint Christopher nodded his head for a good half hour before he came to a stop, and the prince lay down on the threshold and fell asleep.

The next morning the king said, "Indeed you kept watch very well, but I can't give you my daughter yet. Now, I've got a very large forest, and if you cut it down for me between six this morning and six this evening, I'll consider giving her to you."

The king gave him a glass ax, a glass wedge, and a glass mattock. When the prince reached the forest, he began chopping right away, and the ax broke in two. Then he took the wedge and began hitting it with the mattock, but it splintered into tiny pieces the size of grains of sand. This made the prince very downcast, for he thought he would now have to die. So he sat down and wept.

At noon the king said, "One of you girls must bring him something to eat."

"No," said the oldest, "we won't bring him anything. Let the one he watched over last take him something."

So the youngest daughter had to go and bring him something to eat. When she reached the forest, she asked him how everything was going.

"Oh," he said, "things are going very badly."

She told him to come over to her and have a little something to eat.

"No," he responded. "I can't, for I've got to die, and I don't want to eat anymore."

She spoke kindly to him and implored him to try, so he went over to her and ate something. After he had eaten, she said, "Now I'll louse you a little, and then you'll feel much better."

When she loused him, he became so tired that he fell asleep. Then she took her kerchief, made a knot in it, and struck the ground three times with it.

"Workers, come out!" she cried.

Suddenly numerous gnomes appeared from beneath the earth and asked the princess what her command was.

"In three hours' time," she said, "this great forest must be cut down, and the wood stacked in piles."

The gnomes went and called all their relatives to come out and help them with the work. Then they started, and within three hours everything was finished, and they went and reported to the king's daughter. Once again she took out her white kerchief and said, "Workers, go home!" And they all vanished on the spot.

When the prince woke up, he was very happy, and she said, "When the clock strikes six, you're to go home."

He did as she had said, and the king asked him, "Have you cut down the whole forest?"

"Yes," said the prince.

When they were sitting at the table, the king said, "I can't give you my daughter for your wife yet. You must first do something else."

The prince asked what he had to do.

"I have a very large pond," said the king. "You must go there tomorrow morning and clean it out so that it glistens like a mirror, and there must be all kinds of fish in it."

The next morning the king gave him a glass scoop and said, "You must be finished with the pond by six o'clock."

The prince departed, and when he reached the pond, he stuck the scoop into the muck, and the end broke off. Then he tried a pickax, but it broke as well, and he became discouraged. At noon the youngest daughter brought him something to eat and asked him how everything was going. The prince said that things were going very badly, and he was bound to lose his head. "All the tools broke apart on me again."

"Oh," she said, "you should come and eat something first, then you'll feel much better."

"No," he said, "I can't eat. I feel too sad."

But she spoke kindly to him that he finally had to come and eat something. Once again she loused him, and he fell asleep. She took her kerchief once more, tied a knot in it, and struck the ground three times with it. "Workers, come out!" she cried.

Suddenly numerous gnomes appeared and asked her what she desired.

"In three hours' time the pond must be all cleaned up and must shine so brightly that you can see your own reflection in it. Then you must fill it with all kinds of fish."

The gnomes went off and called all their relatives to come and help them. They finished everything in two hours, returned

324 • *The Tempest*

to the king's daughter, and reported, "We've done what you commanded."

Once again she took her kerchief and struck the ground three times. "Workers, go home!" And they all vanished on the spot.

When the prince woke up, the pond was finished, and just as the king's daughter was about to leave him, she told him to go home at six o'clock. When he got there, the king asked, "Have you finished the pond?"

"Yes," said the prince. "Everything's fine."

When they were sitting at the table again, the king said, "Indeed, you finished the pond, but I can't give you my daughter yet. You must first do one more thing."

"What's that?" asked the prince.

"I've got a big mountain with nothing on it but thornbushes. I want them all cut down, and then you must build the most magnificent castle imaginable, and all the proper furnishings must be in it."

When the prince got up the next morning, the king gave him a glass ax and a glass drill to take with him and told him that he had to be finished by six o'clock. At this the prince began to chop the first thornbush with the ax, it broke into little pieces that flew all around him, and the drill also turned out to be useless. Then he became very dejected and waited to see if his beloved would come again and help him out of this desperate situation.

At noon she came and brought him something to eat. He went to meet her and told her everything that had happened. Then he ate something, let her louse him, and fell asleep. Once again she took her kerchief and struck the ground three times. "Workers, come out!" she cried.

Numerous gnomes again appeared and asked her what she desired.

"In three hours' time," she said, "you must cut down all the thornbushes and build the most magnificent castle imaginable on the mountain, and all the proper furnishings must be in it."

They went off and called all their relatives to come and help them, and when the time was up, everything was finished. Then they went and reported to the king's daughter, whereupon she took the kerchief and struck the ground three times with it. "Workers, go home!" she said, and they all vanished on the spot.

When the prince woke up and saw everything, he was as happy as a bird in the air. Since the clock had struck six, they went home together, and the king asked, "Is the castle finished now?"

"Yes," said the prince.

When they were sitting at the table, the king said, "I can't give you my youngest daughter until the two oldest are married."

The prince and the king's daughter were now very sad, and the prince did not know what to do. Then one night he went to the king's daughter, and they ran away together. After they had gone a short distance, the daughter looked around and saw her father pursuing them. "Oh," she said, "what shall we do? My father's after us, and he'll soon catch up. Wait, I'll turn you into a rosebush and myself into a rose, and I'll protect myself by hiding in the middle of the bush."

When the father reached the spot, there was a rosebush with a rose standing there. When he tried to pluck the rose, the thorns pricked his fingers, so he had to return home. His wife asked him why he had not brought back the couple. He told her that he had almost caught them, but then had lost sight of them and found only a rosebush and a rose where he had thought they were.

"If only you had plucked the rose," the queen said, "the bush would have come along."

So he went away again to fetch the rose. In the meantime, the two had made their way far over some field, and the king had to run after them. Once again the daughter looked around and saw her father coming after them. "Oh," she said, "what shall we do now? Wait, I'll turn you into a church and myself into a pastor. Then I'll stand in the pulpit and preach."

When the king reached the spot, a church was standing there, and a pastor was preaching in the pulpit. So he listened to the sermon and returned home. The queen asked him why he had failed to bring back the couple with him, and he replied, "I ran after them a long time, and just as I thought I had caught up with them, I came upon a church with a pastor preaching in the pulpit."

"You should have taken the pastor with you," said his wife. "The church would have come along. It's no use sending you anymore. I'll have to go myself."

After she had gone a long way and saw the two from afar, the king's daughter looked around and saw her mother coming. "We've run out of luck now," she said. "My mother herself is coming. Wait and I'll turn you into a pond and myself into a fish."

When the mother reached the spot, there was a large pond, and a fish was leaping about in the middle of it. The fish stuck his head out of the water, looked around, and was as merry as could be. The mother tried very hard to catch the fish, but she was unable to land it. Then she got so angry that she drank the entire pond dry just to catch the fish. However, she became so sick that she had to spit out the water, and she vomited the entire pond out again. "It's plain to me that I'm helpless against you." So she made her peace and asked them to return with her, which they did. Now, the queen gave her daughter three walnuts and said, "These will help you in your greatest need."

Then the young couple set off again. After they had walked for ten hours, they had approached the castle where the prince came from, and nearby was a village. When they arrived in the village, the prince said, "Stay here, my dearest. I'll go up to the castle first and then come back to fetch you with a carriage and servants."

When he got to the castle, everyone was happy to see him again. He told them he had a bride, who was now in the village, and he wanted to go fetch her in a carriage. They harnessed the carriage right away, and several servants climbed on back. Just as the prince was about to get in, his mother gave him a kiss, and he forgot everything that had happened and everything that he wanted to do. His mother then ordered them to unharness the carriage, and they all went back into the castle. Meanwhile, the king's daughter sat in the village and waited and waited. She thought the prince would come and fetch her, but no one came. Finally, she hired herself out at the mill that belonged to the castle. She had to sit by the river every afternoon and wash the pots and jars. Once the queen came out of the castle and took a walk along the river. When she saw the beautiful maiden, she said, "What a lovely girl! She's quite appealing!" Then everyone around her took a look, but nobody recognized her.

The king's daughter served the miller as maid honestly and faithfully for a long time. Meanwhile, the queen had found a wife for her son, and she came from a country far away. When the bride arrived, they were to be married right away, and crowds of people gathered to see the event, and the maid asked the miller if she might go and watch too.

"Go right along," said the miller.

Before she left, she cracked open one of the three walnuts and found a beautiful dress inside. She put it on, wore it to church, and stood near the altar. All at once the bride and bridegroom arrived and sat down in front of the altar. When the pastor was about to bless them, the bride looked to one side and saw the maid dressed as a lady standing there. Then she stood up and said that she would not marry until she had a dress as beautiful as the lady's. So they returned home and sent servants to ask the lady if she would sell the dress. No, she told them, she would not sell it, but they might be able to earn it. They asked her what they would have to do, and she said that they could have the dress if she could sleep outside the prince's door that night. They said yes, she could do that, but the servants were ordered to give the prince a sleeping potion.

The king's daughter lay down on the threshold and whimpered all night: she had had the forest cut down for him, she had had the pond cleaned up for him, she had had the castle built for him, she had turned him into a rosebush, then a church, and finally a pond, and yet, he had forgotten her so quickly. The prince did not hear a thing, but her cries woke the servants, who listened but did not know what to make of it all.

When they got up the next morning, the bride put on the dress and went to church with the bridegroom. Meanwhile, the beautiful maid opened the second walnut, and she found a dress more splendid than the first, put it on, and wore it to the church, where she stood near the altar. Then everything happened as on the previous day. Once again the maid lay down in front of the prince's door, but this time the servants did not give the prince a sleeping potion but something to keep him awake, and he went to bed. The miller's maid whimpered once more, as she had before, and told him about all the things she had done for him. The prince heard it all and became very sad, for he remembered everything that had happened. He wanted to go to her right then and there, but his mother had locked the door. However, the next morning he went straight to his beloved and told her what had happened and begged her not to be angry with him for having forgotten her for so long. Then the king's daughter opened the third walnut and found a dress that was even more beautiful than the other two. She put it on and went to church with her bridegroom. Groups of children gathered around them and gave them flowers and placed colored ribbons at their feet. After they were blessed at the wedding, they had a merry celebration, but the false mother and false bride were sent away.

And the lips are still warm on the last person who told this tale.

Zora Neale Hurston
Jack Beats the Devil*

Once, there was a very rich man who had two sons. One was named Jim and the other they called Jack. One night, he called the boys to him and told them, "I don't want you sitting around waiting for me to die to get what I'm going to give you. Here's five hundred dollars apiece. That's your share of the property. Take the money and make men out of yourselves. Put yourselves on the ladder."

Jim took his money and bought a big farm and a pair of mules and settled down. Jack took his money and went down the road, skinning and winning. He took from so many men that he had tripled his money. Then he met a man who said, "Come on, let's skin some money on the wood," he said, and he laid down a hundred dollars.

Jack looked at the hundred dollars and put down five hundred and said, "Man, I'm not here just to dig small potatoes. You're playin' with your head out the window. You're fat around the heart. Bet some money!"

The man covered Jack's money and they went to skinning. Jack was dealing when he thought he saw the other man on the turn, so

---

* Roger D. Abrahams, *African American Folktales: Stories from Black Traditions in the New World* (New York: Pantheon, 1985), 255–60. No. 85. Abrahams's source for this story is Zora Neale Hurston's *Of Mules and Men*, first published in 1935. Hurston heard the story told in Eatonville, Florida, and she reproduces it in a regional dialect, which Abrahams has rendered as standard academic English.

he said, "Five hundred more, my ten spot is the best." The other man covered him, and Jack slapped down another five hundred and said, "Five hundred more, you lose this time." The other man never said a word. He just put down five hundred more.

Jack got to singing:

When your cards get a-lucky, oh pardner
You ought a be in a rolling game.

He flipped the card, and bless God, it was the ten spot! Jack had lost himself instead of the other man. Now he was on the spot. He said, "Well, I've lost my money, so the game is through." The other man said, "We can still play. I'll bet you all the money on this table against your life."

Jack agreed to play because he figured he could outshoot and outcut any man on the road, and if the man tried to kill him, he'd get killed himself. So they shuffled again, and Jack pulled a card out of the deck, and it was a three. Then the man got up and he was twelve foot tall, and Jack was so scared he didn't know what to do. The man looked down on him and told him, "The Devil is my name, and I live across the deep blue sea. I could kill you right now, but I'll give you one more chance. If you can get to my house before the sun sets and rises again, I won't kill you. But if you don't, I'll be compelled to take your life." Then he vanished.

Jack went on down the road till he met an old man. He said, "What's the matter, Jack? Why are you looking so down?" "I played skin with the Devil for my life, and he won and told me that if I can't make it to his house by the time the sun rises and sets and rises again he's going to take my life, and he lives way across that ocean."

The old man said, "You sure are in a bad fix, Jack. There's only one thing that can cross the ocean in that time." Jack asked him what it was, and he said, "It's a bald eagle. She comes down to the edge of the ocean every morning and dips herself in the sea and picks off all the dead feathers. When she's dipped herself three times, she rocks herself and spreads her wings and mounts up into the sky and goes straight across the deep blue sea. So if you could be there when she gets through dipping and picking herself and she begins to mount into the sky, if you jump straddle her back, you just might make it. But get yourself a big yearling, and every time she hollers, you give her a piece of that yearling or she'll eat you."

Jack got the yearling and was waiting for that eagle to come. He was watching her from behind the bushes and saw her when she came out of the water and picked off the dead feathers and rocked, ready to spread her wings and fly off. He jumped on the eagle's back with his yearling, and the eagle was outflying the sun. After a while, she turned her head from side to side and her blazing eyes lit up, first the north then the south, and she hollered, "Ah-h-h. Ah, ah! One quarter of the way across the ocean! I don't see anything but blue water. *Uh!*"

Jack was so scared that instead of giving the eagle a quarter of the meat, he gave her the whole bull. After a while, she said, "Ah-h-h, ah, ah! One half way across the ocean! I don't see anything but blue water!"

Jack didn't have any more meat so he tore off one of his legs and gave it to her. She swallowed that and flew on. She hollered again, "Ah-h-h. Ah, ah!" Almost all the way across the ocean! I don't see anything but blue water! *Uh!*" Jack tore off one arm and gave it to her and she ate that. And pretty soon she landed and Jack jumped off and the eagle flew on to her nest.

Jack didn't know which way the Devil lived, so he asked. "The first big white house around the bend in the road," they told him. Jack walked to the Devil's house and knocked on the door. "Who's that?" "One of the Devil's friends. One without an arm and without a leg."

The Devil told his wife, "Look behind the door and hand that man an arm and a leg." She gave Jack the arm and leg and Jack put them on.

The Devil said, "I see you got here in time for breakfast. But I got a job for you before you eat. I got a hundred acres of new ground that hasn't ever had bush cut on it. I want you to go down there and cut down all the trees and bushes, grub up all the roots and pile them and burn them before dinner time. If you don't, I'll have to take your life."

Just about that time, the Devil's children came out to look at Jack and he saw that the Devil had one real pretty daughter. But Jack was too worried to think about any girls. So he took the tools and went on out to the woodlot and went to work.

By the time he chopped down one tree he was tired, and he knew it would take him ten years to clear that ground right, so Jack set down and started to cry. About that time, the Devil's pretty daughter came with his breakfast. "What's the matter, Jack?" "Your father has given me a job he knew I couldn't get done with, and he's going to take my life and I don't wanna die." "Eat your breakfast, Jack, and put your head in my lap and go to sleep."

Jack did as she told him, and went to sleep. And when he woke up every tree was down, every bush—and the roots dug up and burned. It looked as if there never had been a blade of grass there.

The Devil came out to see how Jack was doing and saw that a hundred acres were cleared off so nice. He said, "Uh, huh, I see you're a wise man, almost as wise as me. Now, I got another job for you. I got a well, a hundred feet deep, and I want you to dip it dry. I want it so dry that I can see dust from it and then I want you to bring me what you find at the bottom."

Jack took the bucket and went to the well and went to work, but he saw that the water was coming in faster than he could draw it out. So he sat down and began to cry again.

When the Devil's daughter came along with Jack's dinner, she saw Jack sitting down crying. "What's the matter, Jack? Don't cry like that unless you want to make me cry too."

"Your father has put me to doing something he knows I can't do, and if I don't get through, he is going to take my life." "Eat your dinner, Jack, and put your head in my lap and go to sleep."

Jack did as she told him to do, and when he woke up the well was so dry that red dust was just boiling out of it like smoke. The girl handed him a ring and told him, "Give my father this ring. That's what he wanted to see. It's my mother's ring, and she lost it in the well the other day."

When the Devil came to see what Jack was doing, Jack gave him the ring and the Devil looked and saw all that dust blowing out of the well. He said, "I see that you're a very smart man. Almost as wise as me. All right, you have just one more job for you, and if you do that I'll spare your life and let you marry my daughter as well. You take these two geese and go up that coconut palm and pick them, and bring me the geese when you get them picked and bring me every feather that comes off of them. If you lose one, I'll have to take your life."

Jack took the two geese and climbed the coconut tree and tried to pick the geese. But he was more than a hundred feet off the ground, and every time he'd pull a feather from one of the birds, the wind would blow it away. So Jack began to cry again. By that time, Beatrice Devil came to him with his supper. "What is the matter, Jack?" "Your father is determined to kill me. He knows I can't pick geese on top of a palm tree and save the feathers." "Eat your supper, Jack, and lay down in my lap."

When Jack woke up both the geese were picked and the girl even had all the feathers; she had caught the ones out of the air that had gotten away from Jack. The Devil said, "Well, now you've done everything I told you to, you can have my daughter. You take that old house down the road apiece; that's where me and her mother got our start."

So Jack and the Devil's daughter got married and went to keeping house. In the middle of the night, Beatrice woke up and shook Jack: "Jack! Jack! Wake up! My father's coming here to kill you. Get up and hide in the barn. He has two horses that can jump a thousand miles at every jump. One is named Hallowed-be-thy-name and the other, Thy-kingdom-come. Go hitch them to that buckboard and head them this way and we'll escape."

Jack ran out to the barn and harnessed the horses and headed toward the house where his wife was. When he got to the door, she jumped in and hollered, "Let's go, Jack. Father's coming after us."

When the Devil got to the house to kill Jack and discovered Jack was gone, he ran to the barn to hitch up his fastest horses. When he saw that they were gone, he hitched up his jumping bull that could jump five hundred miles at every jump, and he took off down the road. The Devil was really driving that bull, whipping him, and the froth was coming from his mouth and the fire from his nostrils. With every jump he'd holler, "Oh, Hallowed-be-thy-name! Thy-kingdom-come!" And every time the horses would hear him call, they would fall to their knees and the bull would gain on them.

The girl said, "Jack, he's about to catch us! Get out and drag your feet backward nine steps, throw some sand over your shoulder, and let's go!" Jack did that, and the horses got up and off they went! But every time they heard their master's voice, they'd stop till the girl told Jack to drag his feet backward nine times, and he did it, and they ran away so fast from the Devil that the horses couldn't hear them anymore and they got away.

So they got to this crossroad and decided to hide to see if they could fool the Devil once and for all. The Devil passed a man and he said, "Have you seen a man in a buckboard with a pretty girl with coal black hair and red eyes behind two fast horses?" The man said, "No, I think they must have made it to the mountain, and if they have gone to the mountain you won't be able to catch up with them." But you know, Jack and his wife were right there listening to the Devil. When the daughter saw her father coming, she turned herself and the horses into goats and they were cropping grass. Jack was so tough she couldn't turn him into anything; so she saw a hollow log and she told him to hide inside it.

Now when the Devil looked all around, he saw that log and something just told him to go look in it. He went over and picked the log up and saw there was someone inside. So he said, "Ah, ha! I got you!" Jack was so scared he began to pray to the Lord. He said, "Oh Lord, have mercy." You know there's nothing the Devil hates more than to hear the name of the Lord, so he threw down that log and said, "Damn it! If I had known that God was in that log, I never would have picked it up."

So he got back on his bull and picked up the reins and hollered to the bull, "Turn, bull, turn! Turn clean around. Turn, bull, turn! Turn clean around!" The jumping bull turned so fast that he fell and broke his own neck and threw the Devil out on his head and killed him.

So that's why they say Jack beat the Devil.

Marie-Catherine d'Aulnoy
The Bee and the Orange Tree*

There was once upon a time a King and a Queen who wanted nothing to make them happy but children. The Queen was already aged;

*Marie-Catherine d'Aulnoy, *Fairy Tales by the Countess d'Aulnoy*, trans. J. R. Planché (London: G. Routledge, 1855), 172–97, https://babel.hathitrust.org/cgi/pt?id=nyp.33433068197767;view=1up;seq=218 (accessed April 21, 2017). This story was first published in d'Aulnoy's collection of fairy tales, *Les Contes de Fées*, in 1697. The notes that follow are Planché's, except where indicated that they are mine.

she had lost all hopes of having any—when she found herself likely
to become a mother, and in due time brought into the world the
most beautiful girl that was ever seen. Joy was extreme in the palace; each person was endeavoring to find a name for the Princess
that would express their feeling toward her. At last they called her
Aimée. The Queen had engraved upon a turquoise heart the name
of Aimée, daughter of the King of the Happy Island; she tied it
round the Princess's neck, believing that the turquoise would bring
her good fortune. But the rule failed in this case; for one day, when,
to amuse the nurse, they took her out to sea in the finest summer
weather, all at once there arose so tremendous a tempest that it was
impossible to land, and as she was in a little boat, which was only
used for pleasure trips close in-shore, it soon went to pieces. The
nurse and all the sailors perished. The little Princess, who was
sleeping in her cradle, remained floating upon the water, and was
ultimately thrown by the waves on the coast of a very pretty country, but which was scarcely inhabited since the Ogre Ravagio and
his wife Tourmentine had come to live there: they ate up everybody. The Ogres are terrible people: when once they have tasted
fresh meat (it is thus they term human flesh), they will hardly ever
eat anything else; and Tourmentine always found out some secret
manner of attracting a victim, for she was half a Fairy.

A league off she smelt the poor little Princess; she ran to the
shore in search of her before Ravagio could find her. They were
equally greedy, and never were seen such hideous figures, each with
one squinting eye in the middle of the forehead, a mouth as large
as that of an oven, a nose large and flat, long asses' ears, hair standing on end, and humps behind and before. When Tourmentine,
however, saw Aimée in her rich cradle, wrapped in swaddling-
clothes of gold brocade, playing with her little hands, her cheeks
resembling the white rose mixed with the carnation, and her little
vermilion smiling mouth half open, which seemed to smile at the

horrid monster who came to devour her, the Ogress, touched with pity she had never felt before, resolved to nurse it, and if she did eat it, not to do so directly. She took the child in her arms, tied the cradle on her back, and in this manner she returned to her cave. "Look, Ravagio," said she to her husband, "here is some fresh meat, very plump, very tender; but, by my head! thou shalt not touch it with teeth,—it is a beautiful little girl. I shall bring it up, and we will marry her to our son; they will have some extraordinary little Ogres, and that will amuse us in our old age."—"Well said," replied Ravagio; "thou art wise, as thou art great. Let me look at the child—it seems wonderfully beautiful!" "Do not eat it!" said Tourmentine, putting the child in his great clutches. "No, no," said he; "I would rather die of hunger." Here, then, were Ravagio, Tourmentine, and the young Ogre, caressing Aimée in so tender a manner that it was miraculous.

But the poor child, who only saw these deformed creatures around her, and not her nurse, began to put up its lip, and then she cried lustily; Ravagio's cavern echoed with it. Tourmentine, fearing the noise would frighten her still more, took and carried her into the wood, her children following her. She had six—each one uglier than the other. She was half a Fairy, as I have said before; her power consisted in a little ivory wand, which she held in her hand when she wished for anything. She took the wand then, and said, "I wish, in the name of the Royal Fairy, Trufio, that the most beautiful hind in our forests, gentle and tame, would leave its fawn, and come hither directly, and nurse this little creature that Fortune has sent me." Immediately a hind appeared; the little Ogres welcomed her kindly; she drew near, and suckled the Princess. Tourmentine carried her back to her grotto; the hind ran skipping and gamboling after them, and the child looked at it and fondled it. When she was in her cradle and cried, the hind was always ready to feed her, and the little Ogre rocked her.

Thus was the King's daughter brought up, while they deplored her loss night and day; and believing she was drowned, the King thought of choosing an heir. He spoke to the Queen upon the subject, who told him to do what he judged proper—that her dear Aimée was dead—that she had no hope of any more children—that he had waited long enough—and that, as fifteen years had elapsed since she had the misery of losing her daughter, it would be folly now to expect her return. The King decided upon asking his brother to select amongst his sons the one he thought most worthy to reign, and to send him without delay to him. The ambassadors, having received their credentials and all necessary instruction, departed. It was a great distance off; they were embarked on board some fine vessels. The wind was favorable, and they arrived in a short time at the palace of the King's brother, who was in possession of a large kingdom. He received them very graciously; and when they asked him permission to take back with them one of his sons to succeed their master the King, he wept for joy; and told them that since his brother left the choice to him, he would send him the one he would have taken for himself; which was the second of his sons, whose inclinations were so well suited to the greatness of his birth, that he found him perfect in everything he could wish him to be. They sent for the Prince Aimé (so was he called), and however prejudiced in his favor the ambassadors were previously, they were perfectly astonished when they saw him. He was eighteen years old. Love, the young god of love himself, was less beautiful—but it was a beauty that detracted nothing from that noble and martial air that inspires respect and affection. He was informed of the anxiety of the King his uncle to have him near him; and of the intention of the King his father to hasten his departure. They prepared his equipage. He took his leave, embarked, and put to sea. Let him sail on; let Fortune guide him!

We will now return to Ravagio, and see what is occupying our young Princess. Her beauty increased with her age, and they might well say of her that Love, the Graces, and all the goddesses combined, never possessed so many charms. It appeared, when she was in the dark cavern with Ravagio, Tourmentine, and the young Ogres, that the sun, stars, and skies had descended into it. The cruelty of these monsters had the effect of making her still gentler; and from the moment she was aware of their terrible inclination for human flesh, she was always endeavoring to save the unfortunate people who fell into their hands, so much so that she often exposed herself to their fury. She would have been sacrificed to it had not the young Ogre guarded her like the apple of his eye. Ah! what will not love do? This little monster's nature had become softened by seeing and loving this beautiful Princess; but, alas! what was her grief when she thought she must marry this detestable lover! Although she knew nothing of her birth, she had rightly guessed from her rich clothes, the gold chain, and the turquoise, that she was of good birth, and she believed so still more from the feelings of her heart. She neither knew how to read or write, nor any language; she spoke the jargon of the Ogres; she lived in perfect ignorance of all worldly matters; she possessed, however, as fine principles of virtue, and as sweet and unaffected manners, as though she had been brought up in the most polished court in the universe. She had made herself a tiger-skin dress, her arms were half naked, she wore a quiver and arrows over her shoulder, and a bow at her side. Her fair hair was fastened only by a platted band of sea-rushes, and floated in the breeze over her neck and shoulders. She also wore buckskins, made of the same rush. In this attire, she walked about the woods like a second Diana; and she would never have known she was beautiful if the crystal fountains had not been innocent mirrors for her—which she gazed into without their inducing her to be vain, or think more of herself. The sun had a similar effect upon her complexion, as upon wax; it made it whiter, and the sea air could not tan it. She never ate anything but what she took in hunting or fishing, and under this pretext she often absented herself from the horrible cavern, to avoid looking at the most deformed objects in nature. "Heavens!" cried she, in shedding tears, "what have I done, that thou hast destined me to be the bride of this cruel little Ogre? Why didst thou not leave me to perish in the sea? Why didst thou preserve a life, that must be spent in this deplorable manner? Hast thou not some compassion for my grief?" She thus addressed the gods, and implored their aid.

When the weather was rough, and she thought the sea had cast some unfortunate persons on shore, she would carefully go and assist them, and prevent them from approaching the Ogres' cavern. It had been blowing fearfully throughout one night: she arose as soon as it was day, and ran toward the sea. She perceived a man, who, with his arms locked round a plank, was trying to gain the shore, notwithstanding the violence of the waves, which continually repulsed him. The Princess was most anxious to help him; she made signs to him, to indicate the easiest landing places; but he neither saw nor heard her. Sometimes he came so close, that it appeared he had but one step to make, when a wave would cover him, and he disappeared. At last he was thrown upon the sand, and lay stretched on it without motion. Aimée drew near him, and, notwithstanding his death-like appearance, she rendered him all the assistance she could. She always carried about her certain herbs, the odor of which was so powerful, it recovered anyone from the longest fainting-fit. She pressed them in her hands, and rubbed his lips and temples with some of them. He opened his eyes, and was so astonished at the beauty and the dress of the Princess, that he could hardly determine if it were a dream or reality. He spoke first; she spoke in her turn. They could not understand each other, and looked at one another with much attention, mingled with astonishment and pleasure. The Princess had only seen some poor fishermen that the Ogres had entrapped, and whom she had saved, as I have already said. What must she, then, have thought, when she saw the handsomest and best made man in the world, most magnificently dressed! It was, in short, the Prince Aimé, her cousingerman,[*] whose fleet, driven by a tempest, had gone to pieces on these shoals, and their crews, at the mercy of the winds and waves, had perished, or been cast upon unknown shores. The young Prince, for his part, was astonished at seeing so beautiful a creature, in such savage attire, and in so deserted a country; and the remembrance of the princes and ladies he had so recently quitted, only served to convince him that the being he now beheld far surpassed them all. In this mutual astonishment they continued to talk, without being understood by each other; their looks and their actions being the sole interpreters of their thoughts: when, after some moments, the Princess suddenly recollecting to what danger this stranger was about to be exposed, the deepest melancholy and dejection became expressed in her countenance. The Prince, fearing she was about to faint, evinced great anxiety, and would have taken her hand, but she repulsed him, and endeavored, as well as she could, to impress upon him that he must go away. She began to run before him; then returned, and made signs to him to do so. He accordingly ran from her, and returned. When he returned, she was angry with him; she took her arrows, and pointed them to her heart, to signify to him that he would be killed. He thought she wished to kill him; he knelt on one knee, and awaited the blow. When she saw that, she knew not what to do, or how to express herself; and, looking at him tenderly, "What," said she, "must thou, then, be the victim of my frightful hosts?—must these very eyes,

[*] First cousin. (Ed.)

which now gaze on thee with so much pleasure, see thee torn in pieces, and devoured without mercy?" She wept; and the Prince was quite at a loss to comprehend the meaning of her actions. She succeeded, however, in making him understand she did not wish him to follow her. She took him by the hand, and led him into a cave in a rock, the mouth of which opened toward the sea. It was very deep: she often went there to deplore her misfortunes; sometimes she slept there, when the sun was too powerful to return to the Ogres' cavern; and, as she had great neatness and skill, she had furnished it with hangings of butterflies' wings, of various colors; and upon canes, twisted and passed one within the other, which formed a sort of couch, she had spread a carpet of sea-rushes. She had placed clusters of flowers in large and deep shells, answering the purpose of vases, which she filled with water, to preserve her bouquets. There were a thousand pretty little things she had manufactured, some with fish-bones and shells, and others with the sea-rush and cane; and these articles, notwithstanding their simplicity, were so exquisitely made, it was easy to judge from them of the good taste and ingenuity of the Princess. The Prince was perfectly surprised at it all, and thought it was in this place that she lived. He was delighted to be there with her; and although he was not happy enough to make her understand the admiration with which she inspired him, it already appeared he preferred seeing and living near her, to all the crowns to which his birth and the will of his relations could call him. She made him sit down; and, to indicate that she wished him to remain till she could procure him something to eat, she unfastened the band from her hair, put it round the Prince's arm, and tied him to the couch, and then left him. He was dying to follow her, but was afraid of displeasing her, and became lost in reflections, from which he had been diverted by the presence of the Princess. "Where am I?" said he. "Into what country has fortune led me? My vessels are lost, my people are drowned, and I have nothing left. Instead of the crown that was offered me, I find a gloomy rock, in which I seek a shelter. What will become of me here? What sort of people shall I find here? If I am to judge from the person who has assisted me, they are all divinities; but the fear she had that I should follow her—the rude and barbarous language which sounded so badly from her beautiful mouth, induces me to think something still more unfortunate will happen to me than has already occurred." He then applied himself entirely to reviewing in his mind all the incomparable charms of the young savage: his heart was on fire; he became impatient that she did not return, and her absence appeared the greatest of all evils to him. She returned as quickly as she possibly could. She had thought of nothing but the Prince; and such tender feelings were so new to her, that she was not on her guard against that with which he was inspiring her. She thanked heaven for having saved him from the dangers of the sea, and she prayed it to preserve him from the peril he ran in being so near the Ogres. She was so excited, and she had walked so rapidly, that when she arrived she felt rather oppressed by the heavy tiger's skin that served as a mantle for her. She sat down; the Prince placed himself at her feet, much moved by her sufferings: he certainly was worse than she was. As soon as she recovered from her faintness, she displayed all the little dainties she had brought him; among others, four parrots and six squirrels, cooked by the sun; strawberries, cherries, raspberries, and other fruits. The plates were of cedar and eagle-wood, the knife of stone, the table-napkins of large leaves of trees, very soft and pliable; there was a shell to drink out of, and another filled with beautiful water. The Prince expressed his gratitude to her by all the signs he could of head and of hands, and she with a sweet smile made him understand that all he did was agreeable to her. But the hour of separation having arrived, she made him so perfectly understand that they must part, that they both began to sigh, and hid their tears from each other. She arose, and would have gone, but the Prince uttered a loud cry, and threw himself at her feet, begging her to remain. She saw clearly what he meant, but she repulsed him with a little air of severity; and he felt he must accustom himself by times to obey her.

To tell the truth he passed a miserable night; that of the Princess was not any better. When she returned to the cavern, and found herself surrounded by the Ogres and their children,—when she contemplated the frightful little Ogre, as the monster that would become her husband, and thought of the charms of the stranger she had just quitted,—she felt inclined to throw herself head foremost into the sea;—added to all this, the fear that Ravagio, or Tourmentine, would smell fresh meat, and that they would go straightway to the rock, and devour Prince Aimé. These various fears kept her awake all night; she arose at daybreak, and went to the seashore; she ran, she flew there, laden with parrots, monkeys, and a bustard; fruits, milk, and everything of the best. The Prince had not taken off his clothes, he had suffered so much from fatigue at sea, and had slept so little, that toward the morning he had fallen into a doze. "What!" said she, in awaking him; "I have thought of you ever since I left you; I have not even closed my eyes, and you are able to sleep!" The Prince looked at her, and listened without understanding her. In his turn he spoke, "What joy, my darling," said he to her, kissing her hands; "what joy it is to see you again! It appears an age since you left this rock." He talked some time to her before he remembered she could not understand him; when he recollected it, he sighed heavily, and was silent. She then took up the conversation, and told him she was dreadfully alarmed that Ravagio and Tourmentine would discover him; that she dared not hope he could be in safety in the rock for any length of time; that if he went away she should die, but that she would sooner consent to that than expose him to be devoured; that she entreated him to fly. At this point tears filled her eyes; she clasped her hands before him in the most supplicating manner; he could not understand at all what she meant, he was in despair, and threw himself at her feet. At last she so frequently pointed out the way to him that he understood some of her signs, and he in his turn explained to her that he would rather die than leave her. She was so touched with this proof of the Prince's affection for her, that she took from her arm the chain of gold, with the turquoise heart, that the Queen, her mother, had hung round her neck, and tied it round his arm in the most gracious manner. Transported as he was by this favor, he failed not to perceive the characters engraved on the turquoise. He examined them attentively, and read, "Aimée, daughter of the King of the Happy Island." No astonishment could equal his; he knew that the little Princess who had perished was called Aimée; he had no doubt this heart belonged to her, but he was ignorant if this beautiful savage was the Princess, or whether the sea had thrown this trinket on the sands. He looked at Aimée with the most extraordinary attention, and the more he looked at her the more he discovered a certain family expression and features; and from the particular feelings at his heart, he felt convinced that the savage maiden must be his cousin. She was perfectly astonished at his actions, lifting his eyes to heaven in token of thanks, looking at her and weeping, taking her hands and kissing them vehemently; he thanked her for her generosity, and fastening the trinket again on her arm, signified to her he would rather have a lock of her hair, which he begged of her, and which he had much trouble in obtaining. Four days passed thus; the Princess carried him every morning the food he required. She remained with him as long as she possibly could, and the hours passed quickly away, although they could not converse together. One evening that she returned rather late, and expected to be scolded by the terrible Tourmentine, she was much surprised at being favorably received; and finding a table covered with fruits, she asked to be allowed to take some. Ravagio told her that they were intended for her; that the young Ogre had been gathering them, and that it was now time to make him happy; that three days hence he wished her to marry him. What tidings! Could there be any in the world more dreadful for this amiable Princess! She thought she should die of fright and grief; but, concealing her affliction, she replied she would obey them without repugnance, provided they would give her a little longer time. Ravagio became angry, and said, "What should prevent my instantly devouring you?" The poor Princess fainted with fear in the claws of Tourmentine and the young Ogre, who loved her dearly, and who entreated Ravagio so much that he appeased him. Aimée did not sleep an instant; she waited for daylight with impatience. As soon as it appeared, she flew to the rock, and when she saw the Prince she uttered sad cries, and shed rivers of tears. He remained almost motionless; his love for the beautiful Aimée had increased in four days, more than a common passion would have done in four years; he was dying to ask her what had happened. She knew he could not understand her, and could think of no mode of explanation. At last she untied her long hair—she put a wreath of flowers on her head, and taking Aimé's hand, she made signs, expressing that they intended she was to do so with another. He comprehended the misery that was threatening him, and that they were going to marry her. He felt he should expire at her feet; he knew neither the roads, nor the means of saving her, nor did she. They shed tears together—looked at each other—and mutually signified it would be better to die together than to be separated. She stayed with him till the evening; but as night advanced sooner than they expected it, and being deep in thought, she did not attend to the paths she took; she entered a part of the wood very little frequented, and where a long thorn pierced her foot through and through: happily for her she was not far from the cavern. She had much trouble in reaching it—her foot was all over blood. Ravagio, Tourmentine, and the young Ogres, came to her assistance. She suffered great pain when they took out the thorn; they gathered herbs, and applied them to her foot; and she retired, very uneasy, as may be imagined, about her dear Prince. "Alas!" said she, "I shall not be able to walk tomorrow; what will he think, if he does not see me? I made him understand they intended marrying me; he will think I have not been able to prevent it; who will feed him? However he may act, it will be death to him; if he come to seek me, he is lost; if I send one of the young Ogres to him, Ravagio will know of it." She burst into tears; she sighed; and would rise early in the morning; but it was impossible for her to walk; her wound was too painful; and Tourmentine, who saw her creeping out, stopped her, and said if she took another step she would eat her.

In the meantime the Prince, finding her usual hour for being with him was passed, became distressed and frightened; the faster the time flew, the more his fears increased; all the punishments in the world would have appeared less terrible to him than the anxieties to which his love consigned him. He constrained himself to have patience, but the longer he waited, the less hope he had. At length he determined to die, and rushed out resolved at all risks to seek his amiable princess. He walked on, he knew not whither; he followed a beaten path that he saw at the entrance of the wood; after walking for about an hour, he heard a noise, and perceived the cavern, from whence came a thick smoke; he expected he should obtain some information there. He entered; and he had scarcely taken a step when he saw Ravagio, who, instantly seizing him with immense strength, would have devoured him, had not the cries he uttered in defending himself reached the ears of his dear love. At the sound of that voice she felt nothing could stop her; she rushed out of the hole she slept in, and entered that part of the cavern where Ravagio was holding the poor Prince; she was pale and trembling as though he would have eaten her. She threw herself upon

her knees before him, and entreated him to keep this fresh meat for
the day of her marriage with the young Ogre, and she herself would
eat him. At these words Ravagio was so satisfied to think the Princess would follow their customs, that he let go the Prince, and shut
him up in the hole where the young Ogres slept. Aimée begged to
be allowed to feed him, that he might not get thin, and that he
might do honor to the nuptial repast. The Ogre consented to it; she
took the best of everything to the Prince. When he saw her enter
his joy diminished his wretchedness, but his grief was renewed
when she showed him her wounded foot. They wept together for
some time. The Prince could not eat, but his dear mistress cut such
delicate pieces with her own hands, and presented them to him
with so much kindness, that it was impossible to refuse them. She
made the young Ogres bring fresh moss, which she covered with
birds' feathers, and caused the Prince to understand it was for his
bed. Tourmentine called her; she could only bid adieu to him by
stretching out her hand; he kissed it with transports of affection
which cannot be described, and in her eyes he read the expression
of her feelings. Ravagio, Tourmentine, and the Princess, slept in
one of the recesses of the cavern. The young Ogre, and five little
Ogres, slept in the other, where the Prince was. It is the custom in
Ogreland, that the Ogre, Ogress, and the young Ogres, always sleep
in their fine gold crowns. This is the only pomp they indulge in; and
they would rather be hung or strangled than forego it. When they
were all asleep, the Princess, who was thinking of her lover, remembered, that although Ravagio and Tourmentine had given her their
word of honor they would not eat him; if they felt hungry in the
night (which was almost always the case when there was fresh meat
near them), it would be all over with him; and the anxiety occa-
sioned by this horrid thought, wrought on her to such a degree, she
was ready to die with fright. After pondering for some time, she
arose, hastily threw on her tiger-skin, and groping her way without

making any noise, she entered the cavern, where the little Ogres were asleep. She took the crown from the head of the first she came to, and put it upon that of the Prince, who was wide awake, but did not dare appear to be, not knowing who was performing this ceremony. The Princess then returned to her own little bed. She had scarcely crept into it, when Ravagio, dreaming of the good meal he might have made of the Prince, and his appetite increasing while he thought of it, arose in his turn, and went into the hole where the little Ogres were sleeping. As he could not distinctly see, fearing he should make a mistake, he felt about with his hand, and throwing himself upon the one who had no crown on, crunched him, as he would a chicken. The poor Princess, who heard the cracking of the bones of the unfortunate creature he was eating, was faint and dying with fear that it might be her lover; and the Prince, for his part, who was much nearer, was a prey to all the terrors consequent on such a situation. Morning relieved the Princess of her terrible anxiety; she quickly sought for the Prince, and by her signs, made him sufficiently understand her fears, and her impatience to see him safe from the murderous teeth of these monsters. She spoke kindly to him, and he would have uttered a thousand kinder words to her, but for the arrival of the Ogress, who came to look at her children. She perceived the cavern filled with blood, and missed her youngest Ogre. She uttered horrible shrieks. Ravagio soon found out what he had done—but the evil could not be remedied. He whispered to her, that being hungry, he had chosen the wrong, for he thought he had eaten the fresh meat.

Tourmentine pretended to be pacified, for Ravagio was cruel, and if she had not taken his apology in good part, he very likely would have devoured her. But, alas! how much the beautiful Princess suffered from anxiety! She was always thinking by what means she could save the Prince; and he could only think of the frightful place this amiable girl was living in. He could not make up his mind to go away so long as she was there—death would have been preferable to a separation. He made her understand this by repeated signs;—she implored him to fly, and save his own life; they shed tears, pressed each other's hands, and in their respective languages, vowed to each other reciprocal faith and everlasting love. She could not resist showing him the clothes she had on when Tourmentine found her, and also the cradle she was in. The Prince recognized the arms and device of the King of the Happy Island. At this sight he was in raptures; the Princess remarked his transports of joy, which led her to believe that he had learned something of importance from the sight of this cradle. She was dying to know what it meant—but how could he make her aware whose daughter she was, and how nearly they were related? All she could make out was, that she had great reason to rejoice. The hour for retiring was come, and they went to their beds as on the preceding night. The Princess, a prey to the same misgivings, got up quietly, went into the cavern where the Prince was, gently took the crown from one of the little Ogres, and put it on her lover's head, who dared not detain her, however desirous he was to do so. The respect he had for her, and the fear of displeasing her, prevented him. The Princess could not have done better than putting the crown upon Aimé's head. Without this precaution, he would have been lost. The barbarous Tourmentine started up out of her sleep, and thinking of the Prince, whom she considered more beautiful than the day, and very tempting food, she was so frightened that Ravagio would eat him by himself, that she thought she would be beforehand with him. She glided, without uttering a word, into the young Ogres' cavern; she gently touched those that had crowns on their head (the Prince was of the number), and one of the little Ogres was gone in three mouthsful. Aimé and his lady-love heard all, and trembled with fear; but Tourmentine, having accomplished her purpose, now only wanted to go to sleep; so they were safe for the remainder of the night. "Heaven aid us!" cried the Princess. "Suggest to me what we can do in such a pressing extremity!" The Prince prayed as fervently; sometimes he felt inclined to attack these two monsters, and fight with them; but what hope had he of obtaining any advantage over them?—they were as tall as giants, and their skin was proof against pistol-shot; so that he came to the more prudent conclusion, that ingenuity could alone extricate them from this frightful position. As soon as it was day, and Tourmentine found the bones of her little Ogre, she filled the air with fearful howls. Ravagio appeared in as much despair. They were a hundred times very nearly throwing themselves upon the Prince and Princess, and devouring them without mercy. They had hidden themselves in a little dark corner, but the cannibals knew full well where they were, and of all the perils they had encountered, this seemed the most imminent. Aimée, racking her brains, all at once remembered that the ivory wand which Tourmentine possessed performed wonders; why, she herself could not tell. "If, notwithstanding her ignorance," said she, "these surprising things occur, why should not my words have as much effect?" Filled with this idea, she ran to the cavern in which Tourmentine slept; she looked for the wand, that was hidden in a hole; and as soon as she had it in her hand, she said—"I wish, in the name of the Royal Fairy, Trufio, to speak the language of him I love!" She would have made many other wishes, but Ravagio entered—the Princess held her tongue, and putting back the wand, she very quietly returned to the Prince. "Dear stranger," she said, "your troubles affect me much more than my own do!" At these words the Prince was struck with astonishment. "I understand you, adorable Princess!" said he; "you speak my language, and I hope that you, in your turn, understand that I suffer less for myself than for you; that you are dearer to me than my life, than the light of day, and all that is most beautiful in nature!" "My expressions are more simple," replied the Princess, "but they are not the less sincere. I feel I would give everything in the rocky cavern on the sea-shore,—all my sheep, lambs, in short all I possess, for the pleasure of beholding you."

The Prince thanked her a thousand times for her kindness, and begged her to tell him who had taught her in so short a time to speak, in so perfect a manner, a language till then unknown. She told him of the power of the enchanted wand, and he informed her of her birth, and their relation to each other. The Princess was transported with joy; and as nature had endowed her with extraordinary intellect, she expressed it in such choice and well-turned phrases, that the Prince was more in love with her than ever. They had not much time to lose in settling their affairs; it was a question of flight from these irritated monsters, and speedily to seek an asylum for themselves. They promised to love each other forever; and to unite their destinies, the moment they were able to be married. The Princess told her lover that as soon as she saw Ravagio and Tourmentine were asleep, she would fetch their great camel, and that they would get on it, and go wherever it pleased heaven to conduct them. The Prince was so delighted he could with difficulty contain his joy, and many things, that still alarmed him, were effaced by the charming prospect of the future. The night so long looked for arrived: the Princess took some meal, and kneaded it with her white hands, into a cake, in which she put a bean; then, she said, holding the ivory wand, "Oh, bean, little bean! I wish, in the name of the Royal Fairy, Trufio, that you may speak, if it be necessary, till you are baked." She put this cake in the hot cinders, and then went to the Prince, who was waiting most impatiently, in the miserable lodging belonging to the young Ogres. "Let us go," said she, "the camel is tethered in the wood." "May love and fortune guide us," replied the Prince, in a low voice. "Come, come, my Aimée; let us seek a happy and peaceful abode." It was moonlight; she had secured the ivory wand; they found the camel, and went on the road, not knowing whither. In the meantime Tourmentine, who was full of grief, kept turning about without being able to sleep; she put out her arm to feel if the Princess was in her bed yet; and not finding her, she cried out in a voice of thunder, "Where art thou, girl?" "I am near the fire," answered the bean. "Wilt thou come to bed?" said Tourmentine; "Directly," replied the bean; "go to sleep, go to sleep." Tourmentine fearing to wake Ravagio, ceased speaking; but in about two hours afterward, she again felt in Aimée's little bed, and cried out, "What, thou little jade, thou wilt not come to bed?" "I am warming myself as much as I can," answered the bean. "I wish thou wast in the middle of the fire, for thy pains!" added the Ogress. "I am there," said the bean, "and none ever warmed themselves nearer." They still continued talking, for the bean kept up the conversation, like a very clever bean. Toward the morning, Tourmentine again called the Princess; but the bean was baked, and did not answer. This silence made her uneasy,—she got up very angry; looked about her; called; alarmed everybody; and searched in every direction. No Princess! no Prince! no little wand! She shrieked so loudly, that the rocks and valleys echoed again. "Wake up, my poppet; awake, dear Ravagio; thy Tourmentine is betrayed. Our fresh meat has run away." Ravagio opened his eye, and bounded into the middle of the cavern like a lion; he roared, he bellowed, he howled, he foamed. "Quick, quick; give me my seven-leagued boots, that I may pursue our fugitives; I will catch them, and swallow them before long." He put on his boots, with which at one stride he went seven leagues. Alas! how was it possible to fly fast enough to escape from such a runner? You may be surprised that with the ivory wand they did not go faster than he did; but the beautiful Princess was a novice in Fairy art; she knew not all she could do with such a wand; and it was only in extreme cases that a sudden light broke upon her. Delighted at being together, at understanding each other, and by the hope of not being pursued, they traveled on; when the Princess, who was the first to perceive the terrible Ravagio, cried out, "Prince, we are lost! Behold that frightful monster, who is coming upon us like a thunder-bolt!" "What shall we do?" said the Prince, "What will become of us? Ah, if I were alone, I should not care for my life; but yours, my dear mistress, is threatened." "I am hopeless, if the wand will not aid us," added Aimée, weeping. "I wish," said she, "in the name of the Royal Fairy, Trufio, that our camel may become a pond, that the Prince may be a boat, and myself an old woman, who is rowing it." Immediately, the pond, the boat, and the old woman were there, and Ravagio arrived at the water's edge. "Hola, ho! old mother," he cried, "have you seen a camel, and a young man and woman, pass by here?" The old woman, who kept her boat in the middle of the pond, put her spectacles on her nose, and looking at Ravagio, made signs to him, that she had seen them, and that they had passed through the meadow. The Ogre believed her; he went to the left. The Princess wished to take her natural form; she touched herself with the wand three times, and struck the boat and the pond. She and the Prince became young and beautiful again. They quickly mounted the camel, and turned to the right, that they might not meet their enemy.

While proceeding rapidly, and hoping to find someone who could tell them the road to the Happy Island, they lived upon the wild fruit of the country, they drank water from the fountains, and slept beneath the trees, not without fear that the wild beasts would come and devour them. But the Princess had her bow and arrows, with which she would have tried to defend herself. The danger was not so terrible to them as to prevent their feeling the liveliest pleasure in being released from the cavern, and finding themselves together. Since they had been able to understand, they had said the prettiest things in the world to each other. Love generally quickens the wit; but, in their case, they needed no such assistance, possessing naturally a thousand agreeable accomplishments, and an imagination ever suggesting new and original ideas.

The Prince testified to the Princess his extreme impatience to arrive speedily either at his or her royal father's court, as she had promised, that with the consent of their parents, she would accept him as her husband. What you will have some difficulty perhaps in believing is, that while waiting for this happy day, and being with her in forests and solitudes, where he was at full liberty to make to her any proposals he pleased, he conducted himself in so respectful and prudent a manner, that never in the world has there been known to exist so much love and virtue together.

After Ravagio had scoured the mountains, forests, and plains, he returned to his cavern, where Tourmentine and the young Ogres impatiently awaited him. He was laden with five or six people who had unfortunately fallen into his clutches. "Well," said Tourmentine, "hast thou found and eaten those runaways, those thieves, that fresh meat? Hast thou not saved for me either a hand or a foot of them?" "I believe they must have flown away," replied Ravagio; "I ran like a wolf in all directions without meeting with them. I only saw an old woman in a boat upon a pond, who gave me some tidings of them." "What did she tell thee, then?" impatiently inquired Tourmentine. "That they had gone to the left," replied Ravagio. "By my head, thou hast been deceived," said she: "I suspect it was to them thou didst speak. Go back; and if thou findest them, give them not a moment's grace!" Ravagio greased his seven-leagued boots, and set out again like a madman. Our young lovers were issuing from a wood, in which they had passed the night. When they saw the Ogre they were both greatly alarmed. "My Aimée," said the Prince, "here is our enemy; I feel I have courage enough to fight with him; have you not sufficient to escape, by yourself?" "No," cried she, "I will never forsake you—unkind one; do you thus doubt my love for you? But let us not lose a moment; perhaps the wand may be of great service to us. I wish," cried she, "in the name of the Royal Fairy, Trufio, that the Prince should be changed into a picture, the camel into a pillar, and myself into a dwarf." The change was made; and the dwarf began to blow a horn. Ravagio, who approached with rapid strides, said, "Tell me, you little abortion of nature, if you have not seen a fine young man, a young girl, and a camel pass by here?" "Ah, I will tell you," replied the dwarf; "I know that you are in quest of a gentle Damoiseau,* a marvelously fair dame, and the beast they rode on. I espied them here yesterday at this, disporting themselves happily and joyously. The gentle Damoiseau received the praise and guerdon of the jousts and tournaments, which were held in honor of Merlusine, of whom you here behold the lovely resemblance. Many high-born gentlemen and good knights broke their lances here, on hauberks, helmets, and shields; the conflict was rough, and the guerdon, a most beautiful clasp of gold, richly beset with pearls and diamonds. On their departure, the unknown dame said to me, 'Dwarf, my friend, without longer parley, I crave a boon of thee, in the name of thy fairest lady-love.' 'It will not be denied,' said I to her; 'and I grant it to you, on the sole condition, that it is in my power.' 'In case then,' said she, 'that thou shouldst espy the great and extraordinary giant, whose eye is in the middle of his forehead—pray him most courteously, that he go his way in peace, and leave us alone'; and, therewith, she whipped her palfrey, and they departed." "Which way?" said Ravagio. "By that verdant meadow, on the skirts of the wood," said the dwarf. "If thou liest," replied the Ogre, "be assured, thou filthy little reptile, that I will eat thee, thy pillar, and thy portrait of Merluche."†

---

*A young gentleman before he was knighted. All the answers of the dwarf in the original are written in the language of the Middle Ages and evince Madame d'Aulnoy's study of the Romans and Fabliaux of the thirteenth and fourteenth centuries.

† An intentional contemptuous alteration of the name of Merlusine into that for a stock fish.

"There is no villainy or falsehood in me," said the dwarf; "my mouth is no lying one; living man cannot convict me of fraud. But go quickly, if you would kill them before the sun sets." The Ogre strode away. The dwarf resumed her own figure, and touched the portrait and the pillar, which also became themselves again. What joy for the lover and his mistress! "Never," said the Prince, "did I suffer such keen anxiety, my dear Aimée! as my love for you increases every moment, so are my fears augmented when you are in peril." "And I," said she, "seemed to have no fear; for Ravagio never eats pictures, and I was alone exposed to his fury. There was also little in my appearance that was palatable; and, in short, I risked my life to preserve yours."

Ravagio hunted in vain; he could neither find the lover nor his mistress. He was as tired as a dog; he retraced his steps to the cavern. "What! hast thou returned without our prisoners?" exclaimed Tourmentine, tearing her bristling hair. "Don't come near me, or I shall strangle thee!" "I saw nothing," said he, "but a dwarf, a pillar, and a picture." "By my head," continued she, "it was them! I was very foolish to leave my vengeance in thy hands, as though I were too little to undertake it myself. Here! here I go! I will put on the boots this time, and I shall not speed worse than thou." She put on the seven-leagued boots, and started. What chance have the Prince and Princess of traveling so quickly as to escape these monsters, with their accursed seven-leagued boots! They saw Tourmentine coming, dressed in a serpent's skin, the variegated colors of which were wonderful. She carried upon her shoulder a mace of iron, of a terrible weight; and as she looked carefully on all sides, she must have seen the Prince and Princess, had they not been at that moment in the thickest part of a wood. "The matter is hopeless," said Aimée, weeping; "here comes the cruel Tourmentine, whose sight chills my blood: she is more cunning than Ravagio. If either of us speak to her, she will know us, and eat us up without more ado. Our trial will be soon over, as you may imagine." "Love, Love, do not abandon us!" exclaimed the Prince. "Hast thou within thy empire fonder hearts or purer flames than ours? Ah, my dear Aimée," continued he, taking her hands and kissing them fervently, "canst thou be destined to perish in so barbarous a manner?" "No," said she, "no; I have a certain feeling of courage and firmness that reassures me. Come, little wand, do thy duty. I wish, in the name of the Royal Fairy, Trufio, that the camel should be a tub, that my dear prince should become a beautiful orange tree, and that I, metamorphosed into a bee, should hover around him." As usual, she struck three blows for each; and the change took place so suddenly, that Tourmentine, who had arrived on the spot, did not perceive it. The horrible fury was out of breath, and sat down under the orange tree. The Princess Bee delighted in stinging her in a thousand places: and although her skin was so hard, the sting pierced it, and made her cry out. To see her roll and lay about her upon the grass, one would have thought her a bull, or a young lion, tormented by a swarm of insects; for this one was worth a hundred. The Prince Orange Tree was dying with fear that she would be caught and killed. At last, Tourmentine, covered with blood, made off; and the Princess was about to resume her own form, when, unluckily, some travelers passing through the wood, having perceived the ivory wand, which was a very pretty-looking thing, picked it up, and carried it away. Nothing could be much more unfortunate than this. The Prince and Princess had not lost their speech, but of how little use was it to them in their present condition! The Prince, overwhelmed with grief, uttered lamentations that greatly added to his dear Aimée's distress. He would sometimes thus express himself:—

"The moment was near, when my lovely Princess
Had promised my wishes to crown.
A hope so enchanting—of joy, such excess,
Defied of misfortune the frown!
O Love, who such wonders can work at thy will;

Who ruleth the world with thy dart;
Preserve my dear Bee from each peril, and still
Unchanged to the last keep her heart."

"How wretched am I," continued he, "thus pent up within the bark of a tree. Here I am, an Orange Tree, without any power to move. What will become of me, if you abandon me, my dear little Bee?" "But," added he, "why will you go so far from me! You will find a most agreeable dew on my flowers, and drops in them sweeter than honey: you will be able to live on it. My leaves invite you to couch in them; there you will have nothing to fear from the malice of spiders!" As soon as the Orange Tree ceased its complaints, the Bee replied to him thus—

"Fear not, Prince, that I should range;
Nought my faithful heart can change;
Let the only thought of thine,
Be that thou hast conquer'd mine."

She added to that—"Do not fear that I will ever leave you. Neither the lilies, nor the jasmines, nor the roses, nor all the flowers of the most beautiful gardens, would induce me to commit so much infidelity. You shall see me continually flying around you, and you will know that the Orange Tree is not less dear to the Bee than Prince Aimé was to the Princess Aimée." In short, she shut herself up in one of the largest flowers, as in a palace; and true love, which is never without its consolations, found some even in this union.

The wood in which the Orange Tree was situated was the favorite promenade of a princess who lived hard by in a magnificent palace. She was young, beautiful, and witty: they called her Linda. She would not marry, because she feared she should not be always loved by the person she might choose for a husband; and as she was very wealthy, she built a sumptuous castle, and received there only ladies, and old men (more philosophers than gallants), permitting no young cavalier to approach it. The heat of the day having detained her a longer time than she wished in her apartments, she went out in the evening, with all her ladies, and came to walk in the wood. The perfume from the Orange Tree surprised her; she had never seen one, and she was charmed to have found it. She could not understand by what chance she had met with it in such a place. It was soon surrounded by all the company. Linda forbade any one to pick a single flower, and they carried the tree into her garden, whither the faithful Bee followed it. Linda, enchanted with its delicious odor, seated herself beneath it. Before returning to the palace, she was about to gather a few of the blossoms, when the vigilant Bee sallied out humming under the leaves, where she remained as sentinel, and stung the princess so severely, that she very nearly fainted. There was an end of depriving the Orange Tree of its blossoms; Linda returned to her palace, quite ill. When the Prince was at liberty to speak to Aimée, "What made you so vexed with young Linda, my dear Bee?" said he to her; "you have stung her cruelly." "Can you ask me such a question?" replied she. "Have you not sufficient delicacy to understand that you ought not to have any sweets but for me; that all that is yours belongs to me, and that I defend my property when I defend your blossoms?" "But," said he, "you see them fall without being distressed: would it not be the same to you if the princess adorned herself with them—if she placed them in her hair, or put them in her bosom?" "No," said the Bee, in a sharp tone, "it is not at all the same thing to me. I know, ungrateful one, that you feel more for her than you do for me. There is also a great difference between an accomplished person, richly dressed, and of considerable rank in these parts, and an unfortunate princess, whom you found covered with a tiger's skin, surrounded by monsters who could only give her coarse and barbarous ideas, and whose beauty is not great enough to enslave you." And then she cried, as much as any bee is able to cry. Some of the flowers of the enamored Orange Tree were wetted by her tears, and his distress at having vexed his princess was so great that all his leaves turned yellow, several branches withered, and he thought he should die. "What have I done, then," exclaimed he, "my beautiful Bee? What have I done to make you so angry? Ah! doubtless, you will abandon me. You are already weary of being linked to one so unfortunate as I am." The night was passed in reproaches; but at the break of day a kind Zephyr, who had been listening to them, induced them to be reconciled; it could not render them a greater service. In the meantime, Linda, who was dying to have a bouquet of orange flowers, arose early in the morning, descended to her flower-garden, and flew to gather one. But when she put forth her hand, she felt herself so violently stung by the jealous Bee, that her heart failed her. She returned to her room in a very bad temper. "I cannot make out," said she, "what this tree is that we have found; for whenever I wish to take the smallest bud, some insects that guard it pierce me with their stings." One of her maids, who had some wit, and was very lively, said, laughingly: "I would advise you, Madam, to arm yourself as an Amazon, and follow Jason's example, when he went to win the golden fleece, and courageously take the most beautiful flowers from this pretty tree." Linda thought there was something amusing in this idea, and immediately she ordered them to make her a helmet covered with feathers, a light cuirass, and gauntlets; and to the sound of trumpets, kettle drums, fifes, and hautbois, she entered the garden, followed by all her ladies, who were armed like herself, and who called this fête "the Battle of the Bees and Amazons." Linda drew her sword very gracefully; then, striking the most beautiful branch of the Orange Tree, said: "Appear, terrible Bees, appear! I come to defy you! Are you sufficiently valiant to defend that which you love?" But what became of Linda, and all who accompanied her, when they heard a pitiful "Alas!" issue from the stem of the Orange Tree, and saw that blood flowed from the severed branch? "Heavens!" cried she, "what have I done?—what prodigy is this!" She took the bleeding branch, and vainly attempted to rejoin the portions: she was seized with alarm and an overpowering anxiety.

The poor little Bee, in despair at the sad accident that had happened to her dear Orange Tree, was about to rush out to find death at the point of the fatal sword, in her attempt to avenge her dear Prince; but she preferred living for him, and recollecting a remedy that he needed, she entreated him to let her fly to Arabia that she might bring back some balm for him. After he had consented to her going there, and they had taken a tender and affectionate farewell of each other, she started for that part of the world, with instinct alone for her guide. But to speak more correctly, Love carried her there; and as he flies faster than the swiftest of winged beings, he enabled her rapidly to perform this long journey. She brought back wonderful balm upon her wings, and about her little feet, with which she cured her Prince. It is true, it was not so much by the excellence of the balm, by as the pleasure it afforded him, in seeing the Princess Bee take so much care of his wound. She applied the balm every day, and he had much need of it; for the severed branch was one of his fingers; so had they continued to treat him as Linda had done, he would neither have had legs nor arms. Oh, how acutely did the Bee feel for the sufferings of the Orange Tree! She reproached herself with being the cause, by the impetuosity with which she defended its flowers. Linda, alarmed at what she had seen, could neither sleep nor eat. At last she resolved to send for some Fairies, in the hope of being enlightened upon a matter that seemed so extraordinary. She dispatched ambassadors, laden with handsome presents, to invite them to her court.

Queen Trufio was one of the first who arrived at Linda's palace. There never was a person so skillful in Fairy art. She examined the branch and the Orange Tree, she smelt its flowers, and distinguished a human odor, which surprised her. She did not leave a spell untried, and employed some so powerful, that all at once the Orange Tree disappeared, and they perceived the Prince, handsomer and better made than any other man in the world. At this sight Linda became immovable; she was struck with admiration, and so peculiar a feeling for him, that she had already lost her former indifference, while the young Prince, thinking of his charming Bee, threw himself at Trufio's feet. "Great Queen," said he, "I am infinitely indebted to thee; thou hast given me new life, by restoring me to my original form; but, if thou wouldst that I should owe thee my peace and happiness, a blessing even greater than the life thou hast recalled me to, restore me my Princess!" In uttering these words he took hold of the little Bee, whom he never ceased gazing upon. "Thou shalt be satisfied," answered the generous Trufio. She recommenced her ceremonies, and the Princess Aimée appeared with so many charms that there was not one of the ladies who was not envious of her. Linda hesitated within herself, whether she ought to be pleased or vexed at so extraordinary an adventure; and, particularly, at the metamorphose of the Bee.

At length her reason got the better of her passion, which was only in its infancy; she embraced Aimée a thousand times, and Trufio begged her to relate her adventures. She was under too much obligation to her to refuse what she wished. The graceful and easy manner with which she spoke interested the whole assembly; and when she told Trufio she had performed so many wonders by virtue of her name and her wand, there was an exclamation of joy throughout the hall, and everyone entreated the Fairy to complete this great work. Trufio, on her side, felt extreme pleasure at all she had heard.

She folded the Princess in her arms. "Since I was so useful to you, without knowing you," said she to her, "judge, charming Aimée, now that I do know you, how much I am inclined to serve you. I am a friend of the King your father, and of the Queen your mother: let us instantly go, in my flying chariot, to the Happy Island, where both of you will be received as you deserve." Linda begged them to remain one day with her, during which she made them very costly presents, and the Princess Aimée left off her tiger's skin for dresses of incomparable beauty. Let all now imagine the joy of our happy lovers. Yes, let them imagine it, if they can; but to do that, they should have met with the same misfortunes, have been amongst Ogres, and undergone transformations. They set out at last; Trufio conducted them through the air to the Happy Island. They were received by the King and Queen as the last persons in the world they had ever expected to see again, but whom they beheld with the greatest pleasure. Aimée's beauty and prudence, added to her wit, made her the admiration of the age. Her dear mother loved her passionately. The fine qualities of Prince Aimé's mind were not less appreciated than his handsome person. The nuptials were celebrated; nothing was ever so magnificent. The Graces attended in their festive attire. The Loves were there, without even being invited, and by their express order, the eldest son of the Prince and Princess was named "Faithful Love." They have given him since then many other titles; and under all these various names it is very difficult to find "Faithful Love," such as sprang from this charming marriage. Happy they who meet with him unmistakably.

> Aimée with her lover alone in a wood,
>   Conducted herself with extreme circumspection;
> To Reason she listen'd—Temptation withstood,
>   And lost not a jot of her Prince's affection.
> Believe not, ye fair, who would captivate hearts,
>   That Cupid needs Pleasure alone to retain him;
> Love oft from the lap of Indulgence departs,
>   But Prudence and Virtue forever enchain him.

BIBLIOGRAPHY

Bibliographic information for the folktales in this anthology is given in each story's first footnote rather than in this bibliography.

Artese, Charlotte. *Shakespeare's Folktale Sources*. Newark: University of Delaware Press, 2015.

Ayrer, Jacob. *Comedy of the Beautiful Sidea*. Translated by Thomas Solly. In *Shakespeare in Germany in the Sixteenth and Seventeenth Centuries*, by Albert Cohn. 5–76. London: Asher, 1865.

Basile, Giambattista. *The Tale of Tales, or Entertainment for Little Ones*. Translated by Nancy L. Canepa. Detroit: Wayne State University Press, 2007.

Belsey, Catherine. *Why Shakespeare?* New York: Palgrave Macmillan, 2007.

Brennecke, Ernest. *Shakespeare in Germany, 1590–1700*. Chicago: University of Chicago Press, 1964.

Bruford, Alan. "A Scottish Gaelic Version of 'Snow White.'" *Scottish Studies* 9 (1965): 153–74.

Brunvand, Jan Harold. "The Folktale Origin of *The Taming of the Shrew*." *Shakespeare Quarterly* 17, no. 4 (1966): 345–59.

———. *The Taming of the Shrew: A Comparative Study of Oral and Literary Versions*. New York: Garland, 1991.

Bullough, Geoffrey. *Narrative and Dramatic Sources of Shakespeare*. 8 vols. New York: Columbia University Press, 1957–75.

Burton, Richard F., trans. and ed. *Supplemental Nights to the Book of the Thousand and One Nights*. 6 vols. London, 1886.

Butler, Martin, ed. *Cymbeline*, by William Shakespeare. Cambridge: Cambridge University Press, 2005.

Calvino, Italo. *Italian Folktales*. Translated by George Martin. New York: Harcourt Brace, 1980.

Campbell, J. F. *Popular Tales of the West Highlands, Orally Collected*. 4 vols. London: 1890–92.

Fox, Adam. *Oral and Literate Culture in England, 1500–1700*. Oxford: Oxford University Press, 2000.

Grimm, Jacob and Wilhelm. *Kinder- und Hausmärchen gesammelt durch die Brüder Grimm*. 3 vols. Frankfurt am Main: Insel, 1984.

Hansen, William. *Ariadne's Thread: A Guide to International Tales Found in Classical Literature.* Ithaca, NY: Cornell University Press, 2002.

———. "An Oral Source for the *Menaechmi.*" *Classical World* 70, no. 6 (March 1977): 385–90.

Jacobs, Joseph. *English Fairy Tales.* Illustrated by John Dixon Batten. London: David Nutt, 1890. http://babel.hathitrust.org/cgi/pt?id=hvd.32044024186231;view=1up;seq=60 (accessed July 19, 2016).

Johnson, John H. "Folklore from Antigua." *Journal of American Folklore* 34 (1921): 40–83.

Jones, Steven Swann. *The New Comparative Method: Structural and Symbolic Analysis of the Allomotifs of "Snow White."* Helsinki: Suomalainen Tiedeakatemia, 1990.

Manuel, Don Juan. *Count Lucanor, or The Fifty Pleasant Tales of Patronio.* Translated by James York. New York: E. P. Dutton, 1924.

Roberts, Warren E. *The Tale of the Kind and Unkind Girls: AA-TH 480 and Related Titles.* Berlin: Walter De Gruyter, 1958.

Rollins, Hyder E. *An Analytical Index to the Ballad-Entries (1557–1709) in the Registers of the Company of Stationers of London.* Hatboro, PA: Tradition, 1967.

Shakespeare, William. *All's Well That Ends Well.* Edited by G. K. Hunter. London: Cengage, 2007.

———. *The Comedy of Errors.* Edited by Kent Cartwright. New York: Bloomsbury, 2016.

———. *Cymbeline.* Edited by Valerie Wayne. New York: Bloomsbury, 2017.

———. *Hamlet.* Edited by Ann Thompson and Neil Taylor. London: Bloomsbury, 2006.

———. *King Lear.* Edited by R. A. Foakes. London: Cengage, 1997.

———. *Macbeth.* Edited by Sandra Clark and Pamela Mason. New York: Bloomsbury, 2016.

———. *The Merchant of Venice.* Edited by John Drakakis. London: Methuen, 2010.

———. *Much Ado about Nothing.* Edited by A. R. Humphries. New York, Routledge, 1991.

———. *Narrative Poems.* Edited by Jonathan Crewe. New York: Penguin, 1999.

———. *Othello.* Edited by M. R. Ridley. New York: Routledge, 1992.

———. *The Taming of the Shrew.* Edited by Barbara Hodgdon. London: Methuen, 2010.

———. *The Tempest.* Edited by Virginia Mason Vaughan and Alden T. Vaughan. London: Bloomsbury, 2011.

———. *Titus Andronicus.* Edited by Jonathan Bate. London: Cengage, 1995.

———. *The Winter's Tale.* Edited by Frances E. Dolan. New York: Penguin, 1999.

Skelton, Robin. Introduction to *Four Plays and The Aran Islands*, by J. M. Synge. vii–xiv. London: Oxford University Press, 1962.

Somadeva Bhatta. *The Kathā Sarit Sāgara, or Ocean of the Streams of Story*. Translated by C. H. Tawney. 2 vols. Calcutta, 1880.

Synge, J. B. *The Aran Islands*. Dublin: Maunsel, 1907. http://hdl.handle.net/2027/uc1.31175001609034 (accessed May 15, 2017).

Thompson, Stith. *The Folktale*. New York: Dryden Press, 1946.

———. *Motif-Index of Folk-Literature*. 6 vols. Bloomington: Indiana University Press, 1955–58.

Trenkner, Sophie. *The Greek Novella in the Classical Period*. Cambridge: Cambridge University Press, 1958.

Uther, Hans-Jörg. *The Types of International Folktales*. 3 vols. Helsinki: Folktale Fellows, 2004.

Wilson, Edwin. *Shaw on Shakespeare*. New York: E. P. Dutton, 1961.

INDEX

Notes

* Folktale types are double-posted in the index. They are listed in the entry "Types" by their designation in Uther's *The Types of International Folktales*—which consists of the prefix "ATU" followed by a number (cf. p. 4)—and title of the folktale type (e.g., ATU 890 "A Pound of Flesh"). They are also listed in the index by title, followed by their Uther designation (e.g., "A Pound of Flesh" [ATU 890]).

* Motif types are double-posted in the index. They are listed in the entry "Motifs" by their designation in Thompson's *Motif-Index of Folk-Literature*—which consists of a letter prefix followed by a number (cf. p. 5)—and title of the motif (e.g., J1161.2 "Pound of flesh"). They are also listed in the index by title, followed by their Thompson designation (e.g., "Pound of Flesh" motif [J1161.2]).

* Folktales are double-posted in the index. They are listed by title, followed by a parenthetical indication of culture of origin (e.g., "White Onion" (Chilean story)). They are also listed by the name of the collector of the tale, followed by title (e.g., Pino-Saavedra, Yolando, "White Onion").

* Page numbers in italic type indicate the text of the folktale.

Abrahams, Roger D., "Black Jack and White Jack," 8, 59–61, *76–81*

Afanas'ev, Aleksandr, "The Armless Maiden," 85–87, *124–29*

Alma, Adelaide de, 220n

Alta Silva, Johannes de, "The Creditor," 131, 132, *133–37*

"The Armless Maiden" (Russian story), 85–87, *124–29*

Artese, Charlotte, *Shakespeare's Folktale Sources*, 6–7

Asbjørnsen, Peter Christian, and Jørgen Moe, "The Twelve Wild Ducks," 244–45, 251, *292–99*

"Asleep and Awake" (Arabic story), 12–13, *30–52*

audience, for Shakespeare's plays, 3, 6, 9, 59, 83, 85, 204, 251

Aulnoy, Marie-Catherine d', "The Bee and the Orange Tree," 301–4, *335–64*

Ayrer, Jacob, *The Fair Sidea*, 301–2

Basile, Giambattista
"The Dove," 301, 301n

"The Enchanted Doe," 59, *62–69*

"The Little Slave Girl," 248

"Petrosinella," 301, 301n

"Rosella," 301, 301n

"The Bee and the Orange Tree" (French story), 301–4, *335–64*

Belsey, Catherine, 4

Bense, Marianne, 211n

Berger, Pablo, *Blancanieves*, 4

"Black Jack and White Jack" (Antiguan story), 8, 59–61, *76–81*

Bladé, Jean-François, "The Turkey-Girl," 202–3, *211–20*

"Blanca Rosa and the Forty Thieves" (Chilean story), 248–49, *274–79*

"Bluebeard." *See* "Maiden-Killer"

Boccaccio, Giovanni, *The Decameron*, 155–56, 243

Bruford, Alan, "Lasair Gheug, the King of Ireland's Daughter," 249–50, *283–92*

Buchan, Peter
"The Cruel Stepmother," 85–87, *105–9*
"Green Sleeves," 302–3, *309–19*

Bullough, Geoffrey, *Narrative and Dramatic Sources of Shakespeare*, 2–3

Bushnaq, Inea, "The Sultan's Camp Follower," 175–80

Busk, Rachel Harriette, "The Queen and the Tripe-Seller," 13, 52–58

Butler, Martin, 248

Calvino, Italo
 "Catherine the Wise," 155–58, 167–75
 Italian Folktales, 246
 "The King of Spain and the English Milord," 246
 "Olive," 85, 87, 115–23
 "Wormwood," 244–45, 262–69

"Cap o' Rushes" (English story), 202, 206–10

"Catherine the Wise" (Italian story), 155–58, 167–75

"The Chest" (Scottish story), 242, 242n

"Childe Rowland" (English story), 6

"Cinderella" (story), 1–2, 202–4

Coronado, Francisco, 137

"The Creditor" (medieval story), 131, 132, 133–37

"The Cruel Creditor" (Moroccan Jewish story), 132, 142–46

"The Cruel Stepmother" (Scottish story), 85–87, 105–9

Disney, Walt, 246

Dolopathos (medieval anthology), 131, 132, 133–37, 133n

"Donkeyskin" [ATU 510B], 204–5

Edwards, George B., 76n

"The Enchanted Doe" (Italian story), 59, 62–69

English Comedians theater company, 131, 132

"The Envious Sisters" (Hungarian story), 85–87, 110–15

fairy tales, 7

"Fareed and the Kázi" (Persian story), 131, 132, 146–49

"The Farmwife Is Changed into a Woodpecker" [ATU 751A], 6n7

Fiorentino, Giovanni, *The Dunce* (*Il Pecorone*), 2–3, 132

Flores, Amanda, 274n

folktales
 international similarities of, 8
 relation of modern folktales to stories of Shakespeare's time, 2–3, 8
 Shakespeare's audience's knowledge of, 3, 6, 9, 59, 85, 204, 251
 traditional area of, 8
 types and motifs of, 4–5

"Forbidden Chamber" motif [C611], 5

France, Marie de, *Eliduc*, 248

"The Frolicksome Duke: Or, The Tinker's Good Fortune" (English ballad), 13, 27–30

Garrido, Escolástica, 251n

Geoffrey of Monmouth, *The History of the Kings of Britain*, 203–4, 206

Gerald of Wales, "The Scene of Sorrows," 83–84, 89–91

Gesta Romanorum (anthology), 133

"The Gift of God" (Turkish story), 202–4, 224–28

Ginanni, Luisa, 115n

"The Glass Coffin" (Tuscan story), 249, 279–83

"The Goose Girl at the Spring" (German story), 202–3, 205, 229–40

Graf, Franz, 257n

"Green Sleeves" (Scottish story), 302–3, 309–19

Grimm, Jacob and Wilhelm
 "The Goose Girl at the Spring," 202–3, 205, 229–40
 "The Maiden without Hands," 2, 85–86, 98–104
 "Princess Mouseskin," 205
 "Snow White," 246, 251
 "The Two Kings' Children," 303, 320–29

Grundtvig, Svend, "The Most Obedient Wife," 10, 14–21

"How a Bad Daughter Was Made a Good Wife" (Scottish story), 11, 21–26

Hurston, Zora Neale, "Jack Beats the Devil," 8, 302, 303, *329–35*

"The Innkeeper of Moscow" (German story), 244, *257–61*

"Jack Beats the Devil" (African-American story), 8, 302, 303, *329–35*
Jacobs, Joseph
  "Cap o' Rushes," 202, *206–10*
  English Fairy Tales, 5–6
  "Nix Nought Nothing," 302, *304–9*
Jason (Greek mythological figure), 302
Johnson, John H., "Folklore from Antigua," 76n
Jones, W. Henry, and Lewis L. Kropf, "The Envious Sisters," 85–87, *110–15*

Kennedy, Patrick, "The Maid in the Country Underground," 133, *149–54*
"The Kind and Unkind Girls" [ATU 480], 133
"The King of Spain and the English Milord" (Italian story), 246
Kuka, Meherjibhai Nosherwanji, "Fareed and the Kázi," 131, 132, *146–49*
Kurosawa, Akira, *Throne of Blood*, 4

"The Lady and the Blackamoor" (English ballad), 83–84, *91–98*
"The Lady O'Conor" (Irish story), 1, 246, *269–74*
"Lasair Gheug, the King of Ireland's Daughter" (Scottish story), 249–50, *283–92*
Lee, Vernon. *See* Paget, Violet
"Lord for a Day" [ATU 1531], 12–13, 27–30, *30–52*
Lorimer, D.L.R. and E. O., "The Story of the Two Golden Brothers," 60–61, *69–76*
"Love Like Salt" [ATU 923], 202–6, 206–10, 211–20, 220–24, 224–28, *229–40*

MacLellan, Angus, "How a Bad Daughter Was Made a Good Wife," 11, *21–26*
"The Magic Flight" [ATU 313], 7, 300–304, 304–9, 309–19, 320–29, 329–35, *335–64*

"Maiden-Killer (Bluebeard)" [ATU 312], 4–5
"The Maiden Who Seeks Her Brothers" [ATU 451], 244, 250–51, *292–99*
"The Maiden without Hands" (German story), 2, 85–86, *98–104*
"The Maiden without Hands" [ATU 706], 2, 7, 82–87, 98–104, 105–9, 110–15, 115–23, 124–29, 250
"The Maid in the Country Underground" (Irish story), 133, *149–54*
"The Man Who Deserted His Wife" [ATU 891], 155–59, 159–67, 167–75, 175–80, 180–201
"Marie, the King's Daughter" (French story), 202–4, *220–24*
Mas'udi, "Revenge," 83–84, *88–89*
Medea (Greek mythological figure), 302
Messia, Agatuzza, 167n
"Modest choice: three caskets type" motif [L211], 132–33, 132n
"The Most Obedient Wife" (Danish story), 10, *14–21*
Motifs, 4
  A1958.01 "The Owl Is a Baker's Daughter," 6n7
  C611 "Forbidden Chamber," 5
  H511.1 "Three Caskets," 132–33, 132n, 149–54
  J1161.2 "Pound of Flesh," 130n
  L211 "Modest choice: three caskets type," 132–33, 132n
"Mr. Fox" (English story), 5

Nerucci, Gherardo, 115n
"Nix Nought Nothing" (English story), 302, *304–9*
"The Northern Lord" (English ballad), 246
Noy, Dov, "The Cruel Creditor," 132, *142–46*

Ocean of the Streams of Story (Indian anthology), 155, 301, 302
"Of That Which Happened to the Emperor Frederick and Don Alvar Fanez, with Their Wives" (Spanish story), 11n
"Of What Happened to a Young Man on His Wedding Day" (Spanish story), 11n

"Olive" (Italian story), 85, 87, 115–23
oral tradition, 3, 5–6
"Ortodosio, Isabella, Argentina" (Italian story), 155, 157, 159–67
Ortoli, Jean-Baptiste Frédéric, "Marie, the King's Daughter," 202–4, 220–24
Ovid, Metamorphoses, 82, 87
"The Owl Is a Baker's Daughter" motif [A1958.01], 6n7

Paget, Violet, "The Glass Coffin," 249, 279–83
Perrault, Charles, "Donkeyskin," 204–5
Philomela, rape of, 82–83, 85–87
Pino-Saavedra, Yolando
    "Blanca Rosa and the Forty Thieves," 248–49, 274–79
    "The Wager on the Wife's Chastity," 243–44, 251–57
    "White Onion," 1, 2, 3, 132, 137–42
Pitrè, Giuseppe, 167n, 262n
Pizaro, Marino, 274n
Plautus, Menaechmi, 59–61
"A Pound of Flesh" [ATU 890], 1–4, 130–33, 133–37, 137–42, 142–46, 146–49, 159, 246
"Pound of Flesh" motif [J1161.2], 130n
"Princess Mouseskin" (German story), 205

"The Queen and the Tripe-Seller" (Italian story), 13, 52–58

Ranke, Kurt, "The Innkeeper of Moscow," 244, 257–61
"Revenge" (Arabic story), 83–84, 88–89
"The Revenge of the Castrated Man" [ATU 844*], 82–84, 87, 88–89, 89–91, 91–98

Śāstrī, Saṅgēndi Mahāliṅgam Naṭeśa, "The Talisman of Chastity," 155–57, 180–201
"The Scene of Sorrows" (Welsh story), 83–84, 89–91
"Series of Clever Unjust Decisions" [ATU 1534], 131
Shakespeare, William
    audience for plays of, 3, 6, 9, 59, 83, 85, 204, 251

and oral tradition, 5–6
problem plays of, 155, 159
stories underlying plays of, 2–4, 7–8, 10–13, 59–62, 82–88, 130–33, 155–59, 202–6, 241–51, 300–304
Shakespeare, William, works of
    All's Well That Ends Well, 6, 155–59
    The Comedy of Errors, 7, 59–62, 82
    Cymbeline, 1, 7, 156n, 241–51
    Hamlet, 6
    King Lear, 5–6, 7, 202–6
    Macbeth, 4, 5, 7
    Measure for Measure, 6
    The Merchant of Venice, 1–3, 6, 8, 130–33, 246
    The Merry Wives of Windsor, 6
    A Midsummer Night's Dream, 7
    Much Ado about Nothing, 5
    Othello, 244
    Pericles, 7, 248
    The Rape of Lucrece, 245–46
    Romeo and Juliet, 7
    The Taming of the Shrew, 6, 10–14
    The Tempest, 7, 300–304
    Titus Andronicus, 6, 7, 82–88
    The Winter's Tale, 5, 7
Shaw, George Bernard, 245
Sir Gawain and the Green Knight (British romance), 302
"The Sister of Nine Brothers" [ATU 709A], 250–51
Smiley, Jane, A Thousand Acres, 205–6
"Snow White" (German story), 246, 251
"Snow White" [ATU 709], 4, 7, 241–42, 246–51, 274–79, 279–83, 283–92
Stewart-Murray, Evelyn, 283n
Stich, Josef, 257n
"Story of Śṛṅgabhuja and the Daughter of the Rākshasa" (Indian story), 301, 301n
"The Story of the Two Golden Brothers" (Persian story), 60–61, 69–76
Straparola, Giovanni Francesco, "Ortodosio, Isabella, Argentina," 155, 157, 159–67
"The Sultan's Camp Follower" (Iraqi story), 155–58, 175–80
Synge, J. M., "The Lady O'Conor," 1, 246, 269–74

"The Talisman of Chastity" (Indian story), 155–57, *180–201*

"The Taming of the Shrew" [ATU 901], 10–13, 14–21, 21–26

Tate, Nahum, 206

Tezel, Naki, "The Gift of God," 202–4, *224–28*

Thompson, Stith, *Motif-Index of Folk-Literature*, 5

The Thousand and One Nights, "Asleep and Awake," 12, *30–52*

"Three Caskets" motif [H511.1], 132–33, 132n, 149–54

"The Turkey-Girl" (French story), 202–3, *211–20*

"The Twelve Wild Ducks" (Norwegian story), 244–45, 251, *292–99*

"The Twins or Blood-Brothers" [ATU 303], 7, 59–62, 62–69, 69–76, 76–81

"The Two Kings' Children" (German story), 303, *320–29*

Types, 4

    ATU 303 "The Twins or Blood Brothers," 7, 59–62, 62–69, 69–76, 76–81

    ATU 312 "Maiden-Killer (Bluebeard)," 4–5

    ATU 313 "The Magic Flight," 7, 300–304, 304–9, 309–19, 320–29, 329–35, 335–64

    ATU 451 "The Maiden Who Seeks Her Brothers," 244, 250–51, 292–99

    ATU 480 "The Kind and Unkind Girls," 133

    ATU 510B "Donkeyskin," 204–5

    ATU 706 "The Maiden without Hands," 2, 7, 82–87, 98–104, 105–9, 110–15, 115–23, 124–29, 250

    ATU 709A "The Sister of Nine Brothers," 250–51

    ATU 709 "Snow White," 4, 7, 241–42, 246–51, 274–79, 279–83, 283–92

    ATU 751A "The Farmwife Is Changed into a Woodpecker," 6n7

ATU 844* "The Revenge of the Castrated Man," 82–84, 87, 88–89, 89–91, 91–98

ATU 882 "The Wager on the Wife's Chastity," 156n, 241–46, 251, 251–57, 257–61, 262–69, 269–74

ATU 890 "A Pound of Flesh," 1–4, 130–33, 133–37, 137–42, 142–46, 146–49, 159, 246

ATU 891 "The Man Who Deserted His Wife," 155–59, 159–67, 167–75, 175–80, 180–201

ATU 901 "The Taming of the Shrew," 10–13, 14–21, 21–26

ATU 905A* "The Wicked Queen Reformed by Whipping by a Cobbler," 13, 52–58

ATU 923 "Love Like Salt," 202–6, 206–10, 211–20, 220–24, 224–28, 229–40

ATU 1531 "Lord for a Day," 11–12, 27–30, 30–52

ATU 1534 "Series of Clever Unjust Decisions," 131

Uther, Hans-Jörg, *The Types of International Folktales*, 4

"The Wager on the Wife's Chastity" (Chilean story), 243–44, *251–57*

"The Wager on the Wife's Chastity" [ATU 882], 156n, 241–46, 251, 251–57, 257–61, 262–69, 269–74

Wayne, Valerie, 242n

"White Onion" (Chilean story), 1, 2, 3, 132, *137–42*

"The Wicked Queen Reformed by Whipping by a Cobbler" [ATU 905A*], 13, 52–58

"Wormwood" (Italian story), 244–46, *262–69*

Xenophon of Ephesus, *An Ephesian Story*, 248

TEXT CREDITS